# NO EXCUSES, NO REGRETS

## THE *ERIC WEDDLE* STORY

# NO EXCUSES, NO REGRETS
## THE ERIC WEDDLE STORY

## BY TRENT TOONE

SHADOW
MOUNTAIN

*To Chanel, Brooklyn, Gaige, and Silver.*

*As you live each day to the fullest, may this book inspire
you to go and do something totally amazing.*

ERIC WEDDLE

Visit us at ShadowMountain.com

**Library of Congress Cataloging-in-Publication Data**

Toone, Trent, author.
  No excuses, no regrets : the Eric Weddle story / Trent Toone.
     pages cm
  Includes bibliographical references and index.
  ISBN 978-1-60907-395-4 (hardbound : alk. paper)
  1. Weddle, Eric, 1985– 2. Football players—Biography. 3. Mormon athletes—
Biography. 4. San Diego Chargers (Football team)—Biography. I. Title.
  GV939.W363T66 2013
  796.332092—dc23
  [B]                                                                    2013003186

Printed in the United States of America
Lake Book Manufacturing, Inc., Melrose Park, Illinois

10   9   8   7   6   5   4   3   2   1

"I still remember [my mother's] advice
to me given on that day long ago
when my team lost a football game:
'Come what may, and love it.'"

—JOSEPH B. WIRTHLIN

# CONTENTS

# CONTENTS

# FOREWORD

## BY KYLE WHITTINGHAM

Over the past twenty-five years I have had the opportunity to coach many outstanding college football players. From the all-Americans to the guys who didn't make the headlines, their contributions have brought notoriety and respect to our program at the University of Utah. Many of these former players have gone on to professional careers in the National Football League.

One who ranks among the best to ever don the Utah uniform is Eric Weddle.

In 2001, my recruiting area included Alta Loma High School in Rancho Cucamonga, California. I vividly remember the first time I sized Eric up. He was hardly an imposing figure, at just a shade under six feet tall and weighing maybe 185 pounds, with slicked-back hair. His game film, however, revealed a player who was multitalented and had some of the best instincts of any of the players I had ever evaluated. Eric was all over the field, playing a multitude of positions. He made play after play, and it was no wonder that he would later be named the offensive and defensive MVP of his league.

At that point in time, Eric was drawing moderate interest from several schools in the PAC-10 as well as many other smaller schools, and I put him on my list as a guy that I wanted to follow up on in the fall.

Six months later, I was surprised to learn that not one of the PAC-10 schools had offered him a scholarship. This seemed very strange since virtually every coach in his league raved that he was the best player in the area.

So why hadn't any big-name schools offered him a scholarship? I researched Eric further to make sure there were no character issues or heinous crimes in his past. When all this checked out okay, I was convinced that, regardless of his lack of recruitment by the PAC-10, he would be a great fit for our program. When he visited our campus, we made the scholarship offer and he accepted. Even so, Urban Meyer, our head coach at the time, was a little skeptical that Eric was a guy that could help us win.

It didn't take us long to realize we had a special player on our hands. By the fourth game of his freshman year, Eric had already cracked the starting lineup.

One of Eric's many strong suits was his humility. Even with his early success, he would never boast or brag. He was also a perfectionist. Regardless of his high level of performance, he always felt there was room for improvement. Confidence, character, class, consistency, toughness, competitiveness, intelligence, compassion, the ability to overcome adversity—all are qualities that describe Eric Weddle. He's a guy who does things the right way in both his approach to the game of football and to life.

I have always been impressed with Eric's competitiveness. Following his rookie season with the San Diego Chargers, we invited Eric back to be an honorary coach in our annual Red and White spring game on April 19, 2008. Not only did his white squad win, he also did something that was quintessential competitive Eric.

After the white squad scored a touchdown, we put Eric out there to kick the PAT, which was about the only thing he hadn't done for us in his time at Utah. Perhaps that was a good thing, because his kick was low and was easily blocked. The ball bounced toward the sideline, where it was scooped up by a player from the red squad. As the defensive player began to run it back, Eric, dressed in shorts, a golf shirt, and untied sneakers, with a cell phone on his belt and a hat on backwards, bolted after him. But just before Eric could make the tackle, the defensive player pitched the ball back to one of his teammates. With several thousand Ute fans cheering, Eric took off in pursuit of the player and, some 50 yards later, Eric finally caught him just before he reached the other end zone and playfully fell on top of him.

I was praying the entire time that Eric wouldn't get hurt and that the Chargers would never get wind of the incident. But it was a prime example of Eric's competitive spirit.

During his career at Utah, Eric was always a class act. His generous gesture at the end of the 2006 BYU game typifies his character and what he is all about. At the end of the game, Eric went out of his way to congratulate the Cougars' winning quarterback, even though it had been very difficult for him to lose his final home game as a Ute. Very few players would have had the presence of mind to do what he did in that situation.

As good as Eric is on the field, he is an even better person off. His commitment to his religious beliefs, his family, his friends, and his community are his priorities. During his time at Utah, he visited sick children in hospitals, went to see those with special needs, and spent time talking with troubled youth at juvenile correction facilities. He cares about people.

Another thing I admire about Eric is the love and dedication he has for his family. Eric and his wife, Chanel, are the parents of three adorable children: daughter Brooklyn, son Gaige, and a second daughter, Silver. Eric credits his parents, Steve and Debbie Weddle, with teaching him the life lessons, values, and principles that have helped him become the husband and father he is today. Even with all the praise and accolades he has received for his play on the football field, Eric will be the first to tell you that his family is his greatest source of happiness.

Since leaving the University of Utah for the NFL, Eric has been a great ambassador for our program. He has stayed involved and continues to offer a helping hand when time permits.

It is a privilege to have Eric as a friend, and coaching him was an honor. I continue to watch his career unfold and am elated at the success he is having as a member of the San Diego Chargers in the National Football League. Eric is truly one of the "great ones."

# PROLOGUE

---

# THE SAFETY THAT WAS TOO SHORT

This wasn't the way Eric Weddle imagined it would be.

Growing up about fifty miles east of the UCLA campus, he had often aspired to one day be playing football for the Bruins. Over the course of countless Saturdays, he had religiously watched the great ones such as Troy Aikman, Cade McNown, and DeShaun Foster, then mimicked their moves in Pop Warner ball. He wore a blue-and-gold jersey to school, where his dreams of pigskin greatness helped him survive high school algebra. Honestly, it was more interesting to visualize himself running into the Rose Bowl stadium to the roar of a hundred thousand fans than it was to solve for X and Y. At Alta Loma High School, he had been a three-sport athlete, but football was his passion. As a sophomore he started in the varsity's defensive secondary. As a junior he started at safety and quickly developed into an electrifying wide receiver. That year, he was named the Mount Baldy League's MVP, and recruiting mail poured in from the PAC-10, the Big 12, and even Notre Dame.

While envelopes with official university stationery are fun to receive, there were no scholarship offers. He soon learned the reason why. Notwithstanding his 4.4 speed, elusive moves, and reliable hands, Eric was only five-foot-ten and 175 pounds. Recruiters acknowledged he was one of the top athletes in an area loaded with good football players, but, according to the recruiters, his stature fell short of the prototypical college football player. Many of the top programs around the country were changing to more pass-fancy offenses with taller, faster receivers. As a result, opposing defenses needed taller, faster defensive backs and safeties. It came down to a matter of inches, and Eric didn't measure up to those physical standards.

The harsh reality became evident in the fall of 2002, Eric's senior year, when a recruiter from UCLA quietly came to Alta Loma to visit with Eric's coach, John Kusleika, and to watch Eric's highlight film. Mark Weber, a stout man with a shaved head and broad shoulders, was then the Bruins offensive line coach. He was a friend and longtime coaching colleague of Kusleika. Weber respected the high school coach's eye for talent, and came on his recommendation. Weber was initially impressed with what he saw of Weddle's game film. He admired Eric's speed and unmistakable playmaking abilities. Coach Kusleika vouched for his player's character and academic performance, and Weber agreed to take the tape back to UCLA to show the other coaches. But before he left, the recruiter asked if he could see the kid in person. In keeping with NCAA rules, Weber couldn't speak with Eric at the time, but he wanted to size him up from a distance.

They found the popular senior socializing with his friends in the cafeteria. Kusleika pointed toward Eric and said, "That's him," but all Weber could see was a small, skinny kid in baggy clothes with a hat on backwards. The recruiter gazed intently but

2

failed to see a college football player. "Which one?" Weber repeated several times. Finally, someone crept up a few feet behind
Weddle and silently gestured directly at him. There was no mistake now, yet Weber continued to stare in disbelief. The Mount
Baldy MVP he had witnessed do spectacular things on film was
not the same person he was looking at in the cafeteria. Although
Eric was the best high school football player Kusleika had ever
coached, Weber did not foresee UCLA offering a scholarship to a
scrawny athlete of Weddle's small frame. "I have six-foot-two guys
all over the place," Weber told the high school coach.

The process for signing four- and five-star recruits is fairly
simple for programs like UCLA. Each year, coaches like Weber
compile lists of recruits a mile long. These coaches scrutinize the
list and narrow their choices to the strongest, tallest, and fastest
athletes, the Cadillacs and Rolls Royces of high school football.
Then a limited number of scholarships are offered and accepted
quickly.

"Schools like UCLA get their pick of the litter. If they have
to choose between two guys, they will always choose the bigger,
taller, and faster guy. It's not that they think the other guy [is a
bad player], but you can't take them all," said Weber, currently
the offensive line coach at Utah State University. "Recruiting is
not a science. Eric just didn't fit the prototype. We considered
him and recognized his talent, but he was small."

More than a decade later, the undersized Weddle has achieved
more than 99 percent of what the recruiters dreamed possible
for him. First, he was named a consensus all-American at the
University of Utah. After trading away four picks, the San Diego
Chargers picked Eric in the second round of the 2007 NFL
draft. He became the Chargers' starting free safety in 2008. Since
then, Eric has developed a reputation as one of the NFL's bright,

defensive minds, a fundamentally sound tackling machine, and a reliable last line of defense in the secondary. Prior to the 2011 season, San Diego made Eric one of the highest-paid safeties in league history by signing him a five-year, $40-million contract. Eric proved he was worth the lucrative investment by having the best season of his career. One of the team's elected captains, Eric posted a league-best seven interceptions, made his first Pro Bowl roster, and was named first-team All-Pro by the *Associated Press,* one of the most respected honors an NFL player can receive in a career. He followed that performance up with another all-pro season in 2012.

That's not bad for a player who was supposed to be too short to play college football.

The story that follows started in sunny southern California, with loving family and friends, supportive teammates and coaches, and an unparalleled passion for sports and competition. It's a love story about a boy and a girl who met in high school, their deep friendship and roller-coaster courtship. It's a story about overcoming stereotypes, adversity, and accomplishing impossible dreams. It's about an athlete that surprised his family and friends by joining a church they knew little about, and how his faith has continued to bless his life. It's a story about big games in enormous stadiums, epic wins and devastating losses, confidence and character, taking advantage of opportunities and respecting the game of football. It's a story about a man who values his family above all else. It's a story about attacking the challenges of life with no excuses, and living each day with no regrets. That's Weddle's way.

# CHAPTER 1

## THE PREGAME SHOW

Steve Weddle and his buddies were scrubbing down a fishing boat off the coast of southern California, when he made one of the biggest decisions of his young life.

It was early in the summer of 1976, and for the past few months the adventurous twenty-year-old had been living the carefree life of a fishing boat deckhand. The work was not for everyone. The vessel ventured out early in the morning or late at night and stayed as long as the fish were biting, which usually meant all day. A night's sleep usually lasted around four to five hours. The deckhand made next to no money, usually collecting tips in the five-dollar range from passenger fishermen who felt generous. Sometimes the weather was rough. On top of all that, a deckhand typically worked for twenty or thirty days in a row then enjoyed one day off before going aboard again for another month.

Steve, young and energetic, enjoyed life as a deckhand. Yes, it was an aquatic marathon, but the work was not physically exhausting. Working side-by-side with a few of his high school buddies, Steve spent the whole day catching and filleting yellow-fin tuna, dorado, and various whoppers. He relished the smell of the sea and the ocean breeze in his face—not to mention the scenic sunsets. He loved the adventure of it all.

There was only one problem: He missed Debbie Robles, his high school sweetheart.

They met at a friend's party when he was sixteen and she was fifteen, and there was an instant connection. The following week, the two exchanged valentines and went out again. When he kissed her for the first time, Debbie melted. "He was so happy and outgoing. He was the most handsome boy in the world with his blue eyes and rugged good looks. I was a silly girl, but he was so romantic," Debbie sighed.

They dated throughout their time at Temple City High in the San Gabriel Valley. He was a star on the football and track-and-field teams. She was involved in a myriad of extracurricular activities, including student government, a capella choir, and carrying the banner for the marching band. She was voted as the class prom queen. When they weren't at school activities, Steve was like a member of the Robles family. Debbie's father, Ed Robles, liked Steve because he was an athlete, and the two had similar interests. It wasn't uncommon for Steve to spend the night sleeping on the Robles' living room floor, or to accompany the Robles on a family excursion.

Debbie's parents supported their family with little more than a high school education. For most of their adult lives, Ed worked for UPS, and Debbie's mother, Betty, was a secretary at Temple City High. Debbie became the first in her family to attend college when she enrolled at Long Beach State that fall. Steve registered for classes at Pasadena Community College, and they continued to date in their spare time.

A few years went by as they studied at college and their love for one another deepened. They talked about marriage, and Steve proposed. The engagement didn't last long, however. One night as they discussed wedding plans, Debbie noticed a lack of excitement in Steve.

"You really don't want to get married right now, do you?" she asked bluntly.

"Not really," came Steve's honest reply.

A serious conversation ensued and sharp words were exchanged. With tears flowing, Debbie sealed the breakup with the words, "Don't you call me, don't talk to me. I never want to see your face again."

"He wasn't ready," she said. "And like any girl would, I cried my eyes out."

Debbie continued working toward a degree at Long Beach State, while Steve lost interest in school. He opted to move to San Diego and began working seriously long hours on a charter fishing boat. For the next year there was zero contact between them. Then one day Steve awoke to the realization that the person he was in love with was back at home—and likely dating other guys by now.

On the boat, as he and his shipmates cleaned and prepared to dock at the fisherman's landing, the lovesick young man determined to make a phone call. The life of a deckhand on a fishing boat was enjoyable, but it was time to get real. The woman he loved was more than a hundred miles away at Long Beach State, and as far as he knew she wasn't waiting around for him. If things went well on the phone and she would have him, this fishing voyage would be his last.

When the boat docked at the fisherman's landing and his daily duties were completed, Steve fished in his pocket for some loose change (there wasn't much) and located a phone booth. He took a deep breath, inserted his coins, and dialed Debbie's number. After a few rings, a familiar voice answered, and he prayed his next sentence would prevent her from hanging up.

"Can I just talk to you for five minutes?" he pleaded.

Silence. When she didn't hang up, he took that as a good sign and pushed on, apologizing for his mistakes and asking for forgiveness.

Silence.

He was prepared to find a real job, and, if she would still have him, he was ready to talk about marriage. On the other end of the line, Debbie melted once again.

"Okay, come on up," she told him. Steve sighed with relief. He had finally pulled in the biggest catch of his life—the woman of his dreams. A second marriage proposal quickly followed.

Steve and Debbie were married July 24, 1976. She found a job as an elementary school teacher in the El Monte School District, and Steve accepted employment as a truck driver. Now all they needed was a home. In 1977, the newlyweds heard about houses for sale in a new community called Alta Loma. Steve's parents were already in the area, and Debbie's sister also had a home nearby. The idea of moving there had a lot of appeal. What they didn't have was $3,000 for a down payment. "We had just gotten married and didn't have any money," Debbie explained.

But the bank was willing to work with the Weddles. Using a thousand dollars and the title to Steve's van, a deal was struck, and the couple had a new house. The modest, one-level home with a garage, a green lawn, and a basketball court driveway was located at the end of the street in a nice neighborhood. The home was comfortable and perfect for their needs. Years later, a flag-pole in the backyard would hoist the flags of Los Angeles Lakers purple and gold, University of Utah crimson, and San Diego Chargers blue. The only hard part about their new home was breaking the news to Debbie's parents that they were moving almost an hour away.

The Weddles were happy. It was the beginning of a new life for Steve and Debbie. Within a few years they discussed the idea of starting a family. Shortly thereafter Debbie learned she was pregnant, and they had a baby girl. Kathleen arrived without incident on September 19, 1981, and even though she was a girl, Steve considered naming her Eric. While he loved his daughter, he had also always wanted a son, and he wanted to name him Eric, a name he picked out for his future son when he was a teenager. "It was a strong name," Steve said. "I loved it."

So when Debbie announced that she was pregnant with their second child in the summer of 1984, Steve was determined to name the baby Eric, regardless of its gender. "Whatever came out was going to be an Eric," he said, laughing. The young father would eventually be granted his wish of a son, but he and Debbie would have to pass through a few trials of stress and heartache first.

## A MIRACULOUS BIRTH

Debbie Weddle was in the second trimester of her pregnancy with Eric, early in the fall of 1984, when she awoke to a mother's worst nightmare.

Sometime after midnight, the young mother felt moisture on her sheets and bolted up in bed. A feeling of panic began to rise within her heart as she realized she was sitting in amniotic fluid.

Debbie tossed the bed covers aside and carefully walked to the bathroom to sit on the toilet, where more fluid discharged.

Something felt terribly wrong. Rubbing her weary eyes, she flipped on the light and examined herself, trying to figure out what had happened. As she peered into the toilet, she blinked and stared in disbelief. Pregnancy tissue was floating in the white porcelain bowl. "Steve," she said, "we need to get to the hospital."

In moments the couple was in the midst of a hasty thirty-minute drive to Kaiser Permanente Medical Center in Fontana, California. Steve wonders now why he didn't just dial 911. Both parents feared they may have lost their unborn child.

Upon arriving at the emergency room, they were met by Debbie's mother and examined by a doctor. The news was not good.

"They told me I was going to have a miscarriage," Debbie said, recalling the traumatic experience, "or I could go into labor. The baby's heartbeat was perfect. There was nothing physically wrong with me. They told me to just sit there and wait for the miscarriage to happen."

One possible explanation for the expelled tissue, the doctor told her, was that she had been carrying twins and one had miscarried. But that theory was discarded because a fetus was not found in the tissues. If she didn't go into labor soon, however, a miscarriage would likely happen because the amniotic fluid had flushed out.

A feeling of despair gripped the huddled family. According to the doctors, losing the baby seemed like a foregone conclusion. But not knowing what would happen was the worst feeling of all.

So they waited. But the longer Debbie waited, the more irritated she became. She was frustrated and wanted answers. She remained in the room for several hours before she was allowed to go home and rest, but later returned to the hospital.

A long, scary week slowly passed, with Debbie under close observation in a hospital bed, but, curiously, the miscarriage did not occur. Medical personnel monitored the baby and its heartbeat. Much to the doctor's amazement, mother and baby remained in good health, as if nothing unusual had ever happened. Debbie was sent home and ordered to be on bed rest for the next month. Steve was at his wife's side as often as possible to offer strength and support. Although a small chance of keeping the baby full-term still existed, the doctor's opinion that Debbie would lose the baby didn't budge. "They told us the chances of keeping the baby were slim-to-none. They told us to be prepared for a miscarriage at any time. It was minute-to-minute," Debbie remembered.

While heartbroken by this discouraging development, Debbie found comfort in the kind words of a stranger. While marching defiantly around her room one day, she and her mother were not surprised to see a nurse open the door. What did surprise them, however, was what the woman said. Like an old friend, the nurse advised the distraught women to ignore the pessimistic doctors, because she had seen a friend experience the same symptoms and carry the baby full-term. Those hushed words gave Debbie hope that she and her child would get through this challenging time of her life.

"She said that only God knows what will happen and to have faith," Debbie said. "At that moment my mom and I both cried. We told Steve and, needless to say, I stopped my marching around the room, and I lay down in bed."

Miraculously, Debbie's uterus healed and resealed itself. Fluid mysteriously returned to the womb. Doctors could not explain it. Almost four months later, on January 4, 1985, Debbie delivered a seven-pound, eight-ounce baby boy by cesarean section. Despite what she had already been through, Debbie had originally requested a natural delivery but changed her mind on the advice of her mother.

The delivery was uneventful and a healthy baby boy was born. The little guy had a severe case of jaundice, which required that he lie under a bright light for four days, but Steve finally had a son he could name Eric. The newborn was given the full name of Eric Steven Weddle. Little did they know that surviving the pregnancy to reach Earth was the first of many obstacles he would overcome in his life. Eric proved the doctors wrong then, and years later he would prove many football experts wrong. The love and support shown by his family was also a prelude of things to come.

Looking back, Steve and Debbie have no doubt that their son's survival and birth was a miracle.

"He wasn't supposed to be here. No one knows how everything sealed back up. No one knows how it filled back up with fluid," Debbie said. "In that process you are praying to God every minute of every day, saying, 'I will do anything.' I am not one who asks for favors like that, but I prayed all the time: 'I will do whatever you ask.' So when he was born, we were just so excited. You look at him now and say, 'Here is a kid who wasn't supposed to be here.'"

## A SURE FOUNDATION

Alta Loma, California, where Eric Weddle grew up, was one of three unincorporated areas that became part of the city of Rancho Cucamonga in 1977, the same year his parents bought their home. Set against the south face of the San Gabriel mountain range, Alta Loma, which in Spanish means "high hill," or "high hillside," is one of the more affluent areas in San Bernardino County. Today, most of the community is residential, with tree-lined neighborhoods, plenty of parks, and a comfortable climate. Located forty miles east of Los Angeles and 120 miles north of San Diego, this community of more than one hundred thousand provided an ideal setting for Eric to grow up in during the late 1980s and 1990s.

Steve and Debbie believed in hard work, kindness toward others, and always doing the right thing. They were members of the Lutheran faith and believed in traditional Christian values. These standards were passed down to Kathleen and Eric. While Debbie continued teaching elementary school, Steve eventually formed his own construction business. He wanted his son to do well in school so he wouldn't have to break his back to make a living. He and Debbie expected Kathleen and Eric to perform well in school and each had a list of daily household chores: cleaning the bathroom, loading the dishwasher, taking out the trash, pulling weeds, mowing the grass, and cleaning up after the family dog.

Eric was a good son and brother—very active and always on the go—except when it came time to do those chores. Then he would turn into a little escape artist and quietly disappear. He also had a Tom Sawyer talent for getting his friends to do his work. One time Debbie found Eric loaning his Nintendo to a neighbor boy. She eventually learned Eric had bribed the boy to come over and clean up after the dog in exchange for some time on the Nintendo. "He was a little businessman," she said.

When she was old enough, Kathleen was often left in charge of keeping an eye on Eric while their parents were away. Like a typical brother, he messed with her dolls and teased her in front of her friends, but he also looked out for her. One day when the two were home alone, Kathleen called her mother to say they had heard strange noises in the house. "Mom, Eric got out the shotgun to protect me—we are all right." As calmly as she could, Debbie instructed her daughter to have Eric carefully put the shotgun back where he found it. Eric obeyed. But it wasn't the last time he pulled out a gun to save his sister.

Growing up, Eric described his parents as "strict, but fair." Looking back, he understands they were trying to teach him right from wrong. When it came to punishing little household crimes, Debbie was the enforcer. On those rare occasions when Eric was in big trouble, Debbie pointed to Steve to take charge. Eric's father did what had to be done, but it pained him to physically discipline his son. After the punishment was passed, father and son embraced and tears were shed. "He made me promise to never do it again, then we would cry together," Eric said.

As a young teenager, Eric only remembers challenging his father once, which was all it took. One day, father and son were in the garage. A small disagreement arose, and Eric wouldn't let it go. He can't even remember now how the argument began. Angry words were exchanged, and Eric shoved his father. Steve's father, Norman Weddle, had been a golden-glove boxer who had sparred with Rocky Marciano when he was serving in the army. Norman taught Steve the fundamentals of boxing. In his moment of machismo, Eric wasn't thinking about his father's boxing skills. Steve, however, looked his son in the eye and smacked him in the face, knocking him back against a door. Eric wasn't hurt physically, but "humble pie" had been served. "He put me in my place. That was the last time I did that," Eric recalled.

The worst form of parental punishment, Eric said, wasn't physical. If he got into trouble at school or slacked off academically, Steve didn't have to say a word. Eric's father had a certain penetrating look of disappointment that was ten times worse than getting the belt or being popped in the face. It became Eric's mission and objective never to disappoint his parents, especially his father.

Being kind and charitable toward others was another lesson Eric learned at a young age. When Eric was in grade school, the Weddles became acquainted with an African-American family that lived a few houses away. It became evident that the father of the family was involved with serious issues, including gang activity, drugs, and alcohol. When situations escalated, the two little boys who lived there often escaped to find refuge in the Weddle home. "Dad is chasing Mom with a gun again," was, sadly, a common phrase. Steve or Debbie would call the police, and flashing lights were often seen in the family's driveway. From these experiences Eric learned to appreciate his parents and their willingness to assist others. He gained gratitude for the blessings in his life and learned what it meant to have compassion for someone in a tough situation.

The Weddles were a close-knit clan. Family unity was cultivated with home-cooked meals and wholesome recreation. Eric's fondest memories are of weeklong vacations to Baja, California, and Ensenada and Tijuana, Mexico, where the family camped on the beach, drove ATVs, and fished until they were full. Friends and family loaded into boats and reeled in everything from tuna to sea bass. The day's catch became the evening feast. When possible, Steve took Eric golfing. To this day, Bajamar, about a three-hour drive south of Alta Loma, is Eric's favorite course.

Scott Strohman, a lifelong friend of Eric, said Steve wanted his son to do well in everything he did, but more importantly he wanted him to become a good man. Eric credits his parents with helping him become the person he is today. When he was a child, they taught him the value of hard work, the importance of family, and how to help others, vital lessons he continues to apply now with his own family.

"The thing I love about my dad is he always put our family first. His priorities were never messed up. It was always about us," Eric said. "One of the biggest lessons I learned from my father is that nothing gets in the way of being a dad first. There was never a time when he had something more important. When he went golfing or fishing with his buddies, he always took me along. His redeeming qualities were his unselfishness and love for his family. I know a lot of dads who weren't that way."

Steve and Debbie raised their children in the Lutheran faith, but two things provided a convenient excuse to miss church: their pastor moved away, and Eric started playing Pop Warner football.

As Eric began to play sports, his parents labored to teach him two more essential principles that have fueled his desire to achieve success: First, don't let others tell you what you can and can't do; and second, no matter how good you think you are, there is always someone out there who is better.

# CHAPTER 2

## FEAR THE "WASHING MACHINE"

Expectations were low when coach Dennis Wolcott sent the play in from the sideline. The Rancho Cucamonga Stingrays were losing to the squad from San Dimas La Verne by three touchdowns late in the fourth quarter on a warm Sunday afternoon. The seasoned Pop Warner coach knew it would mean a great deal to his players if he allowed one of his offensive linemen, seven-year-old guard Eric Weddle, to take a few handoffs. The game's outcome was already determined, and there was only one game left in the 1991 season, so what did he have to lose? Why not let the kids have some fun? His co-head coach, Joe Avila, didn't object. So when the orange-cream-colored jerseys broke the huddle, No. 50 lined up in the backfield.

Eric inserted his mouth guard, leaned forward with his hands on his knees, and listened to the quarterback's cadence. His pulse quickened. Seconds later, the ball was snapped, players lunged forward, and pads popped. The quarterback turned and handed the ball to his new tailback. Previously untapped instincts kicked in as Weddle burst forward and made one cut through the line. He felt two defenders graze his shoulder pads and suddenly found himself alone in an open expanse of green grass. With parents and onlookers clapping and yelling, and his mom filming with the family video camera, Eric galloped down the middle of the field 65 yards and stumbled into the end zone to score the first touchdown of his young Pop Warner career. On the sideline, Wolcott was stunned. The veteran Pop Warner coach couldn't believe that the first time he gave the pigskin to Eric Weddle he took it 65 yards to the house. Wolcott's mind raced a moment while he tried to recall the reasoning for sticking Eric on the offensive line. "We were pleasantly surprised," said Wolcott, who has coached Little League for more than twenty-five years. "It was definitely a turning point." Eric's days as a lineman were over.

Having started on the offensive line, Eric learned early to appreciate the role of the players working in the trenches to open holes for their teammates. It was a lesson Wolcott continually preached to his players.

Sporting a full handlebar mustache and a ball cap, Steve Weddle beamed proudly that day in the afterglow of his son's sweet run. Eric's coaches had finally witnessed for themselves the speedy Weddle wheels in action. Steve was not the kind of parent to promote his son's talents or try to influence the team's coaches. Having already coached Eric in baseball and basketball, he knew it was just a matter of time until his Pop Warner coaches noticed Eric's abilities. It was important to Steve and Debbie that their son earn everything he received on his own merits.

Eric came from a pedigree of talented athletes. In addition to his grandfather's golden-glove boxing abilities, Eric's dad starred in football and track and field at Temple City High in the early 1970s. Steve earned the nickname "Hurricane Weddle" as a

100- and 200-meter sprinter. The five-foot-ten Weddle was also proficient in the long jump and pole vault. He won the California Interscholastic Federation (CIF) championship in the long jump his senior year and set the Temple City High School record at 24 feet, 11 inches.

Of course, Steve also played football in high school. As No. 31, he blew out his ACL during his junior year, but he recovered and returned in full force to play running back for the Rams his senior year. The shifty speedster helped Temple City High go 13–0 to win the CIF title, which turned out to be the beginning of a 56-game winning streak for the Rams. Debbie's father, Ed Robles, had also displayed remarkable ability as a multisport athlete. He played high school football in the Los Angeles area in the days of leather helmets.

With Eric playing football in the fall, basketball in the winter, and baseball in the summer, the Weddle calendar filled up fast. His sister, Kathleen, also played softball, so when necessary Steve and Debbie split up so they could support both children. Debbie wanted to be there to see the triumphs—and in the event that one of the kids was injured. Every game was covered.

Erik Avila and Scott Strohman, two of Eric's lifelong friends, said Eric excelled at sports early on because he was quicker and stronger than the other kids. He was the best athlete on the field and the fastest player on the team, and he had the strongest arm. He had "it," Wolcott said. Weddle also had an unparalleled competitive drive, even when it came to playing a game of Ping-Pong.

"He wanted to win at everything he did," Strohman said.

"If it was anything that involved athleticism, he was good at it," Erik Avila agreed.

Upon noticing Eric's talent, many people attempted to persuade Steve and Debbie to look at getting Eric on the roster of a traveling team so he could line up against older, more skilled competition. "Thanks and no thanks," Debbie always replied. "People always told us, 'He needs to play up with older kids.' We said, 'No, he can play with the kids his age. We don't have money. We are working people. He can do what he can.' I just wanted him to get an education, go to college, and get a good job. Playing in the pros was never the end goal," Debbie said.

During these youthful years, Eric also received good marks in the classroom. Ms. Marji Woodhall, his fifth-grade teacher at Deer Canyon Elementary School, knew how to connect with Eric. She helped him unlock a love of learning. He wasn't fond of math or science—watching paint dry was more interesting—but history and English stimulated his brain. Writing was his favorite assignment. In connection with the Drug Abuse Resistance Education (D.A.R.E.) program, every fifth-grader in the school was instructed to write an essay about saying no to drugs. The essays were judged, and the winner was announced in an assembly for the entire school. To his surprise, Eric's name was called.

"I never thought they would pick me," he said. "At the time I averaged Bs, but for a moment, I felt like one of those smart, elite students."

While he felt honored, Eric was also embarrassed because he didn't want to be perceived as a nerd or an egghead. He considered himself to be an athlete and sought attention through sports. Nevertheless, his parents were elated and framed the article in their home. His essay was later printed in the local newspaper, the *Inland Valley Daily Bulletin*. The headline on the article read "Drugs: The Wrong Choice":

> I promise to say no to drugs.
> First, I will promise to my mom and dad. Second, to my grandparents. Third, I will say it to my best friends. I promise

these people to say no to drugs because they care about me and I care about them.

I will keep these promises by doing the right things.

First, I will make good decisions. If I make a good decision, that means I won't get hooked on drugs or do anything bad.

Second, I will always make good friends who don't do drugs and who don't hang with gangs or anything else.

I want good friends who will trust me at all times.

Then if I need help, they would be there for me all through my life.

I promise that I will do these things, and if I do, I will have a wonderful life ahead of me. I think other families should, too!

Keeping this promise is very important to me. I want to be successful in life, but if I do drugs, I won't do anything in life, because I probably would hang out with gang bangers.

Also, if I don't do drugs, I will be able to do anything in life!

For example, in my career I want to be a football player, basketball player and baseball player.

However, if I did drugs, I wouldn't be chosen to be on the teams because they wouldn't want me because I was a druggie.

To conclude, if you want to reach your dreams in life, don't do drugs!!!

(Eric Steven Weddle is a fifth grader at Deer Canyon School)

When he was in the eighth grade, Eric learned a pivotal lesson about the importance of being a good student. During that fall, Eric slacked off in schoolwork, and his grade point average dropped below the required 2.0. The school's team was a few games into the basketball season when a letter was sent to the Weddle residence informing Steve and Debbie that Eric had been ruled ineligible and would be dismissed from the team. Eric knew that when his parents found out, he would be in big trouble, so he didn't tell them. When the letter arrived in the mailbox, Eric intercepted and disposed of it. He thought he had everything under control.

But the secret didn't last long. When his mother showed up at the next game, one of his teammates' parents approached her and expressed concern for Eric, who was officially ineligible following the day's game. Debbie was shocked and dismayed.

After the game, both Steve and Debbie waited for Eric outside the locker room with stern facial expressions.

"You got something to tell me?" Debbie said to Eric, hands on her hips.

"No," the son replied sheepishly.

"You're not going to tell me you didn't make grades? You're not going to tell me you are out for the rest of the season?" Debbie said, with an interrogative tone and piercing eyes.

The eighth-grader was silent.

Steve stood by quietly, utter disappointment written all over his face.

"His joy was working hard all day and then coming to watch me play sports," Eric recalled. "He didn't have much to say. The worst feeling was knowing I had let him down."

Lesson learned. Missing the rest of the season was difficult, but shaming his parents was far worse. The image of his disheartened parents and the overwhelming guilt has remained vivid in his memory. Eric rededicated his academic efforts and ended up pulling straight Bs by the end of the quarter. He never flirted with ineligibility again. "That was a big deal. I learned that education was important," Eric said. "It's unfortunate, but that's what had to happen for me to learn that lesson."

Mentored by coaches and fathers who taught principles of

hard work, discipline, teamwork, and sportsmanship, Weddle used his athletic gifts to dominate the competition and have fun. An injury once threatened to ruin one of Eric's many Little League seasons on the baseball diamond, but there is no such thing as a wounded Weddle. For many years he played on a team called the Mariners. He doesn't remember how it happened, but in the course of one of his games, he hurt his wrist. The pain was enough that Steve took his little slugger to the emergency room. The doctor's diagnosis was a broken wrist, and he instructed Eric to get a cast. But the idea of a cast troubled father and son. The Little League all-star game was coming up, and baseball players can't play with casts. Then football season was scheduled to begin. Steve decided this was a teaching moment in toughness.

"You sure you want a cast?" Steve asked his son.

Minutes later, the Weddles walked out of the hospital. The cast was forgotten. They obtained something a little more suitable for a baseball player. "We get this little wrist brace thinking it will do the job," Eric laughed later. The injury left him unable to pitch or throw, but nothing was more frustrating than sitting in the dugout. He focused on the one position he felt he could play with a broken wrist—catcher—and approached his coach. Soon enough he was figuring out how to put on all the gear so he could get back in the game. "That's how we were. We lived and died for sports," Eric said.

There were enough kids in the Rancho Cucamonga area in Eric's age group to have two Pop Warner teams. Dennis Wolcott and Joe Avila coached the same group of boys for six seasons; from the time Eric was age seven to age thirteen. Initially, games were played at Chaffey College and later were moved to the grassy field of Summit Junior High. After his memorable run against San Dimas, Weddle became the star of the team, and he played multiple positions. He was a virtual Swiss army knife of football skills, and he liked to hit. Popping pads was fun. Wolcott remembers Weddle during those years as a kid with big feet who was always happy and smiling. He was also the team comedian. "He had a tendency to be a little squirrelly, but he was coachable. Sometimes when I had my back turned and heard someone smacking helmets or joking around, I knew it was Eric Weddle. He was always having fun out there. Every once in a while I would have to say, 'C'mon, let's focus,' and then he would be fine."

In the seasons that followed that first epic run, Eric traded in jersey No. 50 for No. 22, after his hero, Dallas Cowboys all-pro running back Emmitt Smith. In one game, Weddle scored six touchdowns. In another game, he took the ball on a reverse and scampered 98 yards for the score. He possessed an uncanny ability to make tacklers miss, and his mother also has video footage of her son running through defenders. Erik Avila recalls one game against Rialto, when Rancho had the ball inside the 5-yard line. Eric's number was called and over the course of one long play, he made all eleven defenders miss before finally reaching the end zone and collapsing in exhaustion. "We went back and watched Debbie's game film," Avila said. "It was amazing for a kid that young. Every kid on Rialto had an attempted miss before Eric finally broke away and scored. We won the game."

Debbie still giggles a little at the memory of her son and his friends making themselves comfortable on the Weddle living room couch to review her recordings of their Pop Warner games. Each week, they broke down the film and analyzed each play as if they were in the NFL. What was perhaps most entertaining for Debbie was to see the boys grill each other for mistakes they made in the game. When blocks were missed or balls were dropped, the boys teased each other relentlessly.

Occasionally when Eric was running the ball, he would leap and spin in the air to elude an opposing player. This signature move earned Weddle the nickname, "The Washing Machine." Coach Joe Avila coined the nickname. To witness the "washing machine" in action was priceless, Erik Avila said. "It was pretty funny. Every player is coached to never leave his feet. Coach kept saying, 'You better stop that. One of these times you are going to get hit and messed up.' But he did it for a few years. Eventually he got out of the habit."

Eric now laughs about his former signature move, which he says came mostly out of instinct. Despite his coach's protests, the "washing machine" helped him spin out of several tackles in his early Pop Warner days.

Steve never forced sports, particularly football, on his son. And when it came to coaching and instruction, he left it to the coaches. What he did stress to his son during those early years of competition was that no matter how good he thought he was, there was always someone out there who was better. Eric found that to be true in his last year of Pop Warner. After coaching the same boys for six years, Dennis Wolcott and Joe Avila decided it would be good for the boys to experience being coached by someone else prior to entering a high school program. Their team was combined with the other Rancho Cucamonga bunch in their age group to form a very talented squad called the Panthers. A handful of players on that team went on to play Division I college football, including Eric and a player named Terrell Thomas, with whom he developed a friendly rivalry. But with the coaching change came a reduced role for Eric. He was relegated to backup quarterback.

"It was challenging for him," Erik Avila said. "Eric was used to being the guy who did everything for us, our whole offense, but the coach had his guys, and Eric really didn't get to play."

"Challenging" didn't quite describe it. Some kids play Pop Warner for the fun of it, some play for the postgame treat, and then there was Eric, who played for the love of competition and victory. He didn't want to watch the game from the sideline—he lived to be on the field, knocking opponents' helmets off. To go from star player to benchwarmer was more frustrating than anything Eric had previously experienced. If he had known how that season would unfold, he wouldn't have signed up to play. "It was the worst feeling ever," Eric said. "I didn't feel part of the team. I didn't want to be there. I wasn't raised to quit, but I hated being a part of it. I would rather have been on a team with less talent and played. It was a waste of time."

The main lesson Eric learned from that season was that you don't always get what you want, even though you may be better than someone else. "You have to learn to deal with rejection and people who don't believe in you," he said. "How will you deal with it? Will you let it affect you?"

Even now, that Pop Warner coach probably has no clue as to how he ignited a firestorm of motivation in Eric. "To this day I want to prove to that coach that he was a moron for not playing me. From that day forward I started keeping a mental list of people I wanted to prove wrong. What were you thinking? Why didn't you play me? I don't know if I would ever say anything to them now. If I saw them I would be respectful and cordial, but in the back of my mind I'd be saying, 'I want to rip your head off because you don't know what you are doing.' That is a side of me that doesn't come out very often, but when it does . . ."

Despite the diminished playing time, Weddle remained loyal

to his team and patiently waited for another opportunity to prove himself. In the final game of the season, Eric was inserted at quarterback and threw for 180 yards and a pair of touchdowns to lift the Panthers to victory. His performance caught the eye of some high school coaches. In the fall of 1999, Eric Weddle also made a significant decision regarding which high school he would attend. Although the reasoning behind the decision was obvious enough, he could not have known at the time that it would impact the rest of his life.

# CHAPTER 3

—

# ALTA LOMA HIGH SCHOOL

In the spring of 1999, high school was just around the corner. Some of Eric's Pop Warner teammates planned to enroll at Rancho Cucamonga High School, one of several high schools in the populated area.

The Weddles lived in the school boundaries of Etiwanda High School. Eric's sister, Kathleen, attended Etiwanda and graduated that spring. But Eric had a different plan. The soon-to-be freshman wanted to attend Alta Loma, another high school in the area, for a few reasons. Primarily, he wanted to play multiple sports. It was his impression that Etiwanda coaches encouraged their student athletes to compete in only one sport. Dedication to one sport may have meant greater individual skill development and fewer potential injuries, but Eric didn't want restrictions or limitations. There was no question he wanted to play football, basketball, *and* baseball. Moreover, Alta Loma's football team carried a long winning tradition. Etiwanda was a basketball school. Eric didn't know anyone at Alta Loma, and all but two of his friends were going to Rancho Cucamonga or Etiwanda High. Erik Avila and Scott Strohman wanted to transfer to Alta Loma. So that was it. Eric Weddle decided to take his talents to 8880 Baseline Road. In order to enroll at Alta Loma, a transfer was required. Fortunately, that wasn't complicated, and Eric's transfer request was approved without a hitch.

In playing multiple sports, Eric continued to do what he had always done. Early that summer, his schedule included playing on a baseball team in the morning and participating in freshman football workouts in the afternoon. He was living the Bo Jackson dream, perfectly content running from sport to sport, practice to practice, and game to game.

The constant activity was exhilarating for Eric, but it soon began to wear on his fifteen-year-old right arm. It wasn't uncommon for him to pitch for several innings in the morning and fire pass routes to receivers for a few hours in the afternoon. Then one day his arm reached its breaking point. After throwing six innings earlier in the day, Eric was participating in seven-on-seven drills with the Alta Loma freshman football squad. Rain drizzled that day, making the football wet and heavier than usual. As he took a snap, dropped back, and threw a deep route, he heard a pop. "The outside bone in my elbow fractured. The two bones in the joint came out. It was the worst pain of all my injuries," Eric recalled. He still winces when telling the story.

His arm was placed in a cast for the rest of the summer, followed by another month of rehabilitation. At that point, his elbow felt functional and there was still time to get ready for freshman football. His doctor cleared him to start throwing again, but on his very first toss, there was another pop. To his dismay, Eric had dislocated his elbow again. Pain and frustration boiled over into tears. "My dad was there and we were both crying," Eric said.

Not only did the injury cause Eric grief, but it also changed his relationship with his freshman football coach. The coach had planned to start Eric at quarterback; following the injury, he gave him the cold shoulder.

Eric repeated the healing and rehabilitation process. He couldn't throw the ball well, but he was given a clean bill of health to play other positions. With a late start to the season, though, Eric missed his chance to earn regular playing time. Instead of playing quarterback and defensive back, the discouraged freshman walked the sidelines in his royal blue jersey. "It was a frustrating year—knowing I could play but couldn't get on the field," Eric said. "It taught me a lot about patience, waiting for an opportunity and seizing it. It also fueled in me that desire to prove some people wrong."

The freshman Braves finished the season 7–3 and were Mount Baldy League co-champs. Eric was proud of the team and the individual successes of his friends, but frustrated that an injury had robbed him of his freshman season. He obviously disagreed with his coach for making him ride the bench. All he had to show for the year was a small certificate of participation. The hollow feeling served as motivation to prove himself as a sophomore.

He brushed the doldrums aside in time for basketball. His arm was now fully healed, and he was ready for layups, jump shots, and the squeak of basketball shoes on a wooden court.

## THE "TEAM" THEME

One important lesson Eric Weddle learned during his freshman year of high school was how to be a team player, which meant putting the team's goals and ambitions ahead of individual success and notoriety.

Ten games into the freshman basketball season, Eric averaged double figures as the starting point guard, and the Braves were winning games. The team had a solid nucleus of players and an effective rotation in place. Then one day, as the freshmen were warming up for practice, coach Rick Secrist pulled Eric aside and wanted to discuss the "Junior Denson situation."

Lionel "Junior" Denson was a five-foot-ten African-American athlete with catlike quickness and skills that could take the Braves to the next level. He lived to play basketball, but his stepfather saw the game as a distraction to his stepson's academic pursuits. So when Junior's grades were not where his stepfather thought they should be, and an isolated incident led to detention, Junior was not permitted to try out for the freshman basketball team. It appeared he would miss the season.

Guy Thomas, another coach in the Alta Loma hoops program, had coached Junior during the summer and knew his basketball potential. Junior was clearly among the top players in the freshman class. Thomas and Secrist discussed how they could get Junior on the squad. It was decided Thomas would approach Junior's stepfather and work on the problem. Eventually a meeting was arranged that included Thomas, Secrist, and Junior's stepfather. The coaches committed to make sure Junior's grades and behavior met specific expectations, the same as every other player on the team. Junior's stepfather finally agreed to allow him to play but made it very clear that if his stepson's grades dropped, he would pull him from the team. The coaches smiled.

Junior worked hard to repair the damage by doing extra chores at home, and he went the extra mile to improve his grades. But his acceptance onto the team was not a done deal just yet.

Thomas and Secrist were concerned about the team's chemistry being disrupted. The Braves had already played several games, and an effective rotation was in place. Thomas proposed the idea of having the team decide Junior's fate. The players voiced their opinions, and the vote came down to its current best player: Eric, the team captain. Eric didn't know Junior personally, but he had seen him play in the city championship and knew he was talented. After a short deliberation, he gave the thumbs-up sign. "The only thing I thought about was how good he was and how he could make us better," Eric said. "I knew he needed to be on the team."

When he was informed he had made the team, Junior gushed with gratitude. He was warmly accepted by the other players and became the starting point guard while Eric, for the good of the team, moved to shooting guard. The two became fast friends, and their chemistry carried over onto the court, where they overwhelmed opponents. Eric said they looked forward to every practice and game because they had so much fun. Winning was easy.

"With both those guys in the backcourt we were pretty much unstoppable," Secrist said.

When they weren't dominating opponents on the basketball court, Eric and Junior played one-on-one in Eric's driveway and engaged in serious video game battles. "He became my brother," Eric said.

The experience prepared Eric for baseball season because he was about to give up his preferred position again.

During spring tryouts for the ninth-grade baseball team, Eric was one of six players to audition at shortstop. Secrist, also the freshman baseball coach, recognized right away that Eric was one of the top players on the team. He was probably the best athlete of the six who auditioned and could easily win the job. The kid had a strong arm, he could run, he could field the ball well, and he could swing the bat. But there were other positions to fill. Two thoughts popped into Secrist's mind: First, given his abilities, Eric would make a great center fielder; second, of the six, Eric had the most maturity to handle the move. He pulled the freshman aside to discuss the switch.

"Are you sure?" Eric asked his coach, a little disappointed.

"I think you would be better suited there," Secrist replied.

Eric pondered this for a moment. The news was disheartening because he really wanted to play shortstop, and he knew he could prove himself. Did his coach think he wasn't good enough for the infield? Something told him that wasn't the case. But in his mind he could hear his father's voice tell him to do as his coach instructed for the sake of the team. He knew what he had to do, but that didn't mean it was easy. He looked his coach in the eye and nodded his acceptance. The issue was settled.

The position change proved to be a good one—Eric excelled in center field. He finished the season among the top hitters on the team, with a batting average of .410. In fifty-six at bats, he recorded twenty-three hits, including four doubles, one triple, three home runs, and seventeen RBIs. Coach Secrist was most impressed by Eric's willingness to put the team before himself. One day Secrist approached the varsity baseball coach to inform him Eric Weddle was the best outfielder in the whole Alta Loma baseball program.

"He laughed because at the time we had a kid named Drew Macias who was eventually drafted by the San Diego Padres," Secrist said. "Drew has had a good career in baseball, but that is how good Eric was at the time. If he had made the decision to play baseball instead of football, I have no doubt he would have been a top draft pick in the major league right now."

## SOPHOMORE REDEMPTION

Eric Weddle made good on his vow to contribute more to the football team's success as a sophomore.

Because he hardly played as a freshman, Eric started at the bottom of the junior varsity depth chart in the summer of 2000. But he was physically ready and knew his assignments. When the team participated in seven-on-seven flag football tournaments, Eric got opportunities to show his skills and performed well enough to climb from third to second-string varsity on the defensive depth chart at safety. In addition to his talent and athletic ability, coaches noticed that Eric carried himself with an air of self-assurance and swagger. They liked that.

More opportunities were presented, and the confident, five-foot-seven, 170-pound Eric Weddle capitalized on them. When the starting varsity safety struggled in another seven-on-seven passing tournament, Eric's number was called. Soon he was making plays and intercepting passes all over the field. Eric continued to impress his coaches and was named the varsity starter going into the fall.

"When he was healthy again, the varsity coaches loved him right away," commented linebacker Erik Avila, the only other sophomore to earn a varsity roster spot. "After that there was no looking back. He got better and better."

With twelve returning starters, an offensive line that averaged around 290 pounds, and two of the Inland Valley's top running backs, the Braves were a preseason favorite to win the Mount Baldy League crown.

Eric emerged as a contributing member of a defense that held opponents to fewer than 13 points per game during the regular season. He took particular pleasure in lopsided victories against his friends at Rancho Cucamonga and Etiwanda.

Under the leadership of head coach Tom Mitchell, Alta Loma posted a 9–3 record, including 5–0 in Mount Baldy League play. In the opening round of the state playoffs, the Braves had a 3-touchdown lead on West Covina High, and Mitchell felt generous. Eric had played a great defensive game, and Mitchell wanted to see if No. 22 could run the football. Just like his first carry in Pop Warner, Eric took his first handoff and scampered 22 yards for the score, sealing a 48–28 victory. Considering how far he had come in a year, it was a surreal moment for Eric. "I got thrown in there and made the most of it," Eric explained. "We had so many great players, guys with Division I talent who were so much bigger than me. I couldn't believe I was playing with all these huge guys. It was crazy to think about. My coaches showed a lot of confidence in me."

With the victory, Alta Loma advanced to play Upland High in the Division II quarterfinals. The Highlanders had defeated the Braves 28–10 earlier in the season, but ALHS was ready for revenge.

Alta Loma trailed by a point in the fourth quarter, when the Braves forced the Highlanders to punt. Eric had been returning punts all game, but at the last second, senior teammate Eric Wilson trotted onto the field in his place. Much to the dismay of the faithful Alta Loma fans, Wilson muffed the punt and an Upland player recovered the football. The turnover turned out to be the critical play in the game. Minutes later, the Highlanders scored and went on to win the game 28–20 and end the season for the Braves. Eric Weddle was named to the all-league defensive team and couldn't wait for his junior season.

## ONE SHINING MOMENT

The junior varsity basketball season jumped off to a fast start with the backcourt tandem of Eric Weddle and Junior Denson picking up where they left off as freshman. Eric said Junior was the Kobe Bryant of the team and started the year scoring more than 20 points a game. Eric was a reliable second option. He averaged around 15 points per contest. "It wasn't fair [for our opponents] because we understood each other so well—we were killing everybody," Junior said.

Apparently the duo was too good. Early in the season, Denson was called up to play with the varsity squad. Eric missed his buddy, but he continued to play well throughout the season, helping his team finish third in league play. At the end of the season, he was invited to join Denson on the varsity squad for the state playoffs.

To begin the playoffs, Alta Loma hosted a Division I-AAA wildcard game against the Esperanza High Aztecs. Both teams played hard, and the score was tight in the fourth quarter. The coach looked down his bench and gestured for Weddle to go in the game. The move surprised Rick Secrist, one of the assistants. Secrist didn't doubt Weddle's abilities, but it didn't seem like the right time to give the sophomore his first significant varsity action.

But once again, Eric was ready. He made an immediate impact as he hit some clutch shots to keep the Braves in the game. With five seconds to go, Alta Loma was down 3 points, and a time-out was called. In the huddle, Thomas drew up a play for Weddle to run his defender through some picks along the baseline and catch the ball in the corner to take the 3-pointer and send the game into overtime. Once again, Secrist was amazed to see Thomas putting the game in the hands of a sophomore that had spent the year with the junior varsity team. "Coach, are you crazy?" Secrist said. "You pull him cold off the bench and expect him to hit the game-winning shot?"

The referee handed the ball to the Alta Loma player, and the pivotal play was set in motion. Fans in the high school gym held their collective breath as the Aztecs hustled to defend the Braves and prevent a final 3-point shot. The play was well executed. Eric ran along the baseline and found himself covered, but his teammate passed the ball anyway. Somehow the pass reached Eric. He caught it as the clock ticked down. With three defenders crowding him, Eric created some separation with a crossover dribble, stepped back, and launched a fade-away three from the corner. The horn sounded as the ball hit nothing but net. The Alta Loma crowd exploded into a state of hysteria.

Junior was the first teammate to hug Eric. Moments earlier Denson had missed two free throws, and Eric's triple bailed Junior out of the depression of knowing he had blown the game. "He saved me. I was upset. Hitting that 3 erased the deficit and gave us a clean slate. It kind of represents our friendship. Regardless of the situation, I know he has my back," Denson said.

Sadly, however, the Braves lost in overtime, 76–74. Junior finished with 16 points and 6 assists, while Eric added 11 in his varsity debut. The team finished the year with a 12–15 record.

For Eric, the buzzer-beating 3-pointer was the highlight of his Alta Loma basketball career. He played varsity his junior and senior years, but nothing was more memorable than hitting that shot in his first varsity game. "It was a cool moment," he said. "I was honored the coach put the game in my hands."

Brian Brown, another member of the Alta Loma High School basketball staff, said Weddle always had a special aura and maturity about him, and he always achieved his goals. Brown said

Weddle always joined the basketball team late after football season, and he was always banged up. "I knew he wouldn't be a complete basketball player through the whole season," Brown said. "But I also knew I could trust him in any game situation, because no matter how much his leg was hurting or his elbow was killing him, he would be diving on the floor, going for the ball, doing whatever it took."

## A BREAK FROM BASEBALL

Eric Weddle loved football, but baseball was the sport he excelled at the most. When Eric established himself as a standout center fielder, freshman baseball coach Rick Secrist imagined Eric would be invited to play varsity as a sophomore. But it didn't happen.

Toward the end of basketball season, the varsity baseball coach began pressuring Eric to start practicing with the baseball team, but Eric declined. Basketball playoffs were around the corner, and he was dedicated to finishing the year. Eric committed to show up for baseball as soon as the Braves either won the state championship or were eliminated from the playoffs. But the baseball coach persisted in pestering Weddle, hinting that if he didn't join practice before the end of basketball season, he wouldn't have a shot at playing varsity.

Eric tired of this and found it ironic that, at the school he had chosen because of the supposed flexibility given to multisport athletes, the coach was now forcing him to make a choice. In a bold move, he notified the coach he wouldn't be playing baseball that year. Little did he realize his decision to miss baseball season would open a new door and ultimately affect his long-term future.

# THE GIRL WITH LONG, CURLY HAIR

One Friday in the spring of 2001, near the end of Eric's sophomore year, he and a group of his friends decided to go to a movie. Eric's friend Erik Avila was interested in a girl on the soccer team named Natalie. The rumor was that she liked him, too. So Weddle, Avila, and a group of guys and girls gathered at the home of a mutual friend before departing for a night of flirting and fun.

As people arrived and the group prepared to leave, Eric noticed an attractive girl talking to one of his friends. She had long, curly hair, just the way he liked it, and she was wearing a long-sleeved shirt with a zip-up vest. He would have sworn that she glowed. There was something different about her, but he couldn't put his finger on it. Eric was not afraid to talk to girls, yet he couldn't force his feet to move in her direction and could only admire her from a distance.

When the party moved to the movie theater, Eric sat between two other girls, a short distance from this dark-haired beauty. He had decided it was best to observe her for a while. He was a guy who liked the chase, and he would eventually talk with her when the opportunity presented itself.

That opportunity came the following week as he was walking down the stairs outside Alta Loma High School. He was surprised when the same girl came up and gave him a playful hug.

"Hey, remember me from the movies?" she asked with a big smile.

She still had the glow. Her name was Chanel Blaquiere, and from that moment they hit it off. In the weeks that followed, they became great friends. In an effort to learn about her, he sought information from friends and acquaintances around the school. What he learned impressed him. Chanel was a junior and a straight-A student. As a freshman, sophomore, and junior, she had lettered in cross-country, track and field, and soccer. She was involved in student government. Needless to say, several universities were interested in offering her athletic and academic scholarships. She was also widely respected by her peers. In addition to being attractive, Chanel was described as friendly, fun, outgoing, intelligent, and modest. To summarize, "she was 'all that,' the cream of the crop," Eric said. "She knew what she wanted and had direction. It was something different and refreshing. She intrigued me. She was someone I wanted to get to know."

The two developed a friendship over that spring and, though Chanel enjoyed Eric's company, she did not share his romantic attraction right away. Chanel found Eric handsome and fun to be with, but it frustrated her to see him flirt with her friends. He was fond of socializing with several girls at the same time, and Chanel found his sporadic attention and inability to focus more exclusively on her to be aggravating.

"He was really immature," she said.

"She will tell you I was very immature. I probably was," Eric said with a grin.

When the school year ended and the summer months began, Eric didn't have a car and cell phones weren't accessible yet, so he and Chanel became involved in other activities with different friends and didn't see each other for a while. Despite this temporary hiatus, the foundation of a friendship that would develop into something very meaningful in the years to come was already in place.

# CHAPTER 4

———

# THE GIRL, THE SEASON, AND THE FASTBALL

When Alta Loma High opened its doors the next fall, Eric was thrilled for two reasons—it meant he would be playing football and seeing Chanel, the most amazing girl in the school. But to his dismay, the feeling was not mutual with Chanel. When he noticed her in the hallways between classes he would make an effort to say hello, only to be ignored.

Why so cold? Chanel still didn't appreciate Eric's flirty nature, especially with her friends. She knew he had kissed a few girls over the summer, and she just couldn't like a guy who was so casual with other girls. "It was really frustrating," Chanel explained. "He always tried to talk to me, but I didn't want to give him the time of day."

"She didn't want any part of me. She had moved on," Eric said. "I like to give hugs. I like to talk to people. And I didn't change that."

He continued to be friendly to Chanel despite her cold shoulder. Then the ice around Chanel's heart suddenly began to melt.

One day she felt guilty and wrote him a letter. "Sorry I have been so rude to you," she penned. "Hopefully we can be friends and start to talk again. Let's start over."

Their mutual admiration began to blossom at the homecoming dance in the fall of 2001—while they were on dates with other people. That night they were part of a large group, and everyone was having a good time. As the night progressed, Chanel noticed that her date, a good friend, was paying more attention to his ex-girlfriend than to her. She began interacting more with Eric, whose date was also socializing with others. Eventually Eric and Chanel were together on the dance floor, and they preferred it that way.

Eric started going over to Chanel's house or talking with her for hours on the phone late into the night. "She would fall asleep, and that's when I would hang up," Eric said. "We loved being around each other, talking, cuddling, watching each other's games. I sort of became her stress outlet from her other extracurricular activities."

Seeing the writing on the wall, Chanel decided it was time to set some rules. If they were going to date, he had to halt the flirting with other girls and show some restraint. He wondered if he could do that, then decided he had no choice if he wanted Chanel to be his girlfriend. She also informed him there would be no serious physical intimacy because she was waiting until she was married. She wanted to marry a member of her church, The Church of Jesus Christ of Latter-day Saints, in a Latter-day Saint temple. Once again, Eric was impressed. He respected her standards and her determination to live them.

Chanel met Eric's parents one Friday night at an Alta Loma football game. Someone introduced Chanel to Steve and Debbie Weddle as Eric's girlfriend. They were pleasantly surprised. They had no idea Eric even had a girlfriend. Steve noticed Chanel was wearing her letterman jacket and said if she was Eric's girlfriend, why not wear his jacket?

"No, thanks," she replied. "I will wear my own. It has more letters and patches."

To understand Chanel, it helps to know her background in The Church of Jesus Christ of Latter-day Saints. She was raised in a home where her father, Ron, was a non-practicing Catholic, and her mother, Sonya, was a Mormon. She attended the local LDS Church with her mother and two brothers. Though not personally interested in joining the Church, Ron respected the LDS faith, appreciated its history, and supported his family's participation so much that his family still refers to him as "an honorary Mormon."

As much as she loved her father, it pained Chanel that he didn't hold the priesthood. In The Church of Jesus Christ of Latter-day Saints, the father is expected to be a leader and an example in living the tenets of the Church. Fathers in the Church are typically asked to accept responsibilities in the local congregation, fill leadership positions, or perform ordinances such as baptism. It is also common for fathers who are ordained to the priesthood to give family members personal blessings of comfort and inspiration. Chanel did not think any less of her father for his religious leanings but wished he could have baptized her or given her a father's blessing. "I decided I wanted that for my kids and family. That was the backbone. I wanted my kids to have the dad I never had as far as the Church goes," Chanel said. "My dad was awesome, and he liked what the Church stood for, but he couldn't provide very much spiritually."

Members of the LDS faith believe in keeping their bodies healthy. One of the ways they protect their bodies is by not participating in premarital sex. They also avoid tobacco in any form, alcohol, illegal drugs, and even coffee or tea.

Chanel despised alcohol. When she was young, she knew and looked up to a single mother in their congregation named Diane Kimball, who had two sons. A drunk driver had killed Diane's husband before he was 30 years old. Because the Kimballs and the Blaquieres lived near each other, the children and the families participated in fun activities together. Diane didn't have a daughter, so she took an interest in Chanel, and Chanel treated Diane like a second mom. Diane's strength and ability to carry on amid difficult times left a lasting impression on Chanel. Because of someone else's careless choices, Diane didn't have a husband, and she associated alcohol with death, tragedy, and grief. Diane's example also motivated Chanel to want a Latter-day Saint temple marriage. The temple is considered the most sacred of buildings, and the Church teaches that couples that marry in the temple have the opportunity to maintain their marriage and relationships with their spouse and children for eternity.

"She wanted to marry a returned missionary, a strong priesthood holder, so she didn't have to be 'the strong one,'" said Sonya, Chanel's mother. "It was really important to her to marry a husband who could take her to the temple and who would go to church."

Chanel invited Eric to attend Latter-day Saint Church services with her family once or twice, and he was intrigued. She liked Eric, but she was careful not to push her religion on him. If he had questions, she answered them but didn't force anything on him. Eric liked the atmosphere and feeling at the LDS worship services, but he wasn't really interested in learning more at that point.

Sonya Blaquiere worked as an instructional aide at Alta Loma High and knew of Eric Weddle's reputation. "All the girls in school wanted to be with him, and all the guys wanted to be him. He had a big head," she said. "When I came home one day and found him at our house, I thought, 'Uh-oh.' I knew he wasn't a member of the Church, and that worried me a little because I had dated outside the Church. I thought, 'Of all the people she could date, why him?'"

One day at school, a coach at the school named Donald Martin approached Sonya and asked if she knew her daughter was dating Eric Weddle. She indicated she knew. The coach informed her he had spoken to Eric and reminded him that Chanel had high standards, was a top student, and that Eric needed to treat her right or he would answer to him. Before he left, the coach added one more thing. "But if they do get married," Sonya remembered him saying, "the school wants their firstborn."

It didn't take Eric very long to win Chanel's parents over. Ron and Sonya were impressed with how Eric's parents kept him on a tight leash. Sonya said Eric was always very polite, and he idolized Chanel.

While spending time with Eric was becoming important, it was not Chanel's top priority. In addition to earning top marks in the classroom, she was the senior class president and always had a flurry of activities to plan and carry out. Chanel continued to excel in running and soccer into her senior year. She started running as a freshman because she saw some friends doing it and decided she would give it a try. Before long she was the top runner in the school. During track season, she set school records in the 400-meter, the 800-meter and the 4-x-400-meter relay. Following her junior year, she had several scholarship offers to run track and cross-country. Her running performance and good grades attracted even some Ivy League programs. But she was never interested in the prospect of college track or cross-country. After her teammates had finished their workouts, her coaches pushed her to do more, but she didn't share their passion for the sport. "It began to be annoying. I didn't like the pressure they were putting on me," she said. "But I wish now I had looked at it a little differently, because I feel like I let my coaches down. They put a lot of time and effort into helping me, although it burned me out."

Chanel began tossing all the running recruiting mail into a drawer and focused on soccer, playing the striker and wearing jersey No. 8. She attended camps at Brigham Young University and considered playing there, but "it didn't feel right." She was offered a recruiting trip to Utah State University and liked the college-town atmosphere of Logan. When she was offered a scholarship by USU coach Jen Kennedy Croft, Chanel countered with another offer. "She [Coach Croft] was married to assistant USU track coach Stan Croft. I said I will come play for you only if you don't tell your husband I ran track," Chanel said. The coach accepted the deal.

Chanel and Eric dated through the rest of her senior year, attending prom and other dances, then broke up as Chanel made preparations to depart for Utah State. Considering the long distance between them and the different directions their lives would take, parting ways seemed to be the best thing to do, although it wasn't easy. Chanel had discussed their relationship with her bishop—her spiritual advisor and the leader of the local Latter-day Saint congregation. He had asked her if she could see herself marrying him, and she said no.

"Then what is the point of being with him?" the bishop asked.

"It was true," Chanel said. "I liked him, and we had grown close during my senior year, but I was going away to school, and I didn't want to be one of those girlfriends who said, 'You can't date other girls.' I wanted him to have his senior year, go to dances, and not worry about a long-distance relationship. And I wanted to date at USU as well. It didn't mean we couldn't still be friends."

Eric knew this day would come but did not realize how hard it was going to be to see her leave. Chanel was his first serious girlfriend, and, despite their youthful ages, he knew he loved her. He also respected her right to go off to college, play soccer, and pursue her education. What drove a dagger into his heart, however, was the fact that she didn't consider him a candidate for marriage. "Knowing we couldn't be together at that point was tough. I couldn't fulfill her needs, and that hurt," Eric said. "She knew what she wanted, and that was one of the reasons I liked her. She had willpower and knew what she wanted out of life. She was everything I wanted in a woman."

Eric was invited to travel with Chanel and her family to Utah State to get her settled, and then Eric and Chanel's brother were taken to Salt Lake City and sent home on an airplane so the Blaquiere parents could visit relatives. The trip was filled with mixed emotions for Eric. He was happy for her new opportunities, but he also noticed the number of guys turning their heads when Chanel walked by, and he wondered if he would ever see her again. He realized that when he returned to Alta Loma he wouldn't have anyone to confide his secrets in or go to the movies with. He did his best to be happy for her.

In spite of all the teenage drama, Sonya Blaquiere didn't believe Eric and Chanel were that serious. Her opinion changed when she saw them exchange an emotional farewell at the airport. "Chanel cried for three days, and I realized it was more serious than I could have imagined," Sonya said. "But she was very stubborn, and, as much as she loved him, she wouldn't lower her standards for him."

Chanel was one of three people who really influenced Eric's junior year of high school. The second person to make an impact was the quarterback of the Alta Loma football team.

## THE QUARTERBACK AND HIS CAMARO

Expectations were sky high as coach Tom Mitchell reloaded at the skill positions in preparation for another run at the Mount Baldy League title.

Among the incoming talent was Ryan Stickler, a six-foot-three, 215-pound quarterback with a rocket right arm. As a junior at Rancho Cucamonga High, Stickler suffered a fractured collarbone during the second game of the year. He attempted to come back in the eighth game of the year against Alta Loma but reinjured his collarbone seven plays into the contest, ending his season. The following semester he transferred to Alta Loma.

Eric Weddle and Stickler's little sister were friends. They had met when Eric was in eighth grade. Eric and Ryan had played a game of pickup basketball in Eric's driveway, and Eric had been king of the court. When Eric learned that Ryan had transferred to Alta Loma, he was thrilled because he knew Ryan was a good athlete. He was about to find out how good.

For the third time in his high school career, Eric was asked to switch positions for the good of the team. Going into his junior season, he was slotted to play running back. Upon news of Stickler's transfer, Coach Mitchell approached Eric with another idea. He said the team had three other good running backs but no wide receivers. He asked if Eric would make the switch, for the good of the team. "Just move me," Eric said. From that point on, Weddle and Stickler began attending weekly summer passing and quarterback camps, including one camp run by "quarterback guru" and Mission Viejo coach Bob Johnson. Johnson's son, Rob, played quarterback for six NFL teams over eleven years. "We went every week with all the Orange County kids, and we became the best tandem. They saw us at all the flag football tournaments, and we were lighting them up," Eric said. "They tried to get me to transfer." The Braves eventually matched up with the Diablos in the state playoffs a few months later, and Eric had his best game of the season.

The chemistry between quarterback and receiver was unmistakable. Over the next few months, Eric and Ryan became inseparable. They ran passing routes and worked out on weekends that other players took off. "When you hang out with someone, you develop a connection," Eric said. "We threw so much in the off-season that I knew what he was doing and he knew what I was doing."

"We developed a relationship of trust, and Eric was one of the best athletes in the area," Stickler said. "We knew we had a good time, and when we rolled into the fall, expectations were extremely high."

Preseason newspaper reports touted the Braves' bruising offensive line, which included six-foot-eight, 305-pound tackle John Parada and six-foot-three, 280-pound guard Blake Bonnet, both major college prospects. The team also returned nine defensive starters, including Eric's buddy, linebacker Erik Avila. In addition to his wide receiver duties, Eric anchored the defensive secondary at safety.

The Braves ripped open the season with eight straight victories and were truly challenged only in the fifth game by the Upland High Highlanders. Alta Loma won 19–14, thanks to a herculean defensive effort. Eric and teammate Josh Smith were part of a critical goal line stand late in the fourth quarter. The two combined to throw the Upland ball carrier for a 2-yard loss on fourth-and-goal at the 2-yard line. An Alta Loma interception in the final minute sealed the victory.

The streak ended with a heartbreaking 24–21 loss to the Cougars of Rancho Cucamonga. After trailing 21–7 at the half, the Braves fought back to tie their crosstown rivals in the fourth, only to lose on a last-minute 37-yard field goal by kicker Jeffrey Essig from the left hash mark. Stickler was solid against his former school, going 14-for-19 for 136 yards, with one touchdown and one interception. Eric played both ways in the game but caught only one pass for 16 yards.

In the eight games leading up to the loss to Rancho Cucamonga, Eric became Ryan's go-to target. Despite missing the third game with a minor ankle injury, Stickler was 69-for-114 for 1,278 yards, with 9 touchdowns and 4 interceptions. Eric was third in the league with 37 receptions for 694 yards and 6 touchdowns. His best game to that point came in a 35–14 win over Paramount. Eric scored 3 touchdowns and recorded 136 yards receiving, including a 78-yard touchdown catch. Stickler admits he merely had to throw the pigskin in the direction of No. 22, and Eric did the rest. "Eric was my highlight tape. I didn't go to college without him being the kind of athlete he is," Stickler said.

Defensively, Eric was always in position to intercept or knock down a pass. He relished the opportunity to blitz the opposing quarterback. In the special teams department, Eric had a talent for returning punts. Against Montclair, he juked a defender, broke a tackle, and sliced his way 67 yards to the house in a 21–0 defeat of the Cavaliers.

Eric and Ryan attributed most of their success during the 2001 football season to their teammates and hard work in the summer, but there was another reason. Following games on Friday nights, when most kids preferred to find a party, receiver and quarterback retired to the Weddle home where they watched film of that evening's game. "We critiqued each other's performances," Stickler said. "I would throw a ball, and he would complain, in a joking manner, that I threw a bad pass. We watched until past midnight, then I slept over. We did it for every game."

Over a breakfast of doughnuts the next morning, the guys would look to see what the local newspapers were saying about the game. Then they'd watch game film a second time with the team. Because they knew what was coming, they continued to jaw back and forth at each other's mistakes.

When the duo needed a break from football, they escaped to the open road in a black 1997 Z28 Camaro that belonged to Ryan's brother. With some modifications, performance enhancers, and a loud engine, it was almost too much car for a couple of southern California teenagers. "The stereo had to be loud or you couldn't hear the music," Stickler said. They had many adventures in that car. From time to time, Ryan and Eric loaded into the Camaro and tested its power on the open roads. The gas meter was faulty, so they could never tell exactly how much gas was in the tank, and one time the hot rod ran out of gas near a rough part of town in Ontario. Ryan started walking for gas, and Eric stayed with the car. While Ryan looked for a way to get some fuel, a stranger stopped and assisted Eric in filling the tank—even gave him an ice-cold Coke. A short time later, Eric pulled up next to his bewildered friend and picked him up. "It was the last place I expected a stranger to help us," Stickler said.

On another Friday night, the two were driving home late after a game. They were driving a little on the fast side but not outright speeding when Stickler noticed flashing lights behind them. A policeman pulled them over, inspected the car, and made sure the boys weren't drinking alcohol. He interrogated the pair, demanding to know where they had been and where they were headed. He called for backup, and another policeman arrived at the scene.

Eric and Ryan had just played a game. They were tired and planned to watch the film and crash at the Weddles' house as was their tradition. "Just trying to get home," said a nervous Stickler as the policeman shone a flashlight in his face.

The patrolman didn't buy it. He pulled the two young men out and sat them on the curb. Stickler knew he had done nothing wrong, yet he was sweating bullets and trying to figure out how he would explain a ticket to his father. The policemen continued to inspect the car for anything they could find, but there was no evidence of booze or drugs. The boys were clean. After fifteen more minutes of searching, the patrolmen had no choice but to release them. Stickler was careful not to spin the tires as he pulled away.

But, oh, how they loved to peel out in that Camaro. On another occasion, Stickler did just that, and a patrolman on a motorcycle appeared in the rearview mirror. Moments later, the boys were parked on the side of the road again. Stickler explained that they were coming home from football practice, and he planned to drop Eric off at his house. Eventually, Stickler did receive a speeding ticket, and for a time his driving privileges were suspended. "That car got us in so much trouble. We had a good time, but we were young and dumb in that car," Stickler said. "It was too fast. We shouldn't have been driving it, but we loved speed."

Life was good for the Braves until late October when Alta Loma was rocked by an announcement that it would be forced to forfeit its five nonleague games. The school had lost an appeal in the eligibility case of a player who was behind on credits and was not on track to graduate. The Braves had won those games by a combined score of 126–31. In terms of football, the forfeitures dropped the Braves—then ranked by the *Los Angeles Times* as number two in the Inland Valley and number twenty in southern California—from 7–0 to 2–5.

Alta Loma rebounded with a 42–8 thrashing of Chaffey. Eric caught 6 passes for 105 yards and 2 touchdowns.

Then the Braves lost to intercity rival Rancho Cucamonga on a 37-yard field goal by kicker Jeffrey Essig in the final two minutes. The Cougars had three future NFL players: Gerald Alexander (Carolina Panthers), Terrell Thomas (New York Giants) and Patrick Chung (New England Patriots). The upsetting loss meant the Braves had to share the league title with their rivals, a team they had previously defeated five straight times.

Despite the loss, Alta Loma still had a state title to play for, and they rebounded with a 42–12 victory over Ontario in the final game of the regular season. In the first game of the CIF playoffs, the Braves whipped Warren 33–6. They followed that victory up with a tight 41–40 squeaker over Ayala High to earn the right to play top-seeded Mission Viejo.

But the CIF Division II semifinals were as far as the Braves would go in 2001. Injuries on the offensive line, combined with near perfect play by the opposing Diablos, resulted in a 41–0 season-ending loss. One newspaper reported the game as a "wholesale crushing." For good measure, Mission Viejo knocked Stickler out with an apparent concussion in the third quarter. "They straight-up overmatched us in every single facet of the game," Eric told one reporter. "We've never seen a defensive line with that kind of speed before. I mean, we've been behind before . . . but they just kept stuffing us."

Eric was the lone positive for Alta Loma as he hauled in 6 catches for 135 yards. He finished the season with 53 receptions for 1,010 yards and 10 touchdowns, averaging 19.1 yards per catch. He also made numerous plays on the defensive side of the ball. He was selected as the Mount Baldy offensive MVP and was named to the all-Inland Valley and CIF football teams.

Stickler finished with more than 1,650 yards passing and 18 touchdowns in an offense that didn't throw the ball very much, perhaps as many as thirty times a game, Stickler estimated. The tall gunslinger also earned several postseason accolades. He was offered scholarships to play at Idaho State, Utah State, and Hawaii. Stickler opted for football in the islands, largely because of the weather, although his college career as a Hawaii Warrior really didn't turn out the way he hoped. He played behind Timmy Chang and was part of a complicated offense. Then a shoulder injury basically ended his career in 2005. Going into his second year, following Eric's senior year at Alta Loma, Ryan tried to convince June Jones to recruit Eric to Hawaii, but the coach offered his one receiver spot to a kid from Mississippi. To the coach's dismay, the player quit three weeks into camp. "Oh my gosh, they had a chance to get one of the best players I have ever seen, and they went in a different direction," Stickler said. "But it turned out to be a blessing for him that he didn't get recruited by Hawaii."

Eric was flooded by mail following his junior season. Schools from the PAC-10, Big 12, and other western regional schools wanted to know more about the all-Inland Valley playmaker. He even received an envelope from Notre Dame. Steve Weddle preserved every letter in a large black garbage bag. Utah assistant coach Kyle Whittingham supervised recruiting in the area and was impressed with Eric but figured he would eventually be snatched up by one of the PAC-10 programs. But there were no offers. Across town at Rancho Cucamonga High, Eric's friend and rival, Terrell Thomas, was offered a scholarship and verbally committed to USC. Thomas, who Eric played with his last year in Pop Warner, was a flashier player, but by the end of their senior year, many argued that Eric was equally talented, if not better.

Transferring to Alta Loma was one of the best decisions Stickler ever made. Not only did he find the team atmosphere more inviting, but he relished his friendship with Eric. "That season was actually one of the best times of my life," Stickler said. "I had a great time. It was pure fun. We were two kids doing what we liked to do, winning games and being successful. It was a great time." Eric also relished their friendship and attributes Stickler as being one of the most influential people he knew in high school.

## A FASTBALL IN THE FACE

Following his exceptional junior season in football, Eric played varsity basketball through the winter and decided to give baseball another try in the spring of 2002. His freshman basketball and baseball coach, Rick Secrist, was now the varsity baseball coach, and he believed Eric was a prospective high-draft pick with a bright future in baseball. Even Eric admits he was better at baseball at that time, and pro scouts agreed.

Because Eric hadn't played baseball his sophomore year, Secrist irritated some parents by naming the junior his starting varsity center fielder. "He was a five-tool player," Secrist explained. He had speed, he could hit for both average and power, he could field the ball, and he had a cannon for an arm. Secrist also admired Eric's energy, intensity, competitiveness, and overall air of confidence. Most important to Secrist, Eric was a coach's player. In nearly two decades of coaching football, basketball, and baseball at the high school and collegiate levels, Secrist has had the opportunity to coach many great athletes, and Eric remains one of his favorites. "Coaching players like him made the job worthwhile," Secrist said.

It's easy, then, to understand the coach's disappointment when Eric's season and career in baseball ended before it had barely begun.

A tradition of trash-talking usually accompanied games between A.B. Miller High and Alta Loma. Prior to one Saturday doubleheader, Coach Secrist warned his players of potential trouble and discouraged retaliation. "I told them that this is one of their tactics to make us lose our poise," Secrist explained. The season was only one game old, and the new coach was trying to establish a reputation of sportsmanship and doing things the right way, although the next several hours proved to be anything but honorable.

It began when the Rebels' starting pitcher breached baseball etiquette and warmed up on the pitcher's mound instead of in the bullpen. "I had never seen this before and thought it very arrogant on their part," Secrist said.

When Secrist and A.B. Miller coach Frank Martinez exchanged lineup cards at home plate with the umpires, Secrist expressed his displeasure with the pitching warm-up. Harsh words quickly developed into a heated discussion, and the umpires were forced to intervene.

In the top of the first inning, Braves starter Phil Yanchura was ahead 0–2 in the count when his third pitch was up and inside, almost hitting the A.B. Miller batter.

"Great 0–2 pitch, Phil," said Alta Loma pitching coach Bobby Sheridan. Secrist's theory for what eventually happened stems from Sheridan's comment being misinterpreted by the

Rebels first base coach as an attempt to bean the batter in retaliation for their pitcher warming up on the mound. He insists it was not.

When Eric Weddle strutted to the mound to lead off for the home team in the bottom of the first, he had no idea the A.B. Miller pitcher might be gunning for him. As the first pitch was fired, Eric eyed the white sphere's rotation and expected it to curve. It did not. Instead, the high fastball sailed straight into his face, smashing against his left eye. There was a collective gasp from the small crowd as Eric went down and then staggered to his feet. Players froze. Eric tried to make his way to first base, believing he could tough it out. While the rest of the team showed restraint by staying in the dugout, Coach Secrist and trainer Mike Elert rushed to attend to the injured player. The swelling to Eric's face came on quickly, and ice was applied. Within minutes, Eric was on his way to the Kaiser Permanente Medical Center emergency room in nearby Fontana.

There was no doubt in Secrist's mind that what the pitcher did was intentional. As he escorted Eric to the dugout, he shouted to Martinez, "Great job, Coach." The opposing coach simply gazed at the ground.

The doctor who examined Eric reported a fractured eye socket, with damage to his lower orbital and cheekbone. His eyeball was pushed back a half inch into his skull, and his eye was swollen shut, colored red and purple. As horrible as it looked, the doctor said Eric was lucky. "An inch to the left or the right and I could have been blind," Eric said. The injury required a month or so to heal.

Back at the first game of the doubleheader, emotions got the best of both teams. When the A.B. Miller pitcher who had hit Eric came up to bat, Alta Loma sophomore Vinnie Grau was seeing his first varsity action on the pitcher's mound. The coach made the signal to hit the batter, but Grau missed the signal and tossed one right down the middle for a strike. His coaches began yelling to get his attention, and the sophomore wondered why they were upset with his strike. Then he figured it out—and anybody who was closely observing the game knew what was coming next. Sure enough, Grau hurled a hard fastball that landed squarely in the middle of the batter's back. The poor kid jumped around in pain. Once again, the teams showed restraint by remaining in the dugouts. The batter trotted to first base as Secrist and Martinez eyed one another and smiled. Things were even. "Unfortunately, they got Eric a lot worse than we got their guy," Secrist said later.

The rest of the first game and the second game were played without incident, although the Braves lost another starting outfielder when he sprained his ankle while running the bases. Secrist visited both players in the hospital after the game.

Eric returned to the lineup by the end of the season, but he was not the same player. His defensive skills were still solid, but mentally, the fastball was still flying toward his face, and he struggled to stay in the batter's box. "I went from being one of the best players, batting .550, to not being able to do it mentally, hitting .200. I thought I was mentally tough," Eric said with disappointment, "but I couldn't hit the ball. I couldn't understand the fear. I worked on it but just couldn't overcome it. I finished out the season, but I quit playing. I've always been able to overcome things, and to this day it still bugs me that I couldn't overcome a ball to the face. But I think things worked out for the best."

His coach patiently worked with his young star but to no avail. "It was a sad day when he moved on," Secrist said. "Obviously, as a baseball coach you are a little possessive. With him making the decision not to play baseball, we were losing a great player who was instrumental in the success of our program overall. It was players like Eric that I was building a proper foundation for our program around, and it would have been nice to have him around for two years. But I wanted to be supportive, and I knew football was the sport for him."

Looking back, the fastball to the face was a destiny-defining event for Eric. He reflected on how things might have gone. "If that pitch doesn't happen," Eric said, "I probably finish out playing baseball, probably end up getting drafted or playing baseball in college, don't end up going to Utah, maybe I don't join the LDS Church, and maybe I don't see Chanel again, although I would like to think some of those things would still come to pass. It's crazy to consider how different life might be if that doesn't happen. It's crazy to think about how it changed the course of my life."

Walking away from baseball was difficult, but Eric had no regrets. He looked forward to making the most of his senior year in football. He wanted a scholarship and a chance to play on a big stage. Achieving those goals would require everything he could give.

# CHAPTER 5

━━━◢

# A SENIOR'S JOURNEY

**W**hile Eric Weddle's left eye was healing, something significant transpired in the Alta Loma High School athletic department. Tom Mitchell resigned as the Braves head football coach in order to pursue an administrative position. To fill the vacancy, the school hired John Kusleika.

A color photo in the September 6, 2002, edition of the *Inland Valley Daily Bulletin* shows the broad-shouldered Kusleika participating in a drill with players during a fall practice. With his shaved dome and goatee, the charismatic coach is a little reminiscent of professional wrestler "Stone Cold" Steve Austin. Kusleika's coaching experience included strength and conditioning work for a season at the University of Connecticut and a graduate assistant position at Fresno State. He came to Alta Loma from nearby Montclair High School, where he struggled to turn the Cavaliers into winners. His record over three years at Montclair was 6–24. When Alta Loma played Montclair in 2001—Eric's junior year—the Braves whipped the Cavaliers in a 42–0 blowout.

Eric returned a punt 67 yards for a touchdown in the lopsided conquest. The offer to come to a higher profile program like Alta Loma was a promising opportunity Kusleika could not pass up.

Once he arrived, however, Kusleika's transition to Alta Loma was rocky. The new coach was greeted with the news that three players were transferring to Upland High. Kusleika didn't take the players' departures personally, although publicly it appeared to be a slap in the face. At least one player, though, stepped up to welcome the new coach. That player was senior Eric Weddle, who had been in on the interview process. Kusleika believed if he could build a strong rapport with Eric and get him to buy into his coaching philosophies, the rest of the team would quickly follow. And it worked.

"I knew that he did a good job with the talent he had [at Montclair]," Eric recalled. "I knew he would do a good job for us."

But morale among the players was low. The Braves had lost seven key players, including quarterback Ryan Stickler, to graduation. Then three players transferred. As the Braves moved from the Mount Baldy League to the Baseline League, the team boasted twenty-five seniors but only six returning starters. The number was reduced to five when offensive lineman Jeff Valladolid blew out his knee on the first day of practice in pads and was lost for the season. Alta Loma's other top offensive lineman, six-foot-seven, 320-pound John Valdez, was returning from anterior cruciate ligament surgery he'd had the previous year. Senior linebacker Erik Avila and defensive lineman King Nunez were expected to anchor the untested defense. The five-foot-nine, 190-pound Avila, also one of the area's top wrestlers, had two years of varsity experience. His vocal leadership would be a key to Alta Loma's defensive success. Kusleika focused on creating a positive atmosphere for his new team, and much of that focus centered on Eric Weddle, the Braves' most talented and experienced skill player. Kusleika said Eric counted as two returning starters because he had played both ways—both offense and defense. Kusleika would later compare Weddle to NFL running back Michael Pittman, a player Kusleika coached at Fresno State and who earned a Super Bowl ring with the Tampa Bay Buccaneers. He said Weddle had a similar competitive tenacity and blue-collar work ethic.

"We were kind of behind the eight ball, but our ace in the hole was Eric," Kusleika recalled. "In my biased opinion, he was the best player in the area. I could tell by watching him run around in just a helmet, T-shirt, shorts and cleats during the summer that he was one of the best high school players I had seen. Maybe not from a height, weight, or speed standpoint, but he could play any position on the field. He was faster than anybody we had. As coaches walking off the field after practice, guys were saying things like, 'Did you see what he did today? Did you see him in that drill?' He could do it all, play literally any position. Obviously we didn't play him on the line—that would have been an absolute waste—but if we had asked him, he would have done it. He was a selfless teammate who wanted to do whatever was best for the team."

Going into the first game of the season against Charter Oak, the defending Division VII CIF champion and one of the better teams Alta Loma would face all season, the game plan called for Eric to start at safety, wide receiver, kick returner, punt returner, and holder for the PATs and field goals. Sophomore Nick Galbraith started the contest at quarterback but struggled in the opening half of his first varsity start. Alta Loma trailed Charter Oak 24–14 at halftime, and Coach Kusleika asked Eric to add quarterback to his list of duties. It was a bold move, considering

Weddle had never taken a live snap in high school, but he embraced the opportunity. Eric could not have known how the position switch would eventually affect his stock among recruiters, but his coach had spoken, and as he had done so many times before, he obeyed for the good of the team.

"I didn't have a quarterback who could throw him the ball . . . so we moved him there. It didn't make much sense to snap the ball to anyone but him because if you want one guy to touch the ball on every play, why not have it be him? If the play went bad, he took off—not many could catch him," Kusleika said. "We snapped him the ball the rest of the year. As Eric went, so went the Braves. When we won, Eric was a big part of it. Teams always knew where No. 22 was lined up."

When the Braves returned to the field, their offense became "the Weddle option": give the ball to Eric and let him make plays. "It was QB right, QB left," Eric said. "The Braves became my team."

So with several thousand fans packed in the stands at Chaffey College, Weddle dropped into the gun and sparked an Alta Loma rally. The player wearing royal blue No. 22 rolled right and rolled left, sometimes firing a pass, sometimes tucking the ball and scrambling for yardage. Charter Oak was not prepared for the Weddle option but did their best to adjust to the new Alta Loma attack.

One of the more memorable plays in the game came when Eric fielded a punt and sliced his way up the sideline for 31 yards. The notable gallop ended when he smashed into a charging Charter Oak linebacker and sent the player's helmet flying into the air. The opposing player was so dazed after the hit he came and stood on the Alta Loma sideline. Eventually the confused tackler was escorted across the field. He didn't return to the action. "The kid got up and didn't know where he was," Avila said. "I heard later he had a concussion. For our quarterback to do that to their linebacker had to be discouraging for them. It was one of the most memorable moments of the season for me."

Kusleika remembers the punt return vividly, but in a different context. The coach noted that in the span of a minute and a half, Eric showcased his talents by making a variety of plays in various positions. "He started by knocking down a pass as the free safety on third down. On fourth down, they punted to him and he returned the ball up our sidelines. He was one foot from stepping out of bounds when he trucked a kid coming at him. Then he got the play from me, called it in the huddle and ended up running for a 17-yard gain as the quarterback on first down," Kusleika said, recalling the sequence. "That showed everything. He meant everything to that team. He did everything we thought he could do."

The comeback was aided by five Chargers second-half turnovers. The third turnover, an interception by Jeff McDonald, set up a 19-yard touchdown run by Eric on a fourth-and-1 with more than six minutes to play in the game, giving the Braves a 28–24 lead. Charter Oak responded with a touchdown of its own to regain a 31–28 advantage with less than three minutes remaining.

Eager to lead his team to triumph, Eric returned the ensuing kickoff but fumbled the ball as he was tackled. Fortunately, the pigskin bounced into the arms of teammate Rubien Brandon, who rumbled 57 yards down the Braves' sideline to the Charter Oak 8, much to the relief and delight of the Alta Loma faithful. Moments later, Weddle handed off to running back Greg Holt, who punched the ball in from one yard out to make it 35–31 for the Braves. Eric redeemed himself in the closing seconds as he intercepted a last-gasp heave by Charter Oak's quarterback deep in Alta Loma territory to seal the victory. Amazingly, the Braves won despite being limited to 6 first downs in the game, including just one in the second half. Charter Oak finished with 18 first downs and outgained Alta Loma, 359–185. Eric finished with 37 yards rushing and 3 touchdowns, 4-of-12 for 96 yards passing, one reception for 9 yards and 2 interceptions. He was named player of the game. As impressive as Eric played, the accolades and statistics were not important to him. The senior was simply happy he could help his team win.

Eric and the Braves played even better the following week in a 31–7 romp over A.B. Miller. As the quarterback and safety, Eric continued to have a major impact as he intercepted a pass, recovered a fumble, scored on a 2-yard run, and caught 3 passes for 43 yards.

Alta Loma stumbled in week three with a 32–16 loss to Palmdale. Eric ran for 81 yards and a pair of touchdowns but was held in check as the Braves' one-dimensional offense struggled to execute.

Alta Loma found ways to win close games, including a pair of back-to-back one-point victories on the road over foes Norco and J.W. North in Riverside. A blocked extra point proved the only difference in Alta Loma's 7–6 win over the Norco Cougars. A Norco fumble recovered by Erik Avila gave the Braves the ball in Cougar territory with less than seven minutes to go. Minutes later, Eric scrambled into the end zone from 8 yards out for the Braves' lone touchdown. Eric then held for the extra point, and the Braves escaped with the narrow success.

The opposing kicker missed an extra point the following week in Alta Loma's 14–13 squeaker over J.W. North. Once again, Eric scored both touchdowns with his feet. He acknowledged his struggles to throw the ball but was satisfied when the team won. "I was getting beat up playing both ways, but it was my senior year, and I had to play through it. I wasn't that good at throwing the ball, but I got better."

At 4–1, the Braves were ready for their Baseline League opener against Claremont. Although his buddy Ryan Stickler was in the middle of his redshirt season at Hawaii, Eric continued the tradition of watching game film at home. The difference was that the whole team was invited to the Weddle home for midweek film and a barbecue. Having his teammates over for games of pool, Ping-Pong, video games, food, and fun made for a tight-knit group of players.

The brotherly bonding helped Alta Loma weather the storm of losing three of their next five games. The Braves were shut out 31–0 by Claremont, rebounded with a 33–14 win over Chaffey, and then lost to Etiwanda, 24–15. They completed league play with a victory over Upland and a loss to crosstown rival Rancho Cucamonga. Despite their late-season struggles, the Braves, at 6–4, qualified for the CIF southern section playoffs and drew one of the top teams in the powerhouse Chino Cowboys, who were 9–1.

As Alta Loma took the field in Chino on Friday, November 22, 2002, the biggest question was whether the wildcard Braves could move the ball on the stingy Cowboys defense, led by all-league defensive tackle Sedrick Ellis, a future USC Trojan and lineman for the New Orleans Saints. Alta Loma didn't have to move it very far. After Chino jumped out to a 10–0 lead, four Cowboy turnovers gave the Braves the ball inside the Chino 20-yard line. Alta Loma cut the lead to 10–7 when Eric found teammate Immanuel Williams in the end zone with a 14-yard touchdown pass. On the next possession, a Chino running back fumbled a lateral, and Eric recovered the ball at the Cowboy 8. A few plays later, Eric handed off to teammate Deon Credle, and the underdog Braves led 14–10.

The teams went back and forth with scoring spurts. Chino bounced back with two touchdowns to go ahead 23–14.

Then it was the Braves' turn. Eric hooked up with teammate Blake Favinger on a 66-yard bomb to score another touchdown. Another Chino fumble gave Alta Loma the ball on the one, and Sione Toki scored on the following play. Despite a blocked PAT by Chino, the Braves held a 27–23 advantage at the half.

The teams traded field goals in the third quarter, and the game came down to a few key plays in the fourth. The first came when Chino's Ellis blocked an Alta Loma punt to give the Cowboys the ball on the Braves' 35. A few plays later, Eric and the Alta Loma defense had Chino facing fourth-and-2. Glabb took the snap, dropped back, and, unable to find his target, began to scramble and buy some time. As white jerseys and blue helmets closed around, the quarterback spotted his tight end in the flat and floated a pass in his direction. From his safety position, Eric watched the quarterback and locked onto the tight end right before the ball left the quarterback's hand. He flew toward the ball, knowing he could pick it off and take it to the end zone. He could taste the sweetness of an upset. But just as his fingers met the leather of the ball, he collided with a teammate, and they both went down. As luck would have it, the ball was tipped right into the waiting hands of the opposing receiver, who caught it and gained the first down.

"If we had stopped them, we would have pulled off a huge upset," Eric said of the game-changing play.

Erik Avila still laments the tipped ball that got away from the Braves. "Eric had an interception for a touchdown. He was gone.

But one of our linebackers, for whatever reason, drops into coverage when he should have blitzed and runs into Eric. They knock each other down, and the tight end catches the ball and gets a first down right at the stick, *at the stick!*" Avila said. "Even if Eric could have knocked it down, we would have gotten the ball and run out the clock."

There is nothing Eric hates more than losing, but sometimes the ball just takes a funny bounce. He doesn't hold a grudge. If anything, he blames himself. "He wasn't my guy, but I read it and went to pick it up. Another guy did the same thing, and we ran into one another and the guy caught it," Eric said. "It could have been the greatest upset in southern California high school playoff history, but we came up short."

Chino scored on the next play to go ahead 33–30, but there was still time on the clock. Executing the two-minute offense, Weddle maneuvered his team into Cowboy territory in the final minute. The Braves lined up for a 45-yard field goal to tie the game, but a Cowboy defender broke through the line and smothered the ball as it lifted off kicker Drew Stapp's foot. The Chino sideline erupted in celebration, and, after running out the clock, the Cowboys stormed the field. Alta Loma's season—as well as Eric Weddle's high school football career—was over.

Ironically, the Chino game was Eric's best passing performance of the year. He was 11-of-24 for 218 yards and 2 TD passes. He also rushed 8 times for 30 yards, recovered a fumble, and recorded 15 tackles. His efforts did not go unnoticed by Cowboys head coach John Monger. "Weddle is one hell of an athlete," the coach said after the game.

Eric, the team captain, completed his final year with 129 tackles, 5 interceptions, 4 forced fumbles, and 5 recovered fumbles. Offensively, he rushed for 587 yards and passed for 965 yards. He scored 22 touchdowns and threw 5 touchdown passes. He was named the utility player on the all-Inland Valley first team. When the all-area Baseline League was announced, Eric was selected as the defensive player of the year and named to the second team offense as quarterback. Name any postseason award or team, and Eric's name was there. He was also invited to play in an all-star game with the best players in the area, including his friend and crosstown rival Terrell Thomas.

Not counting the five vacated wins his junior year, Alta Loma's combined record for Eric's sophomore and junior years was 20–2; the Braves finished his final year at 6–5. Despite the losses, headaches, and bad luck, Eric said his senior campaign was the most memorable of his high school career. He learned how to deal with losses. He learned how to be a leader, a team player, and the kind of teammate who makes others better. Teammates become brothers. "My senior year was all about putting team first, avoiding selfish acts, and learning that not everything comes easy," Eric said. "It was hard to deal with, but that experience helped me grow and become a better person."

## A COUP FOR THE "U"

In its January 13, 2003, edition, the *Inland Valley Voice,* a local newspaper affiliated with the *Los Angeles Times,* ran a feature article about Eric, detailing his high school career and the schools who were interested in his athletic services. The photo that ran alongside the story showed Eric sporting a black Quicksilver hoodie, clutching a football, his black hair slicked back and a fixed, determined look on his face. The dramatic pose effectively communicated how Eric really felt inside. He had worked hard to achieve his accomplishments at Alta Loma. Now he was intent on succeeding at the next level.

Following the loss to Chino, Kusleika and his staff committed themselves to helping Eric Weddle get a Division I scholarship. The dream scenario included UCLA, Eric's favorite team when he was growing up, but no amount of phone calls or highlight videos seemed to make a difference. Eric was disappointed when he heard about UCLA recruiter Mark Weber's visit to Alta Loma. For all the good he was doing on the football field, playing multiple positions and sacrificing his body for the team, he was barely a blinking dot on the recruiting radar, an unheralded one-star recruit. He felt like he had aced an interview, only to find out his dream job had been given to someone else. The rejection was painful, but it motivated him to continue trying. Ignoring the discouragement, he remained optimistic that another opportunity would present itself.

Eric and his coaches reached out to other programs, such as the University of Nevada at Las Vegas, assistant coach Lenny Ware's alma mater, and Utah State, where Chanel was playing soccer. But interest in the two-way standout diminished when his offensive role switched from receiver to quarterback as a senior. Kusleika told recruiters he envisioned Eric as a defensive back at the next level but shared his opinion that Eric could easily play multiple positions in college if a team wanted to use him that way. "Eric played everything for us," Kusleika once told a recruiter. "'He may be able to do all that stuff for you.' Of course the coach laughed. 'Oh, coach, as long as he can play one position for us we will be happy for that.'"

Kusleika continued: "Sometimes recruiters talk to high school coaches, and you can tell they think, 'Yeah, okay, buddy, I'm not exactly sure you know what you're talking about,' but I had coached at the Division I level, and I had seen athletes they had, and Eric was a football player. He was a throwback because he could do it all. He was good at all of it. He was gifted."

Regardless of Kusleika's endorsement, most recruiters thought Eric was too small for a college defensive secondary. "He didn't fit some people's numbers," Kusleika said. "I was worried he wouldn't get the opportunity to show what he could do. He had some I-AA schools who were slobbering all over him, but he really wanted to play at the highest level, and we felt he *deserved* to play at the highest level. . . . They weren't hearing what we were trying to tell all of them, that this is the best high school football player I have ever seen."

Ever determined, Kusleika furiously worked his coaching network. Perhaps he could try a friend of a friend. Earlier in his career, he had worked with some assistants who had coached alongside Urban Meyer at Colorado State. Kusleika had met Meyer when the two sat at the same table during a coaching function in Dallas, before Meyer interviewed with Lou Holtz for a job at Notre Dame. Following the 2002 season, Meyer was hired as the new head football coach at the University of Utah. Kusleika was also aware that Utah defensive coordinator Kyle Whittingham had contacted Eric as a junior but figured the kid would be gone before Utah had a shot to sign him. Kusleika made the calls, and word eventually reached Whittingham that Eric was still available.

Yes, the Utes were in the market for a defensive back. But Whittingham was skeptical. Eric was "lights out" on tape, but why hadn't someone offered him a scholarship yet? "He was a multisport phenom," Whittingham said. "He did so many things naturally, played all positions. The evidence on film was that he was a tremendous player. He had good grades and showed a lot of character. Whatever he did, he excelled at—so why wasn't the PAC-10 all over this guy? Did he rob a bank? What am I missing?

The more I researched, the more I realized I wasn't missing anything. Everybody else was just missing the boat."

Lenny Ware, Alta Loma's wide receivers coach, wanted to see UNLV go after Eric. He hopped in a car and drove to Las Vegas to speak with the Rebels coaching staff and show Eric's film. When he was finished, the UNLV coaches said Eric "didn't fit the mold of where the game is going."

"They were recruiting defensive backs that could compete with tall, fast, lanky receivers that could jump out of the gym," Ware said. "Short, stocky safeties could tackle and hit, but not cover the pass. There was also a stereotype that white kids couldn't compete with the African-American athlete. It was the beginning of an era and he was caught up in that. It made no sense. He was laying people out, then as quarterback, he was running around people like Gerald Alexander, Terrell Thomas, Patrick Chung, and Sedrick Ellis, some of the top athletes in the area. No one could touch Eric Weddle."

As Eric's friends and fellow players were being offered scholarships to various universities, Ware felt Eric was being overlooked. "What did they see in them? Eric was a better football player because he had the intangibles. He was not a speedster, but he was a complete football player. How do you measure that type of player? That is where the oversight came in—they weren't able to measure his true potential, those intangibles."

Ware remembers having a conversation with one of Utah's assistant coaches, although he can't recall a name. "I know Eric is your boy, but is he for real?" the coach asked Ware. "Is this dude for real?"

Without hesitation, Ware replied with a bold prediction: "He will start as a true freshman and be a leader. He could even start on both sides of the ball."

"That is all I need to hear," the coach told Ware.

In early January 2003, Eric took his one and only official recruiting trip to the University of Utah campus in Salt Lake City. As he toured the university and walked the turf at Rice-Eccles Stadium, he felt at peace. Set against the majestic Wasatch Mountains, the campus was scenic and beautiful. Eric felt comfortable with the coaching staff, as if he had known them for a long time. And of course there was another reason Utah appealed to him.

"He called me from Utah and said he really liked the school, and he was thinking about signing there," said Chanel's mother, Sonya. "I told him his parents might not like that. Then he added, 'I need to be in Utah if I am going to marry your daughter.'"

Eric made a decision. By the end of his visit to Utah, he gave Whittingham a verbal commitment then cancelled trips to Wyoming, New Mexico State, and Colorado State, schools that had jumped in late when they caught word of Utah's interest.

Eric especially felt a connection with Whittingham. "He is just a real straightforward guy," Eric said. "The reason I came to Utah was that [Whittingham] was the only straightforward coach who offered me. He told me what I was going to come in here and do, and he just tells you how it is. I felt he respected me. Utah also had a plan for me. Other coaches said they didn't know where I would fit in, but [Utah's staff] told me where I fit in the program—at safety."

When Eric told his parents he had committed to Utah, Steve's first reaction was, "Oh, Utah has a football team, too?" He had heard of Utah's basketball program, but not much about its football program. That was about to change. Steve and Debbie were happy for their son but sad he was going so far away.

Before signing day, however, Utah's new coach, Urban

Meyer, wanted to meet the Weddles. In January 2003, Eric and his parents found themselves sitting across from Meyer and Whittingham. On the table in the middle of the room sat a plate of tortilla chips and Debbie's popular bean and guacamole dip. Even as the dynamic Meyer shared the details of his vision for the Utah football program and his expectations for an incoming freshman, he eyed Eric closely and wondered if this little toothpick could survive a season on the junior varsity squad. Meyer wanted athletes who knew how to work, and he wanted speed. He looked forward to seeing how Weddle would respond in fall camp. A scholarship was offered and accepted. The coaches concluded their business, dipped one last chip, and said good-bye before moving toward the door.

But Meyer's doubts continued to linger as the coaches clicked on their seat belts in the rental car.

"Are you sure about this kid?" Meyer asked his new assistant coach.

"I'm sure. Trust me on this one," Whittingham replied confidently, knowing Meyer hadn't seen Weddle's highlight film, while he had studied it closely. "I know he looks like a thousand other guys out there—that he doesn't really look imposing, but he's a special player."

Eric was among several local prep stars to sign letters of intent on February 5, 2003. Aside from Sedrick Ellis and Terrell Thomas, who both signed with USC, very few names are well-known. A few players went on to great college careers and the NFL while many did not.

With the benefit of hindsight, observers are left to wonder why the player who went on to become one of the highest paid safeties in NFL history went virtually unnoticed by most Division I programs. Mark Weber has seen numerous examples of such

overlooked players in more than two decades as a coach and recruiter. Weber was an undersized lineman who played college
football at Cal-Lutheran, a Division III program in Thousand
Oaks, California.

"Recruiting is not a science," said Weber, the UCLA recruiter
who sized up Weddle in the school cafeteria and now coaches at
Utah State University. "When you are young, you don't always
understand it. But there is a place for each person, and as long
as you don't lose faith or hope and say 'forget it,' there is a right
place. It may not be the place you hope for, but things happen
for a reason."

As an example of his point, Weber loves to tell the story of
Ryan Wendell, an offensive lineman he tried to recruit to UCLA
out of Diamond Bar High School. But UCLA had many prospects to choose from and considered the six-foot-two, 275-pound
Wendell to be "undersized." When UCLA coach Bob Toledo was
fired in December 2002, Weber accepted a job at Fresno State
and recruited Wendell to be a Bulldog, where he went on to become a freshman all-American. He signed as an undrafted free
agent with the New England Patriots in 2008 and eventually
worked his way from the practice squad to the active roster in
2009. From there he developed into the Patriots' starting center.

As it turned out, the stars aligned for Eric at Utah, Weber
said. "He could have gone to UCLA and probably worked into
the starting lineup eventually. Things probably would have
worked out," Weber said. "Some kids don't get what they want
and they let it get to them. Eric allowed his experience to motivate him. He started as a freshman at Utah. Given the timing
of his college career and his unique abilities, where else could he
have gone and showcased his talents by playing multiple positions? How rare is that?"

After basketball season, Eric focused his efforts on improving his speed and agility doing drills with assistant football coach Lenny Ware. Training with Ware, who had become a friend and mentor, went a long way in preparing Eric for his freshman year at Utah.

## THE MENTOR

Perspiration dripped from Eric Weddle's brow as he crouched into his starting position on the high school track. In the next lane, his twenty-four-year-old coach and friend, Lenny Ware, took a similar position. As the sun bore down on the two athletes, they prepared for another race. "This time," Eric thought to himself, "this time I will beat him."

The two had spent the afternoon talking serious Xs and Os, lifting weights, and doing drills to improve their agility. Now it was time to work on speed. Both athletes had aspirations to play football at the next level—Eric in college, Lenny in the pros. To work their running technique, they prepared to run the forty-yard dash. In previous races, Eric had fallen short, and it hurt to lose, even to Lenny. His competitive nature never took a day off, not even in a game of Uno with his grandpa; any loss was a shot to the gut.

"Ready, set, GO!" Both runners fired out of the blocks. Pumping his arms and stretching his legs, Eric used a natural burst to take a slight lead, but he couldn't hold it for long. Halfway through the race, Lenny found his stride and pulled even with his young protégé. Eric was giving his all, even as Lenny smiled, "See ya!" and pulled away in the final ten yards. As Ware crossed the finish line a few lengths ahead of Eric, he lifted his arms in triumph.

"I could always get out in front of him when we raced because

I was quicker," Eric said, "but he had this nice, smooth stride where he would just eat up the ground because he had these long chicken legs against my short little spurts. I always knew he was coming up behind me, and he would pass me. Even though I lost, it made me try even harder."

They rested a few minutes before Eric challenged his coach again. The result was the same, and Eric began to lose his confident swagger. Eric was consistently running a time of 4.4, a speed many skilled players in college football would die for, but it didn't matter to Eric unless he beat Lenny. They raced a third time, and Eric finally lost his cool.

"He got so mad he almost cried," Ware recalled. "He said, 'This is stupid. I quit.' He went home. He was mature for his age, but I had to remember he was still an adolescent."

Both of them knew Eric would be back. He hated losing at anything, so it was frustrating to fail so many times. At some point he knew it would be different. "If we raced today, I would beat him," Eric said. "But then I couldn't."

Ware was one person who influenced Eric greatly toward the end of his high school years. Like a sponge, Eric absorbed as much as he could from the man. Ware's wisdom and experience helped Eric significantly, especially during his freshman year at Utah.

"I looked up to him in a lot of ways," Eric said. "He played in college and the NFL and knew what he was talking about. He was in great shape and could still play. I gravitated toward him. His personality was 'win at everything.' I measured myself against him in everything I did."

Ware's journey to Alta Loma High School in 2002 had many twists and turns. But that process underscores how he became a mentor to the younger Eric Weddle.

Ware grew up in Pomona, California, where he lived with an elderly father who earned a meager living as a cook at two local restaurants. His father was rarely around. Lenny never knew his mother because she left the family when he was around a year old. He met a stepsister when he was eleven. "Not the most functional family," Lenny admits. "I was a product of my environment."

Because his father was rarely around, Lenny was left to fend for himself. He found his first odd job at age twelve. But with no supervision, especially in the evenings, he became associated with area gangs and consistently stayed out past two or three a.m. He became interested in girls and fathered his first child, a daughter, at age sixteen. "Nothing good happens in Pomona after nine p.m.," Lenny explained. "I thought I was an adult and started making adult decisions. I made a lot of really poor decisions."

If there was one bright spot in his teenage years, it was sports. He could run and catch a football. Had it not been for his athletic talent and a few caring coaches, Ware would not have successfully emerged from the streets of Pomona. Most mornings his coaches at Montclair High tracked him down and gave him a ride to school. He barely remained academically eligible for football. Even so, he excelled on the gridiron, and a miracle, he said, occurred when UNLV offered him a scholarship.

Getting a full-ride to college didn't help him grow up, however. He went through the motions academically and sometimes skipped class. At age nineteen, he fathered a second child, this time a son.

"How did I make it? What was I thinking?" Ware reminisces today. "Living like that, with a child, you would think I would wake up and say, 'I got to get my life together.' But I was on autopilot and never made the connection. Whatever someone suggested we do, I was like, 'Sounds great!' It didn't matter that I had kids to support. I had no goals."

Despite his personal problems off the field, Ware found he had the confidence to play college football. The biggest hurdle came when he was a freshman. When he arrived for fall camp he realized he was dressing in a locker room with twenty-one- and twenty-two-year-olds, some of whom were ex-convicts. Many had full beards. He quickly noticed how much bigger, stronger, and faster their bodies were in comparison to his 165-pound frame. "It was very intimidating, and I would be lying if I say I wasn't scared," Ware said. "I thought, 'Whoa, I don't belong here.'" A blessing came in the form of a redshirt year, giving him the chance to attend school and practice with the team without losing a year of eligibility. It was during that first year that he developed the confidence in his ability to play at the collegiate level. "I realized I could do this, I could compete with these twenty-two-year-olds," Ware said.

The once-troubled youth worked hard to improve his skills, and football became his life.

Of the forty-four games UNLV played from 1996 to 1999, the Rebels won only seven, but it wasn't due to a lack of offensive production. Quarterback John Denton took turns throwing to Ware, his roommate Damon Williams, Carlos Baker, and Todd Floyd. By the end of their careers, each receiver was near the top of the school's all-time receiving list. Williams is currently third on the list, Ware is fifth, and Baker is sixth. Lenny finished his career at UNLV with 161 receptions, 2,322 yards receiving, and 16 touchdowns. He also made his mark with the most 100-yard games receiving and at one point held the freshman record for receptions. During his senior year, he served as team captain and won the R.E. "Doc" Tobler Award for the senior who brings the highest credit to himself and the university. He was presented with the Arthur Ashe Award for outstanding contribution in athletics.

Ware was not drafted but signed as an undrafted free agent with the Tennessee Titans in 2000. On his first NFL training camp play, Ware ran a pattern, caught a ball from all-pro quarterback Steve McNair, and blew out his knee. He was placed on injured reserve and cut at the end of the year.

It was hard to adjust to life without the game he loved. He felt sorry for himself. Had it not been for his girlfriend and future wife, Amanda, he would have made more bad decisions. The Titans paid Lenny a total of $120,000 while he was on injured reserve. He blew through the first $50,000 in no time and admits he would have wasted it all had it not been for Amanda. After he was cut, the couple moved back to Las Vegas, and Amanda encouraged Lenny to save his money, buy a house, and get a job. She wanted to help him grow up and take some responsibility for his disoriented life. Ware was several credits short of earning his communications degree, but having never considered life after football, he wasn't even sure what he would do with a degree. He continued to miss the glamour of being a college football star. He wallowed in self-pity and depression for six months while Amanda worked full-time to support the couple. One day she found him moping around and finally had enough. She gave him the motivational speech of his life. "'You are in a bad place right now and you need to get your s— together,'" Ware recalled Amanda saying. "And, finally, something clicked."

"My spirit broke," Lenny explained. "There is something about your soul and mind hitting rock bottom, and you realize, I either make it or I don't. I have been put in situations where I either make this catch or we lose. They are the ultimatums of life.

If you can come out on the positive side, the winning side, you can have the confidence to succeed in life. That was what really started it for me."

Because he still loved football, he looked for a way to stay involved. He started calling his old high school coaches and asked for advice. They suggested he come home to California to coach football and become a teacher. He wasn't ready to be a teacher, but he agreed to coach and be a teacher's aide. The couple rented out their home in Las Vegas and moved to California. Going into the 2002–2003 school year, Ware joined Kusleika's new Alta Loma staff as a wide receivers coach. One of the first players he met was Eric Weddle.

Because Ware had NFL experience, Weddle and his high school teammates were naturally drawn to him. When Ware spoke, he had the players' full attention because they respected what he had to say. When he spoke, "their eyes were huge," Ware said. He quickly developed a love for teaching young people through his own experiences. He knew he was in the right place.

Lenny recognized special talents in Eric from the beginning. He watched film of Eric's junior year and was impressed with Eric's athletic ability, maturity, likable personality, and teachable attitude. Because Lenny saw so much potential, he took extra interest in working with Eric. It became Lenny's personal project to help Eric develop his remarkable skills. Like a big brother, Lenny taught Eric everything he knew about the game of football and never had to explain anything twice. The prize pupil immediately applied everything his coach taught him. Lenny also appreciated that Eric overlooked his inexperience as a teacher. "[Eric] was gifted physically and mentally," Lenny said. "I challenged him a lot, and he always met those challenges."

The pair typically met in the weight room or on the practice field after school. They lifted weights and ran through cone drills, catching drills, and drills to improve footwork, hip swivel technique, and positioning against a defender. Because Eric had an insatiable football mind, Lenny took Eric to the chalkboard and broke down complex college and professional football schemes. From his experience as a receiver, Lenny quizzed Eric about how to recognize when a defense was in man-to-man coverage versus zone coverage, how to counter different schemes, and how to escape a cornerback's jam at the line of scrimmage. They also discussed defense. "This is how I am going to beat you as a receiver," Lenny would say before scripting a scenario. These in-depth sessions—Ware's crash course in college football schemes 101—helped Eric digest Kyle Whittingham's defense much faster than the average freshman. They also talked about overcoming life's obstacles, the importance of academics, and doing things right.

Ware wasn't just a coach with a whistle. He still harbored aspirations for a comeback in the NFL. The extra work with Eric was beneficial in helping Ware return to top form. As he trained with this goal in mind, he was grateful he could work with someone as talented as Eric because the seventeen-year-old pushed him to the limit. Lenny became convinced of Eric's NFL potential. "He challenged me," Lenny said. "I was fresh off the NFL, and he jammed me at the line like an NFL cornerback. I was stronger, but he could beat me technique-wise. I knew he could play both ways in college."

But the teenager couldn't beat his mentor in the 40-yard dash. Although Eric lost his composure on at least one occasion, Lenny admired Eric's poise and his ability to control his emotions.

A willingness to make sacrifices also set Eric apart from the typical teenage athlete. One Friday night, Ware and Weddle were lifting weights in the Alta Loma weight room when two cars of Eric's friends arrived. His friends told Eric he worked too hard and tried to persuade him to join them for dinner at a local hamburger restaurant.

"Nope, I'm working out with Coach," Weddle told them. The friends persisted, but Eric stood firm. He was willing to sacrifice his social life in order to reach his goals.

"It helped having a guy like Lenny to coach me," Eric said. "I didn't want to just be a good high school player; I wanted to go to college ready to play right away. I knew Lenny could get me there if I would just listen and do what he told me to do. All the friends and parties were put on the back burner. That wouldn't make me successful. Working out and getting my mind right were going to help me be successful. I was committed, and my friends understood that."

"He was one of those types," Lenny continued. "He was focused. He never lost sight of his goals and never wavered, even though a lot of schools weren't interested [in signing him]. He found the confidence. He was like, 'I know I can do this.'"

The education and insight Eric gained from Lenny pushed him years ahead in the college game, and Eric said he will always be supremely grateful for his time with the young coach. "He had a huge influence on me and coached me up," Eric said. "He took me under his wing, taught me what to expect and how to be mentally tough. 'Players in college will be four or five years older than you,' he would say. 'You have to be ready mentally and physically. Take someone's job. Play as a true freshman.' He was constantly beating that into me. He taught me the difference between high school and college ball. He told me what coaches would watch for. He told me about life in the NFL. He got me in the mentality of setting a goal and not letting anything get in my way. He was a wealth of knowledge and the main reason I had such focus and determination."

As much as Lenny helped Eric, Eric also helped Lenny. Mentoring Eric and seeing him succeed touched Lenny's heart and fueled his desire to continue coaching and teaching. After Eric left for Utah, Lenny took an interest in another Alta Loma athlete. The kid was a five-foot-seven redhead with braces. "He was slow as molasses but had the heart of a lion. He was pigeon-toed and not a receiver, but I worked with him. He had a willingness to learn," Lenny said. "By the third game of his sophomore year, he was starting varsity and became our best receiver."

The player's father was grateful for Lenny's interest in his son and gave him a book titled *Crunch Time: What the Game of Football Can Teach You about the Game of Life* by James E. Grassi. The book uses football metaphors, terms, and analogies to teach religious lessons and principles. Lenny had never read a book cover to cover, but he had so much respect for this athlete and his father that he opened the book. He was quickly hooked. It was as if a lightbulb turned on in Lenny's mind, and he found direction and purpose in his life. "My goodness, it blew my head off and got me to the place I needed to be," Ware said. "From that point on, there was no stopping me."

He married Amanda. They wrote down goals. He wanted to finish his bachelor's degree and earn a master's. He wanted to be in a classroom. He was drawn to kids with special needs and disabilities. He also wanted to catch one more touchdown pass.

Arena football was popular at the time, and Las Vegas had the Gladiators, so the couple moved back to Nevada. Lenny trained to play in the AFL using principles he gleaned from another book, *Think and Grow Rich*, by Napoleon Hill. Less than thirty minutes into his tryout with the Gladiators, the coach,

Frank Haege, motioned Ware over, pulled out a contract, and said, "I don't need to see any more. Camp starts in January." The six-foot-one, 195-pound receiver and defensive back played one season with the Gladiators and caught that touchdown pass. He also realized he could do whatever he put his mind to.

In 2004, while his wife pursued her goal of a master's degree in social work, Lenny coached as an assistant at Bishop Gorman High School and worked on his master's degree. He graduated in 2006 and is now working toward a doctorate degree. He works at the Nevada Childhood Cancer Foundation as director of education, helping children with chronic illnesses, cancer, HIV and AIDS, and renal disease continue their education while going through various medical treatments. Today the couple lives in Henderson, Nevada, with their three children. Lenny has also rekindled relationships with his two oldest children. His daughter, Kaylen, graduated from high school with honors, and his son, Christian, is an excellent student with aspirations of playing Division I college basketball. Lenny is amazed at how far he has progressed, especially in his relationship with his kids. His feelings of gratitude almost leave him speechless.

"To grow up like I did," Lenny said, "I can't stress it enough, how truly blessed I am, and in so many ways. . . . It wasn't what I did for Eric, it was what he did for me."

Eric is equally grateful for the impact that Lenny has had on his life. He's also certain he could beat the old receiver if the two lined up for a race today.

As the two parted ways in the spring of 2003, Eric was embarking on a journey that would change his life both athletically and spiritually. The next four years at the University of Utah would shape Eric's life in ways he could not have predicted.

# CHAPTER 6

＿

# THE PUNK FRESHMAN

The snow-capped Wasatch Mountains, named "mountains of many waters" by the Paiute Indians, tower over Salt Lake City, Utah, on the westernmost edge of the Rocky Mountains. These 11,000-foot peaks provide a majestic backdrop for the 1,500-acre University of Utah campus nestled into the hillside overlooking the Salt Lake Valley. Peering west from the school, one can admire the picturesque Oquirrh Mountains, the expansive Great Salt Lake (the world's second largest inland body of salt water), and Utah's capital, Salt Lake City.

One of the most prominent landmarks on campus is Rice-Eccles Stadium. When it was announced in 1995 that Salt Lake City would host the 2002 Winter Olympics, one of the city's top priorities was upgrading the University of Utah's Rice Stadium. The next year, Utah athletic director Chris Hill announced plans to renovate the old stadium into a facility that would be up to Olympic standards. Initially, the project was going to take three years, but $20 million in donations, including a gift of $10 million from the George S. and Dolores Dore Eccles Foundation, accelerated the process. The new $50-million stadium, renamed Rice-Eccles, was completed in time for the Utes' 1998 home opener. The athletic department's new digs included a six-story press box and enough seats for more than 45,000 fans. In June 2003, the next piece was put into place when local businessman Larry H. Miller and his wife, Gail, donated $1.6 million for a video display system and new scoreboards. FieldTurf, complete with the word "Utah" painted in white block letters in each end zone, eventually replaced the artificial turf that had been the playing surface in the old Rice Stadium.

The Dee Glen Smith Athletics Center and adjacent Thomas K. McCarthey practice fields were located southeast of the stadium on Guardsman Way. Before it was demolished to make way for a new facility in 2012, the Smith Center was home to the Utah football team. Following the 2004 season, the Spence Eccles Field House, a 74,000-square-foot indoor practice building, was erected just south of the Smith Center.

From 2003 to 2007, these key locations in the shadow of the Wasatch Mountains became Eric Weddle's home away from home. With one duffel bag of clothes and another filled with video games, Eric moved into the dorms and became roommates with Martail Burnett, a defensive end from Los Angeles. Eric drove a used Honda Accord. His first college class schedule included courses such as food and nutrition, earthquake and volcano studies, and, of course, English. But settling in as a young freshman wasn't going to be easy.

When Urban Meyer announced his 2003 recruiting class, the fanfare centered on heralded recruits at the time such as Thomas Huff, Tony Castaldi, and local product Kyle Brady.

Huff was a lanky six-foot-four receiver with 4.3 speed from

Camelback High School in Phoenix, Arizona, where he was a star on the football field and won a state track championship in the 110-meter hurdles. Several schools in the PAC-10 were all over Huff, but he opted for the University of Utah. Meyer loved Huff's speed and called him the "frosting" on his first recruiting class. The new coach hinted that Huff would get a chance to play that fall. "I expect good things early from . . . Thomas Huff," Meyer said at the time. "A prototype receiver is tall and fast, and that's Thomas Huff."

Meyer also praised Castaldi, a six-foot-three, 235-pound defensive lineman out of Simi Valley, California. Meyer said of Castaldi, "Tony is a tough, hard-nosed, physical player, which is what you want on the defensive line. He was highly recruited, and good defensive linemen are hard to find."

The only Utah player signed by the Utes in 2003 was Class 3-A MVP Kyle Brady, a six-foot-two, 210-pound wide receiver from Tooele High School in Tooele, Utah. Meyer expressed gratitude in signing Brady because so many in-state players had already committed by the time Meyer's new staff started making visits. "Kyle is an extremely versatile player and will have a great career here," Meyer said. "We managed to get a great one in Kyle."

Barely mentioned on signing day in February 2003 was the five-foot-eleven, 185-pound defensive back from Alta Loma, California. Alphabetical order placed Eric Weddle's name at the bottom of Utah's 2003 recruiting list. With his confident grin and slicked-back black hair, some of his teammates teased the southern California recruit by calling him a pretty boy who belonged on the cast of *Beverly Hills 90210*. But Eric was all business. From the moment he stepped on campus, he was determined to make the most of his opportunity. Lenny Ware's advice and encouraging words were still fresh in his mind, and Eric was prepared to do whatever was necessary to earn a starting spot on the defense. He also carried a huge chip on his shoulder: he wanted every school to regret the day it had passed on him. He drew inspiration from a quote by former Baltimore Ravens coach Brian Billick, who, during Baltimore's playoff run to Super Bowl XXXV, had said: "When you go into the lion's den, you don't tippy-toe in. You carry a spear. You go in screaming like a banshee. If you go in any other way, you're going to lose."

"My mindset was that I wasn't trying to make friends," Weddle explained. "People didn't like me because I didn't take any garbage. A lot of guys thought I'd bow down to them, but I wasn't like that. I was just trying to play football and do my thing. I wanted to be the best, and I was going to outplay anyone out there. I've always been that way."

It didn't take long for Eric to make his presence known. As fall camp got under way, the energetic freshman attacked each drill with dramatic fury, as if it were his last, even when the players were instructed to go half-speed. In team meetings, Eric was not afraid to speak up by asking questions or providing answers to questions posed by coaches. "Eric prided himself in being first," said Morgan Scalley, a teammate who became a close friend.

Like most incoming freshmen, Eric started out at the bottom of the depth chart. Scalley, a junior, was the starter at free safety, and senior Dave Revill was the strong safety. Senior Anthony White and junior Kawika Casco were listed second at each respective position. As a senior, Revill took pride in speaking up at team meetings, especially when the questions came from safety coach Bill Busch. When upstart underclassman Eric Weddle began beating him to the punch, Revill began to ask, "Who is this punk freshman? Who does he think he is?"

The closest thing to a confrontation took place on a blistering August afternoon during two-a-days on the practice field. The safeties had gathered for what was supposed to be a light, low contact drill focused on improving fundamental tackling technique. It was not full speed. Players wore helmets and dressed in practice jerseys, shorts, and cleats. Revill took charge by demonstrating the drill. One player was the running back with the ball and the other guy was the safety. They were supposed to jog toward each other and the safety's job was to wrap up the ball carrier and go to the end of the line. Simple enough. "It was a mellow little warm-up. All of us who had been there forever knew what it was about," Revill recalled with a tinge of irritation in his voice. "Eric thought it was full speed, and he started juking people. He was going all out on everybody like he was Rudy [Ruettiger]."

On his first rep, Eric sidestepped Scalley. To save face, Scalley then did the same thing to Revill, "so Morgan wouldn't look bad," Revill said. "Everybody was like, 'Hey this is warm-ups, freshman. Stop. Chill. Simmer down.'" When Eric faked his way past another teammate, Revill was finally fed up. "I said screw that, give me the ball, and I juked him."

Eric respectfully refused to back down. "If someone talked down to me, gave me guff, gave me any 'I am a senior and this is my team' garbage, I wouldn't stand for it," Eric said. "If we had to fight or yell, I was going to fight and yell. I was not going to let them push me around. My whole focus was to play ball and start."

Jay Hill, a defensive graduate assistant at the time, described Eric the freshman this way: "He was extremely confident. . . . He came across as a young, cocky, California egotistical kid, and a lot of older teammates were turned off by it. But he quickly earned people's respect."

While he may have rubbed some players the wrong way with his assertive attitude, Eric did subtle things to gain the respect of other teammates. Toward the end of a team barbecue at the home of Coach Meyer, teammate Justin Hansen remembers, the freshmen were ordered to help clean up the mess. "There was a lot of bickering. Some guys were picking on the freshmen," Hansen said. "Then there was Eric. He grabbed a garbage bag and starting going around, asking if guys were done and picking up trash. I was impressed with his humility in doing that the way he did."

Eric also impressed the coaches, especially when it came to understanding the Xs and Os. It had taken Revill most of his college career to learn Utah's complicated defensive schemes. He said Eric comprehended the defense before he came to Utah. "He was so knowledgeable," Revill said. "He knew the packages and everything else. I knew he would start by the middle of the season. It was unbelievable how much knowledge he had about the game."

"It was apparent from day one," said Kyle Whittingham, then Utah's defensive coordinator. "He was head and shoulders above everyone else in that class in our agility tests and practices. He was the best safety, best wide receiver, the best everything."

Initially, Eric was going to redshirt his first year. But his hustle and aggressive nature impressed the coaches. In the team's first scrimmage in mid-August, the freshman managed to get on the field against the first-string offense and made the most of it. He picked off a Brett Elliott pass and broke several tackles on his way to a 65-yard touchdown return. The play was featured that night in a team meeting at the Smith Center. Kyle Gunther, a fellow freshman, said the coaching staff always compiled the day's best and worst plays. "They either embarrassed you or made you look good," said Gunther, now a sports radio talk show host in Utah. That night he was seated toward the back of the room with the underclassmen, none of whom wanted to redshirt. When Eric's interception return hit the screen, the room went silent. "Here is this freshman picking off our starting quarterback and making the offense look stupid," said Gunther. "He was unstoppable. He spun away from two guys, broke five or six tackles, and had his own little highlight film. That just doesn't happen. Freshmen don't get highlights like that in team meetings. Urban Meyer stood up and said, 'You guys better start praying to Eric Weddle, 'cause this kid is going to play this year.'"

A season-ending injury to Casco solidified the team's need for another defensive back, and going into the first game of the season at home against in-state foe Utah State, Eric had earned the right to start on special teams. He was assigned to the kickoff, kickoff return, and punt return teams. His parents traveled to the game and, just like in Pop Warner and high school games, Debbie Weddle had her home video camera loaded with a blank tape. Every time Eric jogged onto the green turf, Debbie's finger hit the "record" button. There was Eric, in red game jersey and pants with a black stripe down the side. The block numeral 32, in white, stood out in sharp contrast against the red jersey. His feet were clad in white turf shoes. A long-sleeved red shirt covered his arms, complete with white sweatbands above both elbows. Gloves protected his hands. Officially looking the part, Eric the freshman lined up on the front line of the kickoff return team and did his best to engage his assigned USU player. On kickoffs, the team huddled until the last possible moment when the kicker signaled for the players to spread out. This made it harder for the opposing team to figure out which man to block. Eric made a tackle on his second kickoff, and when his name was announced on the

Rice-Eccles public address system, the small Weddle section in the north end zone clapped and cheered.

Because Utah dominated Utah State that night, Eric and the kickoff team were on the field often. With the Utes winning 34–10 late in the fourth quarter, Eric saw his first action in the Utah defensive backfield. When a player is inserted in the fourth quarter of a blowout, it's referred to as "garbage time." Eric didn't expect the Aggies to do much at that point. The freshman was wrong. On the third play of his college career, Eric misread a receiver pattern and got burned for a 50-yard touchdown bomb. "I jumped a short route, and they ran a backside post," Eric said. "I saw the ball go up, and I just started walking to the end zone."

The touchdown was inconsequential because the game was already in the bag, but his teammates and coaches were very displeased with Eric's body language after the mistake. Several individuals let the freshman hear about it when he came off the field. Whittingham was first in line. "It was not laziness as much as it was thinking too much, but he wasn't going full speed, and I told him he was never going to play here with that kind of effort," Whittingham said. "I ripped him pretty good after that play."

Hill, now Utah's cornerback coach, followed Whittingham. "He wasn't in position and got a chewing out like no other," the assistant coach said. "We put the kid in his place."

Revill and Scalley also took their turns. "He quit on the play. He loafed, just didn't care to go after the ball," Revill said. "I sat with him and told him it was fine, don't worry about it. Correct the mistake and move on."

"Welcome to college football," Scalley said.

Eric learned from the experience. "I was rarely scored on in high school, so it made me realize I needed to get with it. There's no chewing out like Coach Whit's chewing out. But I knew he wanted the best out of me," Eric said.

Whittingham loved the fact that Eric seldom made the same mistake twice. He moved on quickly.

Eric continued to contribute on special teams for the next two games, a 28–26 loss at Texas A&M and a 31–24 win over California on national television. Going into the fourth game at Colorado State, however, a new opportunity presented itself. During a team meeting, Scalley and Weddle were informed they would compete for the starting right cornerback position. Freshman Shaun Harper started the first three games at that position, but the coaching staff felt Eric could do a better job. Eric had never played cornerback before, yet he was willing to give it a shot if it meant playing time and helping the team. That day in practice the two defensive backs took turns going one-on-one with receivers. Coach Hill remembers the competition well. "Scalley had the instincts of a safety. Weddle had the hips to play corner and had some interceptions and knockdowns," he said. "We knew we had something special."

So Eric got the nod and moved to right cornerback while Scalley remained at free safety. Meyer and Whittingham hoped Eric could bolster a secondary that had been shaky the previous year. During the 2002 season, Utah's cornerbacks were burned by big plays that led to losses in four games. Eric drew on his own experience at wide receiver to understand the dynamics of his new position. "At corner you are out there on an island by yourself, in your own little world, battling with the receiver. You can't talk to anyone, and you can't worry about anything else but playing the receiver," Eric said. "Even though I was raw, I knew the routes and what the receivers were looking for, and it really helped me in the long run."

Debbie Weddle dreamed her son might start one college game by the end of his senior year. But in the third week of September 2003, Eric called his parents with the news that they needed to find a way to get to Fort Collins, Colorado, for the upcoming weekend.

"Why?" Steve asked.

"Because I'm starting," Eric the freshman replied nonchalantly.

"So we did," Steve said years later. "We felt like it was a once-in-a-lifetime thing."

One of the first wide receivers Eric was assigned to cover was Colorado State's David Anderson. Eric did his best to ignore the 29,000 rowdy fans watching in Hughes Stadium and focus on Anderson. With Utah ahead 14–0 in the second quarter, Eric lost track of Anderson along the back of the end zone. The CSU receiver pulled in a 4-yard touchdown to put the Rams on the board. Eric vowed not to give up another touchdown pass in the game, and he didn't, although Anderson finished with eight catches for 85 yards.

The game ended dramatically. The Utes and Rams were tied 21–21 and CSU was driving for the game-winning score when Revill made one of the biggest plays of the season. As Colorado State running back Marcus Houston took a handoff around the left side of the Utes defense, Revill aimed his helmet at the ball and collided with Houston, popping the pigskin into the air, and it landed in the arms of teammate Arnold Parker. The senior raced 80 yards for the game-winning score. Utah won 28–21.

In his first college start, Eric posted six tackles, including one for a 3-yard loss. But he was just getting started. Over the next five games, Weddle played like a senior and made significant contributions.

**October 3, 2003**: In the fifth game of the 2003 season, nearly 45,000 boisterous fans and a national television audience were watching the Utes cling to a 17–13 lead against the 19th-ranked Oregon Ducks in the middle of the fourth quarter. The tension in Rice-Eccles Stadium was increasing each down as Oregon quarterback Jason Fife marched the Ducks into Utah territory with less than five minutes to play.

Weddle was making just his second start at cornerback. In full Utah getup, Eric had spent most of his energy defending Oregon receivers Demetrius Williams and Samie Parker. Parker was a sprinter with world-class speed. As the final five minutes began to tick away, Fife scrambled for 14 yards and went out of bounds, giving the Ducks first-and-10 at the Utah 38-yard line.

But that was as far as the Ducks would go. Whittingham signaled in a play that called for the freshman to come on a blitz. Seconds after the ball was snapped, Weddle dashed around the Oregon tight end and into the pocket where he pummeled Fife and knocked the ball loose. Unaware of the fumble, other Utah defenders swarmed the fallen quarterback. That allowed Weddle enough time to pounce on the ball. Moments later, when the referees uncovered the pile, No. 32 emerged with the pigskin, sending the crowd into a frenzy. The sack-and-fumble-recovery by Weddle eliminated the Ducks' final scoring threat and all but sealed the victory for the Utes.

**October 11, 2003:** In a 27–6 victory over San Diego State (another California program near Eric's hometown that didn't recruit him), Eric blitzed and sacked the quarterback, then prevented a late SDSU score when he intercepted the ball in the end zone.

**October 18, 2003:** Against UNLV, Eric had 6 tackles, a sack, 2 pass breakups, and a forced fumble. Ware attended the game and reminded the Rebels coaching staff how they had missed out on the Alta Loma kid. "The defensive coordinator exclaimed, 'You didn't tell me he was that good!'" The score: Utes 28, Rebels 10.

**October 25, 2003:** At home against New Mexico, Eric contributed nine tackles, a sack, and another interception in Utah's only conference loss in 2003.

**November 1, 2003:** One week after a thrilling 45–43 triple overtime win against Air Force at Colorado Springs, Colorado, Utah continued its winning ways with a 47–17 thrashing of Wyoming in Salt Lake City. Eric played his best game of the year with 10 tackles, a forced fumble, and a pass breakup.

In order to win their first outright conference title in forty-six years, Utah had to defeat archrival BYU, whom Meyer to this day refers to as "that team down south." The players suited up in front of more than 64,000 fans at LaVell Edwards Stadium on a snowy, frigid afternoon in late November. To say it was "freezing" doesn't begin to describe the conditions that day.

"When you tackled someone, your body became all wet and eventually numb," Eric said. "My hands were like icicles, and I couldn't feel my feet. For someone from southern California, it was awful."

Nevertheless, Weddle endured the chilling conditions and made two critical plays that helped lead Utah to the win. After Utes kicker Bryan Borreson booted a 41-yard field goal through the snowflakes to give Utah a 3–0 margin in the second quarter, Eric stepped in front of a pass by BYU's Jackson Brown, made the interception, and fell out of bounds near midfield to halt a Cougars drive before the half.

The second critical play came with less than five minutes remaining in the fourth quarter. On fourth-and-11 from the Utah

36, Mat Kovacevich punted to BYU's senior wide receiver Toby Christensen. The Cougars player fielded the punt and managed to get 9 yards before a hit by Weddle jarred the ball loose. Weddle's teammate Casey Evans was in the right spot and recovered the pigskin. The Utes ran out the clock and walked away with a 3–0 victory. The team was presented with the Mountain West Conference championship trophy in the visiting locker room and celebrated by singing Utah's old fight song, "Utah Man."

Following the game, Coach Whittingham extended an open invitation to any players who wanted to enjoy a victory party at his parents' Utah County home. Eric and a dozen other players accepted. The shutout win was especially meaningful to Whittingham because of his deep ties to BYU, and because his father, a former Cougar coach, had passed away a month earlier. He appreciated Eric and others who came to share that victory with him. "As the defensive coordinator, it was gratifying to shut BYU out," Whittingham said. "They're our biggest rival, and it had been a difficult time for me with my father's passing, so it was special to be surrounded by friends and family as we celebrated that victory."

Covering Toby Christensen had been one of Weddle's top priorities in the big game, and, with the help of the elements and his teammates, Eric limited the senior wide receiver to 2 catches for 26 yards. While disappointed with the loss, which marked the end of his college career, Christensen came away singing Weddle's praises. "I remember thinking, 'Wow, Utah must really like this kid because he is following me everywhere I go.' It didn't take me long to realize he was an outstanding player."

While taking note of Weddle's physical abilities, Christensen was also impressed by his demeanor on the field. At one point in the game, Christensen made a shifty move to shed Weddle at the line of scrimmage then ran a corner route and caught a pass for a 19-yard gain. "I am used to hearing cornerbacks trash talk about my mother or tell me how badly I play," said Christensen. "There is not a thing I haven't been called—if you can think it, someone has said it." He recalls how Eric didn't trash-talk him after his successful play. Instead, "Eric said to me, 'That was a really nice move.' That shocked me."

Following his career at BYU, Christensen, the son of former BYU and NFL tight end Todd Christensen, signed as an undrafted free agent with the Houston Texans. While in Texas, Christensen sized up cornerback Dunta Robinson, Houston's first-round pick out of South Carolina. Robinson had 4.2 speed, but in Christensen's opinion, he was no Eric Weddle. "Eric may not have been as fast, but he was a better football player. I have nothing but good things to say about him. After I saw what he [Eric] did to [Georgia Tech wide receiver] Calvin Johnson [in the 2005 Emerald Bowl] and San Diego State [in 2006], I don't feel bad that he shut me down."

The season culminated with Utah's 17–0 triumph over Conference USA champ Southern Mississippi in the 2003 Liberty Bowl. The Utah defense finished the season without giving up a point in ten straight quarters. The 10–2 season established a new era of winning and prominence for the Utes football program.

Eric completed the year with stellar numbers: 60 tackles (29 solos), with 4 sacks, 4 forced fumbles, and a fumble recovery. He deflected 4 passes and recorded 3 interceptions. He had earned a reputation as one of the hardest hitters in the league, as well as a reliable cover corner. He was named a freshman all-American by the *Sporting News* and was an all-Mountain West Conference honorable mention selection. His first year of college football may have surprised some, but it was only a glimpse into Eric's potential. His best years were yet to come. While talent and tenacity had carried him through his freshman season at Utah, faith and a spiritual awakening would play a central role in his future success. At the end of his freshman year, Eric moved into a house off-campus with a group of teammates, a few of whom happened to be Latter-day Saint returned missionaries.

# CHAPTER 7

# A SPIRITUAL EDGE

The freshman's poker face made it hard to tell if he was bluffing or just being polite.

Practice and team meetings were over for the day, and a matchup with Conference USA champion Southern Mississippi was looming in the 2003 Liberty Bowl. Rather than expend energy in downtown Memphis, Tennessee, several members of the University of Utah football team were huddled around a table in a hotel room playing Texas Hold 'em and swapping stories.

When the conversation turned religious and Eric Weddle mentioned he had once attended Latter-day Saint Church meetings with his old girlfriend, his Mormon teammates perked up.

"Really," said Justin Hansen, a walk-on tight end and roommate of Eric who had served a two-year LDS mission to Buenos Aires, Argentina. "You should come over to our house and meet the missionaries."

Eric accepted the invitation with a poker face. "Yeah, sure

thing," said the freshman. Cards were shuffled, and the game continued.

Eric's response was so nonchalant that Hansen wasn't sure if the freshman cornerback was genuinely interested or not. He decided to ask again later. At that point, Hansen could not have predicted that six months down the road he would directly participate in Eric Weddle becoming a member of the LDS Church.

Soon after arriving at the University of Utah, Eric recognized that roughly half of his teammates were Mormons—members of The Church of Jesus Christ of Latter-day Saints—and about a third of the team were older players like Hansen who had served two-year missions for their church. Eric was raised in the Lutheran faith but respected his teammates and felt a mutual respect in return. He was comfortable around the other players; they were all good guys, whatever their religious affiliation. Aside from attending worship services once in high school with Chanel, Eric didn't know much about the LDS Church. But he wasn't afraid to ask questions when he was curious. Eric asked Morgan Scalley about his days as a missionary in Germany. He asked Hansen about his daily routine and the people in Argentina, and he posed similar questions to linebacker Spencer Toone about his service in Australia. He learned that Coach Whittingham was a practicing Mormon. Urban Meyer was not a member but had developed a friendship with LDS Apostle Elder Joseph B. Wirthlin, who had been a Utah running back in the 1940s. Wirthlin was a member of the Church's Quorum of Twelve Apostles, a group of Church leaders considered by faithful members to be the modern-day equivalent of the apostles in the New Testament. The Church leader made an impression on the young freshman when they met at a team function. "When you talked to him, he looked you right in the eye," Eric said of Wirthlin, who died in 2008. "He was the most humble, sincere, and genuine person. He had an aura about him. He was pretty amazing to be around."

Eric noticed a similar aura with teammates like Hansen, Toone, and Scalley. They seemed to have something extra, a characteristic or quality that was palpable to Eric, but he couldn't put his finger on exactly what it was.

When the first off-season winter workout after his freshman season rolled around, Eric arrived at the school's indoor athletic facility with his teammates about 5:30 a.m. He tried not to imagine the warm, comfortable bed he had just left. He was not really in the mood for one of Meyer's brutal conditioning sessions. When Meyer was coach at Bowling Green, he became famous for chaining up the doors from the inside, covering the windows with black paper and having players run until they threw up in plastic garbage cans conveniently placed along the field. Running, weight lifting, and other unorthodox methods were used to help players get in shape. "It was one of the toughest things a human could go through," Eric said of winter workouts.

It was during these torturous sessions that Eric noticed Morgan Scalley with a smile on his face, as if he were actually having a good time. Scalley's cheerful disposition boggled Eric's mind. "He was jumping around, laughing and yelling like it was fun. Why was he so happy?" Eric said. "I learned there was something more to him, something special."

As a team leader, Scalley knew most players didn't relish getting out of bed early, so he decided to liven things up. "Our workouts were pretty grueling, so we tried to make it fun by singing and dancing," Scalley said. "It would wake people up and get them going. We were able to have fun in different ways. Eric was very observant. He started to search out how we lived our lives and why we did the things we did. It was a good reminder as a member of the Church that people are always watching you, whether you recognize it or not."

Eric observed similar behavior with other Mormon team-mates as well. The more he was around them, the more they in-trigued him. He admired their positive demeanor and respected the way they carried themselves. They were self-motivated, driven to achieve goals, and they treated him like a brother. At the same time, he also began to feel emptiness in his own life. Something was missing, and it troubled him.

"I was an all-American and had a great future ahead of me, but something didn't feel right," Eric said. "I didn't know where I was going or why I was here. Why are they different from me? What do they have that I don't? It made me start to think about what I was missing in life. I should have been the happiest guy in the world, but I wasn't. Other people had the gospel, and that in-trigued me. I needed something to make me complete, and even-tually I realized it was the gospel."

It was about this time that Hansen extended a second invita-tion for Eric to meet the missionaries. The idea interested Eric, and a meeting was arranged at his teammate's place. Among those in attendance were two fellow students who, like Eric, were not Mormon—a female student secretary in the athletic department and another football player Eric didn't know well. The group also included Eric's teammates Hansen, Toone, and Scalley, as well as two male missionaries aged nineteen and twenty years old.

Eric's first meeting with the Mormon missionaries was both disastrous and momentous, depending on who is recalling the story. His Mormon teammates thought it was a failure. Things started off well enough with some pleasant introductions, then things began to unravel for the young men in white shirts, ties, and black nametags. One of the elders was brand new. He was

German, and he spoke very little English. His American companion, a more experienced missionary, struggled to communicate with his foreign partner and at times lost his patience. Toone recalls a verbal spat between the two at one point. "They didn't get along that well. There was some tension," Toone said. "One would leave the other hanging, and their frustration showed." Eric's buddies figured he would bolt as soon as the meeting was over and never want to hear about the Church again.

Eric, however, was oblivious to their concerns. He focused intently on the message, which hit a mark in his heart. "I was as happy as can be," Eric said. "It was the calm feeling I felt. It felt like what they were saying was true. It could have been a little kid teaching me, because I was ready for it. It was from the heart, and that was what mattered."

That peaceful, reassuring feeling stayed with Eric as he continued to meet with the missionaries and his teammates. "He was very intent on learning," Scalley said. "He took the scripture study very seriously, and he was dead set on finding out if it was true." When he had questions, his teammates eagerly offered their insight and experience, and in such a way that Eric never felt that he was being pressured to join the Church. The more he learned and felt, the more he wanted the Church in his life.

Eric was already living the Mormon lifestyle in many ways, so it was easy to accept what he was being taught. Eric liked the Church's health code, known as the Word of Wisdom, which prohibits the use of addictive substances such as drugs and alcohol, encourages balanced eating habits, and promises health, wisdom, and knowledge to those who follow it. He had tasted alcohol a few times in high school, but at this point in his life he was more interested in taking care of his body.

Latter-day Saints are taught to avoid using profanity and

foul language. Eric had never been one to swear. He liked the emphasis on discipline and education. Honesty, daily habits of prayer and personal scripture study, as well as being kind and serving others, were all aspects of the religion that impressed him. Most of all, Eric was drawn to doctrines and principles about the importance of protecting the family unit. Eric loved his family dearly.

Another element of the Church that captivated Eric's interest was the Book of Mormon. Eric usually watched television or played video games before going to bed in the evenings, but at some point he noticed his roommate, Justin Hansen, in their bedroom reading his Book of Mormon. Eric asked what he was reading, and Hansen described the book's stories with great imagery and detail. These readings played a big role in Eric's investigation of the Church.

"Justin had a talent for telling stories and explained things in a way that was really easy to understand," Eric said. "As he told the story, I could envision the scene in my mind. I was interested and would go in and listen to him most nights."

LDS Church members believe the Book of Mormon contains the history of God's dealings with a civilization that lived in the Americas between approximately 600 B.C. and A.D. 400. According to Mormon doctrine, the records were compiled onto gold plates by a prophet named Mormon and then hidden for centuries in a hillside in upstate New York. In 1827, Church founder Joseph Smith Jr. obtained these ancient records, translated them through divine inspiration, and published the record as the Book of Mormon. Mormons believe the Book of Mormon is a companion to the Bible and consider it "another testament of Jesus Christ."

The battles of two rival societies figure prominently in the book. The Nephites, who often considered themselves devout followers of Jesus Christ, spent much of their time trying to convert or defend themselves against the imperialistic advances of their mostly heathen rivals, the Lamanites. The Book of Mormon ends with the tale of a last great conflict between the Nephites and the Lamanites.

Eric believed in the Bible but had never really cracked one open. When his buddies began sharing stories from the Book of Mormon, especially stories that involved soldiers and battles, he was fascinated. Coach Meyer often motivated the team by talking about dangerous missions, handling intense situations well, and being a strong, courageous and loyal soldier, so the stories from the Book of Mormon resonated with Eric. Captain Moroni, a soldier in the book, was so respected and revered for his character and loyalty in defending his people that he was named chief commander of the Nephite army at age twenty-five. Captain Moroni devoted many years to defending his people from the bloodthirsty, power-hungry Lamanites. Captain Moroni would have made a great team leader for the Utes, Eric thought.

One of Moroni's officers, Teancum, led Nephite forces into battle against a Nephite dissenter named Amalickiah. During the night, Teancum bravely crept into the enemy's camp and stabbed Amalickiah through the heart with a javelin while he slept. Teancum later killed Amalickiah's brother and royal successor, Ammoron, in similar fashion, although this time the covert operation cost Teancum his life. Amalickiah and Ammoron were the two leading instigators of destruction against the Nephites during the tenure of Captain Moroni. The story of stealth assassination missions reminded Eric of blitzing off the corner and blindsiding a quarterback.

Later in the book, a group of Lamanite converts buries their weapons of war and covenants with God never to fight again. Facing attack and certain destruction from their Lamanite compatriots, 2,060 sons of these Christian converts volunteered to fight so their parents could remain true to their promise. The Book of Mormon describes the 2,060 sons as "exceedingly valiant for courage, and also for strength . . .—they were men who were true at all times in whatsoever thing they were entrusted. . . . They were men of truth and soberness, . . . and they did obey and observe to perform every word of command with exactness." These young men became known as the stripling warriors. Despite their youth and inexperience, they returned from several fierce battles without a single death among their ranks. Eric appreciated and connected emotionally, both as a football player and a person, with the Book of Mormon stories of bravery, faith, dedication, and redemption.

Eric also had a real-life example to look to in teammate Ben Moa. The gospel of Jesus Christ changed Moa's life.

Moa's earliest years were spent in San Bernardino, California, where he was raised by a single mother and baptized a Latter-day Saint at age eight. Because his mother worked, Ben was often left without supervision. One of the few positive influences in Moa's early life was his maternal grandfather, Sione Hafoka Moa, a proud Tongan and a devout Mormon. "My grandpa always took me to church when I was younger and told me I was special," Moa said. "But I raised myself, and I chose my uncles, brothers, and gangs."

By age ten, Ben was recruited into a Tongan gang. Soon he was engaging in stealing cars, burglary, selling drugs, drinking, and fighting. While visiting Utah relatives in 1993, the twelve-year-old helped steal a car and fired shots in a drive-by shooting. The police eventually captured him and his cousins, and he was sent to live at the Mill Creek Youth Corrections Center in Ogden for almost four years. At age sixteen, he was released and sent to live with relatives in Ogden, where he became a star athlete at Ogden High. Moa was recruited by then-Utah coach Ron McBride to play at the University of Utah, but he failed to qualify academically as a freshman. He remained on the team and attended classes despite not being eligible to play football. At the university, Moa met his future wife, Christina, a fellow student from Modesto, California. As their relationship deepened, her uplifting influence helped Moa get his life headed in a positive direction. They married prior to the 2000 season.

Despite his efforts, Moa's past continued to haunt him. While attending a family gathering at the National Guard Armory in West Jordan that August, rival gang members showed up for a fight. Moa tried to break it up but instead was hit with a 9mm bullet in his right side, collapsing one of his lungs. He nearly died, but a week later, Moa's condition had improved enough that he attended football practice. In attempting to play catch with a teammate, he tore open his wound and nearly died a second time.

Missing the season frustrated Moa and led to another moment of weakness. In November, he stole a teammate's wallet and was suspended from the team. He decided to quit football.

Moa and his wife moved to Modesto to start over. Christina convinced him to get his life in order. He began attending church again so he could "get things right with the Big Man upstairs," Moa said. They made a goal to be sealed as a couple in the Oakland California LDS temple, an ordinance Mormons believe makes it possible for family relationships to continue beyond death. In order to enter the temple, members must strictly follow Church guidelines prohibiting drugs, alcohol, and the types of activities that had derailed his life in the past. The Moas attended the temple for the first time together on Valentine's Day 2002. Christina also persuaded Ben to try football one more time. He enrolled at Modesto Junior College, pulled decent grades, and became a Junior College All-American tight end in the fall of 2001. Offers came from USC and Oregon, but Moa felt he had some unfinished business in Salt Lake City. He returned to the U of U.

Moa didn't have much of an impact as a junior in 2002, catching only 14 passes for 126 yards. But he was a good fit for Urban Meyer's spread offense. The six-foot-two, 260-pound senior played tight end and some running back during the 2003 season. He made several big plays for the Utes in 2003 but is best remembered for his heroic performance at Air Force. Playing without starting tailback Brandon Warfield, Coach Meyer called upon Moa to fill the void. In the third overtime, nationally ranked Air Force scored to go up 43–37 but failed a 2-point conversion. On fourth-and-one at the goal line, Moa took the direct snap and plunged into the end zone for the touchdown. College overtime rules forced Utah to go for 2. This time Moa took the shotgun snap, faked the run, and floated a pass over the Falcons defense and into the hands of wide-open teammate Matt Hansen. Utah won 45–43.

After his senior year at Utah, Moa spent time with the Miami Dolphins, NFL Europe's Berlin Thunder, and the New York Jets. The Moa family now lives in Ogden, where Ben sells insurance and helps coach local youth sports.

Late one night in the spring of 2004, Christina and the kids were asleep while teammates Ben and Eric played a game of Texas Hold 'em. Because Eric had been meeting with the missionaries, he asked Moa about his conversion and his path back to activity in the Church. Moa responded by sharing a spiritual experience he had when he and his wife were living in Modesto and preparing to attend the Oakland Temple.

After Ben and Christina committed to go to the temple, Ben was bombarded with opposition and questions from friends who advised him to read anti-Mormon material. He began to doubt himself, and confusion set in. One night while he was thinking about his life and family, Ben felt impressed to say a prayer. He went into the bathroom where he could be alone, fell to his knees, and tilted his head upward in supplication to the Lord. He asked God if he was doing the right things for himself and his family. As he continued to pray, he began to notice a powerful, reassuring feeling entering his heart and stirring his emotions. As tears streamed down his face, Moa remained motionless on the bathroom floor. He felt an energy surge within his soul and knew he had received his answer. The Moa family followed through on their plan to be sealed together in the temple. This experience also inspired Ben to return to Utah to redeem his name and finish his college football career.

Moa's experience left an impression on Eric. "For a guy with his stature and background to open up to me and share that spiritual moment was a big thing for him and meant a lot to me," Eric said. "Hearing his experience made me really want to find out if the Church was true."

In the days that followed, Eric had an increased desire to pray and read the Book of Mormon. There is a promise in the final pages of the Book of Mormon that invites readers to personally ask God if the book is inspired scripture: "And when ye shall receive these things, I would exhort you that ye would ask God, the Eternal Father, in the name of Christ, if these things are not true; and if ye shall ask with a sincere heart, with real intent, having faith in Christ, he will manifest the truth of it unto you, by the power of the Holy Ghost. And by the power of the Holy Ghost ye may know the truth of all things." Eric accepted the challenge and put forth the effort. One night, he opened his paperback copy of the Book of Mormon and began reading. As Eric studied the words, his mind felt enlightened. He became immersed in the book and kept turning pages. At one point he stopped and realized he had read more than twenty pages in a matter of minutes. Before, he had struggled to understand what he was reading, but at that moment he recalled details and everything made sense. "Something overtook me," Eric said. "This was the answer to my prayer. It felt right. I knew it was true. I made the decision to get baptized."

When Eric shared the news with his buddies, coaches, and teammates, support from them was abundant. His parents, however, had a different reaction.

"Are you crazy? What are you doing? We leave you for eight months and you want to join this church?" they asked, incredulous at Eric's news.

Eric's parents knew very little about the LDS Church. Debbie knew about the young men in white shirts because they had knocked on the Weddles' door several times over the years, and she usually invited them in and gave them something to drink. She wasn't interested in their message, however. Now Eric wanted to be baptized. She had a million questions and didn't know where to start. One of his parents' biggest concerns was that Eric's conversion might alter their relationship in some way. They worried that their son might not think as highly of them. "We drink and celebrate. Can we be part of your services?" Debbie wanted to know.

Eric patiently answered their questions and did his best to reassure them he still loved them. "I am what I am because of you.

If you weren't included, it wouldn't be worthwhile." He promised he would not get baptized without their blessing.

For several weeks, Eric answered more questions, provided his parents with information about the Church, and explained why the gospel was important to him. Each evening, as Steve and Debbie talked, they discussed their son's religious investigation of the LDS Church.

"In the end, we decided we should do what was best for Eric. We also considered how this might affect his relationship with Chanel," Steve said. "We decided that if this was what Eric wanted, then we would support him."

Back in Salt Lake City, Eric fasted and prayed for his parents' approval. Finally, one morning, his parents surprised him with a call to say they were coming to Salt Lake City for his baptism.

A large crowd of teammates, coaches, friends, family, Church leaders, and even a few curious nonmembers gathered at the LDS institute building on campus for Eric's baptism on June 24, 2004. The service was relatively short in length. Chanel attended the service and offered the closing prayer, even though the two hadn't really spoken in months. The congregation sang a hymn, and several Church leaders offered brief remarks. The group then moved to the baptismal font for the baptismal ordinance. Eric and Justin Hansen, both dressed in white, stood in waist-deep water. Hansen raised his right arm to the square, pronounced a short prayer, then lowered Eric completely under the water and raised him back up. As Eric emerged from under the water, he did something many have never witnessed at a baptism. He pumped his fist in the air and yelled, "Yeah!" The crowd smiled and shared a light chuckle. Many felt the gesture perfectly illustrated Eric's enthusiasm for his religious conversion.

"That was a vintage Eric Weddle move. I'm surprised he didn't flash the 'U' as he came out of the water," Coach Whittingham said later. "It was great to see him take that step in his life. You could see he was at peace with himself. Attending his baptism was a great spiritual experience."

Toone and Hansen agreed the event was one of the more memorable baptisms they had ever attended. "It was special," Toone said. "You have baptisms on your mission, but when you have one at home it means a little more."

"To see the light come into his life, to see the change it made in him and how happy he was—it was special to be part of that," Scalley said.

Steve and Debbie, who came along with Eric's grandparents, described the occasion as "emotional" and "very appropriate." They said they were treated well by those they met and never felt pressured by anyone to join the Church. Most important, they were happy for Eric.

"A mother knows her son. She knows when he is hurt on the field. To see him after he received the Holy Ghost, [his face was bright,] white as a sheet. I knew he had felt something," Debbie said. "It affected us all."

Steve also enjoyed the service but worked in a subtle jab at Scalley. "He came up to me and said, 'When I said take care of him, I didn't mean this,'" Scalley laughed.

When Eric's parents began to grasp an understanding of the basic teachings and practices of the Mormon Church and realized they weren't losing their son, they relaxed and accepted his new lifestyle. In reality, it wasn't much of a change from the life he had been living. "He had always been a good kid," Steve said.

"To this day, joining the Church has been the best decision I have ever made. I have never looked back," Eric said. "Ultimately I became a better teammate, leader, and overall person. Having the gospel makes a difference. You enjoy life and the people around you more. It has put me in a position to have direction, love, and what I want most for my family. Football isn't everything in life. When I am ninety and people look back, they aren't going to look at how many touchdowns I scored. They will want to know if I helped someone out or changed a life, if I was a good husband or father. I can't base my life on whether or not I was a good football player. So I try to keep that in perspective and know I can do so many greater things in life."

Debbie still feels a tinge of guilt for letting Pop Warner games edge out her family's attendance at their Lutheran church services. But she's certain the Sundays spent on the football field served their own purpose. "Who are we to say how God will use Eric? He has a special calling in life," Debbie said. "God will use him."

# CHAPTER 8

⟋

# *THE PERFECT SEASON*

When Chanel Blaquiere left Eric Weddle's baptismal service, she was sincerely happy for him. "Good for him," she thought. She had seen a glow in his countenance and felt a tinge of satisfaction knowing she had played a small role in introducing him to the LDS Church. The gospel of Jesus Christ was her life's main source of happiness. She had prayed he would join the Church for the right reasons and not just because of "a pretty face." At that point, she considered him a dear friend but nothing more. In her opinion, they were not likely to ever get back together. She had soccer, school, and other guys calling for dates.

After arriving at Utah State University for her freshman year in 2002, Chanel embraced her role with the women's soccer team and relished the college town atmosphere she found in Logan. Chanel wore No. 18 and played forward for the Aggies. She saw action in every game and scored three goals to help USU to an 8–9–3 record in her first year. As a sophomore in 2003, she scored two goals, and the team won ten games, lost seven, and tied twice.

Academically, Chanel became fascinated with the field of social work and made it her major.

Although she maintained occasional contact with Eric, she spent her freshman and sophomore years dating four young men at different times. Two left school to serve Mormon missions, and she wrote letters to both of them. In the meantime, two other young men pursued her, both recently returned from the mission field. Chanel didn't consider any of the four relationships to be serious.

Eric knew Chanel was having fun socially, but he was patient and persistent. "He kept telling me he knew I was 'the one.' He said he knew from the beginning," Chanel said. "Well, I didn't, so I dated other people. I had dated only Eric [in high school], so I wanted to date some others and see what was out there. I wanted to date someone like me [a Mormon] because they say you marry the kind of person you date. He kept saying, 'I will wait around for you. I will wait around.'"

But waiting around didn't exactly mean Eric wasn't socializing with other girls. He had invested in a few relationships, but none of them were serious. What bothered Chanel was that he wasn't forthcoming about his other female acquaintances. She didn't mind that he was spending time with other girls, but why not be open about it? It felt like high school again, she thought. Chanel was also bothered that her mother, Sonya, adored Eric and wanted her to take him back. These circumstances motivated her to go in a different direction.

Chanel worried about even attending Eric's baptism, since her mere presence would make things awkward. Originally, she was asked to speak at the service, but she agreed to offer the closing prayer instead. She didn't want people to think she and Eric were anything more than friends.

In the weeks and months following his baptism, Eric continued to send friendly "how are you" text messages to his old girlfriend in Logan, but she didn't respond. Chanel hoped he would get the hint that it was time to move on. As the fall of 2004 began, any chance of a romantic relationship between Eric and Chanel appeared on the brink of collapse. When Sonya asked Chanel if she and Eric might get back together, Chanel replied, "I am not going to, nor will I ever, marry Eric."

Fate intervened on September 2, 2004.

The Utah State women's soccer team was in Spokane, Washington, that Thursday night for a Friday match with Gonzaga. Chanel was relaxing in her hotel room when some teammates came into the room and asked if she had heard the news.

"What news?" Chanel asked.

"Eric got hurt. He's on crutches," a teammate informed her.

"No way!" Chanel said as she reached for the remote and found ESPN.

More than 725 miles away, in Salt Lake City, the University of Utah was hosting Texas A&M in the 2004 season opener. Eric started the game at strong safety, and, early in the first quarter, Terrance Murphy, a wide receiver for the Aggies, hurled his 193 pounds into Weddle's left leg during an attempted block. The impact sprained the medial ligament in Weddle's left knee. He limped off the field and spent the rest of the night on the sidelines.

Eric carried his cell phone to the bench in the third quarter so he could communicate with his parents. He assured them everything would be fine. Then his phone buzzed with a surprise message.

"Hey, I'm watching your game with my teammates and noticed you were hurt," came the thoughtful text from Chanel. "Hope you are doing okay."

Chanel was equally surprised when a reply arrived minutes later. Eric reported he was fine. He asked if they could talk after the game. She agreed.

Hours later, the Utah State soccer player and the University of Utah football player dialed up and reconnected. They lost track of time as they spoke of their families, school, sports, and church. As they talked and teased one another, Chanel's heart softened, and she realized she still wanted to be with Eric. "As nice as the other guys were, they weren't Eric," Chanel said.

Eric may have dated other girls at the U, but Chanel was the only girl he had ever loved. "I needed something to soften her heart so she'd come talk to me," Eric said. "If I hadn't gotten hurt, we wouldn't be married today."

## YEAR OF THE UTE

With a new spiritual balance, Eric found a new passion for life and football. He continued to work hard and impressed his coaches during spring drills. As a result, the coaching staff did as Eric's other coaches had done: changed his position. Because they had a flock of talented cornerbacks, they returned the sophomore to his original position as safety, to share the defensive backfield with senior Morgan Scalley. "He's a very, very versatile kid," Whittingham said of Eric at the time.

As he had done many times before, Eric embraced the change. "I'm all for it," said Eric, the sixth-leading tackler on the team in

2003. "I'm excited. It gives the whole defense more versatility, and it gives me more opportunities to make plays."

The coaches were clearly pleased with Eric's development, but there was still plenty of room for improvement. Jay Hill, then a defensive graduate assistant, said that when Eric was young he wasn't always the hardest worker in practice. "He was so talented and instinctive. He saw things faster than others did. Things came easy for him," Hill said. "So he was a little frustrating to coach because he could be lazy and get away with some things that others couldn't. But his practice habits improved."

Gary Andersen was Utah's defensive line coach in 2004 before being promoted to defensive coordinator in 2005. "Eric Weddle was a guy I had to prod day in and day out," said Andersen, now head coach at the University of Wisconsin. "He needed to be prodded on the practice field or he would get a little content. But he grew and developed and became a tremendous player."

Scalley shared a room with Eric on road trips, and the two became close friends on and off the field. "I took him under my wing, and we connected," Scalley said. "We knew each other's strengths, and we played off that. He was a better cover guy, and I was better in the post. I think that was the reason we had so much success together. We both knew the defense well. If I wanted to disguise a play, we both knew what the other was thinking. Being roommates also helped because we could talk about the game plan and what we wanted to do."

A knee injury was a difficult way to open the remarkable 2004 season for Eric, but he was grateful things weren't worse. The cut block by Murphy caused Eric to miss Utah's second game at Arizona. "It was the first time I wasn't able to play in a game in any sport. It was tough," Eric said. "I just thought to myself, 'This could be it, you know,' but it wasn't. The trainers for the school helped me out tremendously just to get me ready for the games. I was lucky and blessed that I came back from it and had a good rest of the year."

Although Eric was never one hundred percent the rest of the season, the sophomore played through the pain. The Arizona game was the only one he missed in his college career. But there was no way he was going to miss any more action. After going 10–2, earning their first outright conference title since 1957 and winning the Liberty Bowl, the Utes were eager to get back on the field for an encore. Utah returned 17 starters, and the players often mentioned the word "undefeated" in preseason interviews until coach Urban Meyer, a fanatic for focus, quashed any further talk on the subject. He even advised members of the media not to bring it up.

But the Utes coaches knew they had a talented group, and expectations were high. Shane Hinckley, who authored a history of the Utah football program, told of a preseason meeting in which Meyer asked the stadium staff if they were prepared for the fans to tear down the goalposts after Utah's first home game against Texas A&M. No, they were not, came the shocked response. The idea had never occurred to them. They were also appalled by Meyer's confidence, as if the game was already in the bag. While the goalposts didn't come down, Utah dismantled the Aggies, 41–21, much to the delight of more than 45,400 raucous fans. Utah moved up to seventeenth in the *Associated Press* poll.

The Utes followed up with a 23–6 win in Tucson, Arizona, and a 48–6 brotherly beat-down of Utah State in Logan. Just like that, the Utes were 3–0. Eric recorded two tackles in his return to the lineup against USU.

The next two opponents—MWC foes Air Force and New Mexico—were more competitive. Air Force got out to a 14–0 lead in the second quarter, but Utah scored 35 unanswered points. The Falcons pulled to 35–28, but in the fourth quarter, Utah running back Marty Johnson scored the last 2 of his 4 touchdown runs as the Utes pulled away for a 49–35 victory, the first over AFA in Salt Lake City since 1995.

Eric finished the game with 10 total tackles but contributed in another important way. The Utes were struggling in the punt return department. "We're inadequate at that spot," Meyer told reporters. The head coach wanted a north-south runner who could consistently get 10- to 15-yard returns. So receivers Steven Savoy and Paris Warren were out, and Eric was in. Weddle had not returned a punt or kick for the Utes and had been wearing a brace on his knee since the injury, but he got the job done against the Falcons. His first return covered 15 yards—more than triple the Utes' season average going into the game. He ran his second return back 31 yards and finished the day with 4 returns for 65 yards. "I was just waiting for them to give me a shot," Eric said. "I loved it."

Utah then avenged its only 2003 conference loss against New Mexico. The Utes limited the Lobos to 157 yards of total offense and 8 first downs in a 28–7 pounding. Eric led the defense with 7 tackles and returned 3 punts for 22 yards, but he was replaced as punt returner the next day due to a sore back. When the Associated Press poll came out the following week, 5–0 Utah was ranked number fourteen.

Most observers thought the North Carolina Tar Heels would be the season's toughest test for Utah, but the Utes posted 699 yards, the second largest yard total in the school's history, and won in a blowout, 46–16. Utah's defense smothered the Tar Heels, allowing just 221 yards rushing for a team that came in averaging 396.

Despite his nagging injuries, Eric played his best game of the season to that point. The stalwart sophomore recorded 11 tackles, 1.5 tackles for loss, and one interception. But Eric was more thrilled about a goal line stand in the third quarter. Following a fumble by Utah running back Marty Johnson, North Carolina had the ball first-and-goal on the Utah 1.

On first down, linebacker Grady Marshall stuffed the North Carolina runner.

On second down, defensive lineman Sione Pouha swatted away a pass.

On third down, cornerback Gerald Fletcher broke up a second pass.

On fourth down, with one of the largest crowds in Rice-Eccles Stadium history going wild, it was Eric's turn. He broke up a pass and turned the Tar Heels away.

The Utah defense almost repeated the feat a few minutes later on another series, but a pass interference penalty helped North Carolina score on third down from the 1-yard line.

"We just came together as one," Eric said of the goal line stand later. "We worked on it in practice, and we just know we can't budge when we get down there."

Team unity and a feeling of brotherhood among the players off the field was a major reason why the team executed so well on the field. The bonding began after Meyer's arrival in the 2003 season. During a cookout at the Meyer household, the coach and his wife noticed something odd. As the players dined, they were grouped by ethnicity, race, or religion.

"The married LDS kids were sitting over here, the black kids sitting over here, the Polynesians over here, the Hispanics over here," Meyer said in his biography. "Nobody's talking. They couldn't stand each other. I looked at Shelley and we said, 'What is this!?'"

"This has got to stop," Meyer announced to them, and he quickly broke up the divisiveness. Many of the players didn't realize they were doing it. Cliques were eliminated, and, at Meyer's insistence, the Ute players began to find out the family backgrounds of their teammates—their hometowns, their high schools, their hobbies, and so forth. If they didn't have a correct answer, they had to put in some running time. Little by little, a group of individuals became a team. When Meyer saw Scalley rushing off to a Polynesian pig roast, he told his wife, "Unless I screw this up, we will win every game we play next year." His prediction came to pass.

Eric Weddle was one player who connected well with teammates of various backgrounds. "A lot of people were drawn to Eric, from the high-profile guys to the guys who didn't see a down [of playing time]," Scalley said. "He had strong relationships with a lot of guys. He was observant and a good listener." Because Weddle was so well-respected, he became one of a group of players elected to the Utah Football Leadership Committee for the 2004 season. Being a member of the leadership committee provided Eric with opportunities to reach out and serve his teammates.

Marty Johnson was one player who really grew to appreciate Eric's friendship that year and beyond. Johnson came to the University of Utah in 2001 after brief stints at Boise State and Butte Junior College. He showed flashes of greatness, but injuries parked him on the sideline. He drowned his discouragement in alcohol. His trouble started in October 2002 when he crashed into a parked car, left the scene, and was arrested for driving under the influence. His blood-alcohol level was twice the legal limit.

Coach Meyer took a special interest in Johnson and welcomed

him into his family circle. Johnson became a regular at the Meyer home and attended family activities, and life improved for the problematic running back. Then, in the spring of 2003, Johnson failed to earn the starting tailback job and injured his foot again. He went drinking with some friends and had a minor accident on the way home. He was charged with a second DUI. When Meyer found out, he was furious and suspended Johnson indefinitely. He was ready to kick him off the team for good, but his wife, Shelley, persuaded her husband to reconsider. Johnson's mother had been murdered, and he had no real family. The Meyers reasoned that if Johnson lost football at this point, it might result in more DUIs and eventually a fatal accident. The matter finally went before the team's leadership committee. His teammates decided to give Johnson one more shot, provided he could meet a list of about fifteen conditions, including alcohol counseling, curfews, community service, passing random urine tests, and earning his college degree. The day after Thanksgiving 2003, Johnson stepped into a jail cell for a month while the team prepared for the Liberty Bowl. His desire to play football again, and not to be remembered as the talented player who screwed up, served as hope and motivation for him to come back. "It was a wake-up call," Johnson said. "I was willing to do anything. Give up clubs, drinking—I just wanted to play."

Eric was among those who reached out to Johnson. "I got close to Eric my last year because Coach Meyer had designated that I should change who I hang out with because I was getting in trouble," Johnson said. "Eric and Morgan Scalley were probably the main guys I started to hang around with. Scalley was married, so I spent more time with Eric. We played video games, cards, or just hung out. He helped me through a real tough time. We would talk about life and just doing things right. I am older and bigger, but I looked up to him, like a big brother-little brother thing. He was always there, just a good person. Hanging around him helped change my decisions and behavior."

Eric said the feeling was mutual. "I wanted to be a friend, and over the years we have stayed in touch. 'Friends and people pass through this life,' I told him, 'but I will always be there for you. No matter what, you can count on me,'" Eric said. "I was proud to see him turn his life around."

Johnson knew this was his last chance. He met the leadership committee's requirements and worked his way back onto the team. With his life back on track, Johnson became a major contributor to Utah's offensive success in 2004. Against Arizona, he ran for 105 yards and a touchdown. In the win over Air Force, he tied a school record with 4 rushing touchdowns. He also found the end zone in the North Carolina victory and a 63–28 crushing of UNLV.

Eric continued to thrive in the defensive secondary. He had 11 tackles against the Rebels and picked off passes against the Aztecs and Rams. He started returning punts again during this three-game stretch.

He also learned to play with pain. Against CSU, Eric separated his shoulder and played the rest of the season following a routine of little or no contact during the week then receiving a large shot of painkiller in the shoulder before games. There was a partial dulling effect from the shot, accompanied by an intense throbbing the rest of the time. He bore this burden without complaint.

"It was hard," Eric recalls. "I was in constant pain. I couldn't sleep the night after a game. Every time I hit someone, it caused a sharp pain. But it's just something you have to deal with. You're playing football, out there with the guys you love, guys you want to help, playing a game you love. It's a contact sport. I was glad when the season ended to just let it heal. It was a relief to get all that pain over with."

Going into the final regular season game against rival BYU, Utah was sixth in the BCS, a ranking high enough to qualify for a coveted BCS bowl game with a win over the Cougars. One of Meyer's concerns going into the game was the speed of BYU's receivers. Eric compared Todd Watkins to Oregon's Samie Parker. "Fastest receiver we faced in 2003," Eric said. On the other side, there was true freshman Austin Collie, who led the Cougars at that time with 50 receptions, 697 yards, and 7 touchdowns.

Weddle and the secondary felt prepared for the test, having learned lessons in games with other talented receivers such as San Diego State's Jeff Webb, Wyoming's Jovon Bouknight, and Malcom Floyd, a future teammate with the San Diego Chargers, as well as Colorado State's David Andersen. "We're up to the task," Eric told reporters in the days leading up to the game. "It will be great to see how we do against a great group of receivers."

The atmosphere was festive on the day of the game as fans braved the single-digit cold to show support during the live early-morning ESPN *College GameDay* show in the parking lot west of Rice-Eccles Stadium. Holding Fiesta Bowl signs and wearing Mexican sombreros, Utah fans went wild when ESPN's Lee Corso donned the Utes mascot head at the end of the show to predict a Utah win.

The veteran coach and sports broadcaster was right. The Utes thrashed the Cougars 52–21 to win their second consecutive MWC championship. Utah broke open a 21–14 game with 31 points during the second half. The Utes defense allowed the Cougars to compile only 294 total yards and one touchdown in the second half. Eric and the secondary limited Watkins to 4 catches for 41 yards and a touchdown. Collie caught 3 passes for 74 yards and one score. Collie also threw Eric an interception. With less than seven minutes to go in the third quarter, John Beck took the shotgun snap, turned, and fired a lateral pass to Collie near the 50-yard line. Collie launched a long pass down the sideline to a teammate, but at the last second Eric leaped in front of him and intercepted the pass before stepping out of bounds. He had now picked off passes in back-to-back years against BYU, something he was quite proud of.

As the clock ticked down the final seconds, sombrero-wearing fans spilled over the concrete barriers and stormed the field to bring down the goalposts. Meyer's prediction was only ten games late. A short time later, it was announced that Utah, at 11–0, would become the first non-BCS conference school to earn a BCS bid. The Utes were sent to the Fiesta Bowl in Tempe, Arizona, to face Big East champ Pittsburgh.

The forty-one days from the victory over BYU to the historic bowl game were tumultuous and eventful for the Utah program. Several schools wanted Meyer to be their head coach, and a media circus ensued. Florida was very interested, and then Notre Dame administrators arrived one evening in a private jet. Media speculation was wild as reporters scrambled to find sources with information on where Meyer would go. When the dust settled on December 4, Meyer accepted a multimillion-dollar contract to be the next head coach at the University of Florida.

The search for Meyer's replacement began. Dr. Chris Hill, Utah's longtime athletic director, wanted Kyle Whittingham, the Utes' proven defensive coordinator for the previous eleven seasons. But BYU entered the picture and offered Whittingham their head coaching position. He said the decision was one of the hardest of his life. Torn between his alma mater and Utah,

Whittingham lost several pounds in a matter of days because he couldn't eat while pondering his choice. Whittingham visited his father's grave, seeking inspiration. At one point, Scalley, Weddle, and several other players drove to the Whittingham home and pleaded with the coach to choose Utah.

"That was a very touching, emotional moment," Whittingham said. "That display of players voicing their opinion of wanting me to stay was one of the primary factors in my decision."

Finally Whittingham called the Utah team captains to inform them he was staying. Scalley was among the first to get the call. Whittingham's first words also happened to be the first line of the school fight song, "I am a Utah man, sir." In his history of Utah's football program, Shane Hinckley wrote of Whittingham's decision: "In one of the biggest recruiting battles ever waged between Utah and BYU, the Utes had their man."

Eric was happy for Coach Meyer and accepted his departure. "I have a lot of respect for him," Eric said. "He started a great thing here, a winning attitude, got the program on the map. His coaching philosophies have carried over to me as a player and as a person. Our relationship meant a lot to me, but I couldn't talk to him like I talk with Coach Whittingham. He was the reason I came to Utah. He was the only straightforward coach who offered me."

As the team prepared for the game with Pittsburgh, it was decided that Whittingham and Meyer would serve as co-head coaches for the Fiesta Bowl. The pressure was on Utah to prove that they deserved a BCS bid by beating the 20th-ranked Panthers.

But Pittsburgh was the unwanted team among the eight BCS squads. The Panthers automatically qualified for one of the four elite games as Big East champions, even though they were only twenty-first in the BCS rankings. Fiesta Bowl officials had no choice but to invite the 8–3 Panthers. Pitt was also in a state of transition. Like Meyer, coach Walt Harris was leaving for Stanford after eight seasons with the Panthers.

Utah had one advantage before the game even started. At least three-fourths of the sold-out Sun Devil Stadium's 73,519 fans were cheering for the Utes, creating a stunning sea of crimson in the stands for the national TV broadcast. It was likely the largest gathering of Utah fans ever assembled. Coaches and players later said the atmosphere felt like a home game. And the fans did not leave disappointed.

Behind the cool efficiency of quarterback Alex Smith, the fifth-ranked Utes used their fast-paced spread offense and an underrated defense to thoroughly dominate the Panthers 35–7. All of Utah's receivers and running backs got a chance to touch the ball as Smith threw for 328 yards and 4 touchdowns. Wide receiver Paris Warren set a Fiesta Bowl record with 15 receptions for 198 yards, and both Warren and Smith were named co-offensive MVPs.

The defense recorded a Fiesta Bowl-record nine sacks and allowed just 17 yards rushing. Nose tackle Steve Fifita was named the game's defensive MVP. Eric led the team with 11 tackles, a sack, and a pass breakup.

The four-touchdown rout of the Panthers concluded a 12–0 season, the first perfect record for Utah since 1930. The BCS-busting Utes finished number four in the AP's final poll.

## THE CHERRY ON TOP

How do you top a BCS-busting, undefeated season? For Eric Weddle, it was having his sweetheart accept his marriage proposal.

Following the Texas A&M text and late-night phone call, Chanel warmed up to Eric, and they began to talk again. Because of the distance between Logan and Salt Lake City, they only spoke on the phone for the next month. Then came an opportunity for a date, and the relationship deepened. "We went down to Temple Square and had a fun time," Chanel said. "At that point, we knew we wanted to date again. We both knew that if we started dating again we would talk about getting married. He was a member of the Church now, and we had so much chemistry. We set some goals and talked about what we wanted to be different this time."

They had two main goals. They wanted to be morally clean so they could be married in the LDS San Diego Temple. This meant not engaging in any sexual relations before their marriage. To avoid previous drama, parents and friends would not be granted front-row seats in the relationship. "It was not hard once we were committed to each other and made the temple our top priority," Chanel said. "We knew how important it was and were careful not to put ourselves in certain situations. We were still affectionate, but we didn't want anything to get in the way. Everything else was little stuff. Later on, I gave him a few other guidelines. No proposals on birthdays, holidays or at a sporting event. Absolutely not!"

At some point around this time, Eric called Chanel's parents and asked if he could pay them a visit. His purpose was to ask for permission to marry their daughter. To obtain Ron Blaquiere's blessing, Eric had to provide evidence that the couple could make things work financially. Sonya said Eric pulled out a piece of paper displaying dollar figures. "He said, 'This is our plan. This is how we are going to make it work.' Of course, everything was in Chanel's handwriting. Ron asked if Eric was sure, and he was. From then on they were inseparable."

On Chanel's birthday, February 25, 2005, the couple looked at engagement rings in Logan. The following week, Eric called and asked Chanel for a semi-formal, "dress-up" date. She was stressed with midterms to prepare for, but given the previous week's ring shopping, she didn't feel that she could turn him down. A marriage proposal might be forthcoming. This night with Eric might change their lives.

But when her man arrived to pick her up, she noticed Eric was flustered and moody. Something was not right. When she asked what was wrong, he confessed he had planned an elaborate evening to ask her to marry him, but the jeweler wasn't ready with the ring. She showed compassion and tried to comfort him. "He was very frustrated," Chanel said. "I told him it was okay. He totally had me faked out."

He had her fooled for the moment, but inside, Eric had a serious case of butterflies. He had gone to great lengths to plan an evening he hoped Chanel would always remember and one day brag about to her girlfriends, but questions of uncertainty lingered. Yes, they had talked about marriage and looked at rings, but what if he asked her to marry him and she turned him down? Where would the relationship be then? What if she thought his proposal was corny? He tried to calm his nerves by saying a little prayer that everything would go smoothly.

They drove up Sardine Canyon to Sherwood Hills, a resort tucked away in the Wellsville Mountains not far from Cache Valley, where they enjoyed a secluded, romantic dinner. It was a Wednesday night, and there were only two other couples at nearby tables. She ordered spaghetti, and he was so hungry he ordered two meals for himself. As they dined, they savored the moment and relished the rare night together. When a waiter approached and asked about dessert, Eric surprised Chanel by saying he would love dessert, even though he had finished only one of his meals. She didn't notice Eric exchange a glance and a nod with the server. Moments later, a silver platter was delivered. As Eric removed the lid, Chanel's eyes doubled in size and her hands flew over her mouth.

On the platter was a sparkling diamond ring.

He asked the question, and she melted in his arms. Tears flowed as the couple shared a tender kiss and embrace. She would find out later that he had sacrificed and saved nearly six scholarship checks, approximately $3,500, to purchase the ring.

"I was so excited," she said. "I wanted to show everyone—but I had to study all night for midterms."

Eric practically floated back to Salt Lake City. The girl of his dreams had accepted his marriage proposal. The Utes had just gone undefeated. It doesn't get much better than this, he thought.

In the LDS culture, it's very common for young college students to get married and start families. But the idea was somewhat foreign to Steve and Debbie Weddle. They supported their son but expressed parental concern. They were still trying to wrap their minds around Eric's conversion to the Church. Now this?

Sonya recalled the night when Eric, Chanel, and both sets of parents went to dinner at Lucille's Smokehouse BBQ in Rancho Cucamonga to celebrate the engagement. Wedding plans were being discussed—then someone asked Eric and Chanel if they knew how many kids they wanted to have. "Eric replied they wanted a lot of kids," Sonya said. "His parents asked, 'How many is a lot? Two or three? Four or five? Six to eight?' Chanel didn't say a word, and Eric smiled. Steve and Debbie were still adjusting to the whole concept of Eric and Chanel getting married at a young age. It was hard for them to understand. Steve said to the waiter, 'Get me another beer.'"

Eric and Chanel were married in the San Diego Temple on July 22, 2005, followed by a honeymoon in Puerto Vallarta, Mexico.

Going into the 2005 fall semester, the couple made their first big decision together. Chanel wasn't willing to sacrifice her scholarship and senior year of soccer at Utah State to transfer to the University of Utah and was about to complete her social work degree. Eric respectfully declined to transfer to USU to be an Aggie. So they compromised by finding a place in Riverdale, Utah, roughly the middle point between Logan and Salt Lake. She would commute north, and he would commute south. They moved into a modest two-bedroom apartment for $550 a month.

The compromise was one of many ways Eric and Chanel would learn to work together and lean on each other during the next few years as they started a family and Eric continued his football career. Both had learned from past mistakes, and now they carried a newfound commitment to each other that would develop into an unbreakable bond through unselfishness and personal sacrifice. Chanel was willing to help Eric pursue his NFL dream, even if it meant feeling like a single parent many times in the years to come, and he would do his best to be sensitive to her needs, desires, and dreams.

Eric admits he would not be where he is today without his sweetheart, Chanel. "I always felt she was the one for me," Eric said. "She has so many amazing qualities and complements me better than any person I've known. She is everything I want in a woman. I am a blessed man."

# CHAPTER 9

─

# LEADERSHIP, MARRIAGE, AND EMERALDS

By Eric Weddle's junior year at the university, Utah coach Kyle Whittingham had his star defensive back all figured out.

"All you have to do is throw a challenge at Eric, and he'll respond," Whittingham said. "He's the ultimate competitor. Challenge him on something and question whether he can do it or not—that is the best way to motivate him. Boy, that fires him up."

So when Utah learned it would play 24th-ranked Georgia Tech in the 2005 Emerald Bowl, Whittingham gave Eric the assignment of going one-on-one with Tech's Calvin Johnson, a six-foot-five, 235-pound wide receiver and future NFL star. Whittingham reasoned that if Eric could handle GT's all-American, other Utah defensive players would be able to inflict damage on Georgia Tech in other ways, and the Utes' chances of winning would be greatly increased.

As the game got under way and Utah's defense lined up on

the muddy field against the Yellow Jackets offense for the first time, Whittingham watched Utah's No. 32 line up across from the imposing figure that wore Georgia Tech's No. 21. The Utah coach couldn't help but notice his player's five-inch, thirty-pound disadvantage. Even so, Whittingham believed in Eric. In the weeks leading up to the bowl game, the junior defensive back had prepared himself as well as any football player Whittingham had ever seen. In a few hours, 27,000 fans in AT&T Park and those watching on ESPN would understand why he wasn't worried. Eric's performance in that game would become one of the signature moments of his college career.

## THE DEAN OF SAFETIES

Coming into the 2005 season, twenty-year-old junior Eric Weddle was suddenly one of the most experienced players on the Utah roster. With the graduation of Morgan Scalley, the 2004 Mountain West Conference co-defensive player of the year, Eric became the lone defensive back with more than twelve games of experience. Whittingham said that Eric, at three-quarters speed, was better than most players at full speed, and the coach considered his star safety an NFL prospect. Whittingham was pleased with Eric's work ethic and decided it was time for the junior to step into a leadership role. The coaching staff charged Eric with providing guidance, insight, and other mentoring to fellow safeties Casey Evans, Steve Tate, Tim Harris, and Antonio Young.

"He's the dean of safeties back there and actually in the secondary," Whittingham told the press at fall camp. "He's the guy back there with the most experience, and we rely on him a bunch."

Gary Andersen, Utah's defensive coordinator, said Eric was like a coach on the field. "When you play safety in this [Utah's] defense, you have to know a lot about where people fit, what's going on, and the whole big picture. Eric has a very good grasp of the picture, of our whole defense. He's going to get the guys lined up in the right spots," Andersen said. "He's an unbelievable play-maker. He's just one of those kids who has a knack for making plays. Now he has to be a leader off the field, too, for our defense, and I think he has accepted that role."

Eric appreciated his coaches' confidence and trust and didn't want to let them down. Once again he was elected to the team's leadership committee. Eric also had his priorities in order academically, having made the dean's list the previous semester with a 3.5 grade point average. Being a leader at this point in his football career took some getting used to, but he welcomed the challenge.

"It just feels like yesterday I was coming out of high school," Eric said that fall. "Now I'm the guy who has to bring all the young guys along, be the leader, and do everything right. I like that role for this team and for my position."

The best way to fill his role, Eric figured, was to carry on the tradition and high standard of performance started by former safeties Dave Revill and Morgan Scalley. They had called it "safety pride."

"If you have safety pride," Eric explained, "you have an unquestioned work ethic, you are accountable, and you have a true understanding of what it means to be a team player. You are always prepared, but ultimately it comes down to what you do out on the field. You continue to have the kind of reputation started by guys like Revill and Scalley. You are a teammate who can be counted on to make plays. You are a leader."

The message was very effective. Tate defined safety pride as "an unbreakable bond and a legacy to live up to. If you swear on safety pride, there is no going back. It's like swearing on your father's grave," Tate said. "I still text the words 'safety pride' to Eric before his NFL games."

In addition to his leadership duties, the coaches allowed Eric more freedom at his safety position. Instead of playing strong safety or free safety, the coaching staff wanted him to use his unique combination of versatility and athleticism to be a run-stopper and pass defender—in other words, a one-man wrecking crew for opposing offenses. "Basically, they just want me to be around the ball," Eric said.

They also wanted Eric around the ball on special teams. In addition to returning punts, they asked him to hold the ball for the kicker on field goals and extra points.

Eric somehow carried all these responsibilities, including extra time in the film room, despite living more than forty-five minutes from campus. This distance worried Utah safeties coach Derrick Odum at times. "That's a long drive," Odum said. "That's a big commitment to be on time. I thought for sure he was going to be late to some meetings. He was never late."

As Utah prepared to open the 2005 season at home against the University of Arizona, Eric was prepared to play, but in his estimation he was only ninety percent healthy. He still felt occasional pain in the shoulder he separated against Colorado State in 2004. He also felt a pop while running conditioning drills in February and suffered an excruciating hamstring tear. "It was the worst pain I ever felt, except for my elbow when I was fourteen," Eric said. By August, he was mostly healthy again and prayed he could avoid injuries in 2005.

After a stellar BCS-busting, 12–0 season in 2004, the University of Utah's marketing campaign for the 2005 season was "Keep It Rolling," and the Utes won their first two games. Utah celebrated a 27–24 victory over Arizona in Rice-Eccles Stadium, and Eric started the season on a high note with 10 tackles, including a hit for a 4-yard loss on running back Mike Bell, who went on to play for five years in the NFL. Eric forced a fumble, and his most exciting contribution came when he intercepted a pass by Arizona quarterback Richard Kovalcheck and returned it 24 yards for a touchdown. His main motivation was helping Coach Whittingham to win in his debut as head coach. For his efforts, Weddle was named the Mountain West Conference defensive player of the week.

Utah State, the U of U's next opponent, was scheduled to play Nicholls State on September 3, but the game was cancelled because of Hurricane Katrina's impact on the Gulf Coast. This meant the Utes coaching staff didn't have any game film of the Aggies under new head coach Brent Guy. Determined to keep his game plan secret, Guy closed practice the week before the game. Early in the week, however, the new coach was shocked to find a car with University of Utah license plate frames and a Utah athletic department sticker sitting just outside the locker rooms at USU's Romney Stadium. At first he thought it was a joke, then he seriously wondered if there were a spy on campus. After some investigation, Guy discovered the suspicious car belonged to Chanel Weddle, a senior on the USU women's soccer team, and now the wife of Utah safety Eric Weddle.

Chanel was minding her own business in the training facility next to the stadium when someone associated with the USU football team charged in, demanding to know whose "Utah" car was parked outside. At first, Chanel was worried she was getting "booted" for parking illegally, but that worry turned to curiosity when she was asked why she had a University of Utah license plate frame. "Because my husband goes to the U," she calmly replied. The man scowled, turned, and departed without an explanation.

Chanel figured he just really didn't like the University of Utah. It wasn't until later, when she read about the incident in the newspaper, that she realized she was almost accused of being a spy and a traitor. When she told Eric about the "USU Spygate" episode, he thought it was hilarious. "It was funny that he made such a big deal about the car," Eric said. "That shows you how seriously football coaches take these games. They don't want to give up any possible advantage."

Even if Chanel had been a double agent, it wouldn't have helped the Aggies' cause. Utah defeated Utah State in Salt Lake City 31–7 to set a new school record with its eighteenth consecutive win, dating back to 2003.

The historic winning streak was snapped, however, the following week when Utah blew a 10-point lead in the third quarter, losing to Texas Christian University in overtime 23–20 in Fort Worth, Texas. As the Horned Frogs celebrated the game-winning touchdown, several Utah players hung their heads and sat deflated on the field. Eric walked among them and encouraged them to get up and head for the locker room.

"He was leaving but looked back and saw his teammates on the field," said Dirk Facer, longtime Utah beat writer for the *Deseret News*. "Although they were sad to see the streak end, Eric showed leadership by going back and getting everyone up and off the field. Every kid he approached got right up. He didn't make a scene. It's like he was saying, 'If we are going to suffer, let it be in the privacy of our own locker room, not on the field.'"

Utah responded to the TCU loss with a better performance at home against Air Force. Eric played really well at times but also made costly mistakes. In the second quarter, the junior muffed a punt, and the Falcons recovered. It didn't matter to him that he was hit just as the ball touched his hands. No one was harder on

Eric than himself. "It was a bonehead mistake by me that I wish I could take back," Eric said in the postgame press conference.

Two series later, Eric made up for his mistake by recovering an Air Force fumble deep in Falcon territory to help the Utes build a 28–14 halftime lead. Then in the third quarter, the roving safety drilled an Air Force player as he dove for a pass going out of bounds, and Eric was flagged for a late hit. Whittingham thought it was a bad call. But Eric didn't let the penalty get him down. Three plays later he intercepted a Falcon pass to stop a promising AFA drive. When the dust cleared at the end of the fourth quarter, Utah escaped with a 38–35 win.

The Utes emerged from the month of September with a respectable 3–1 record, but adversity was waiting in October. The first loss came against the University of North Carolina, at Kenan Stadium in Chapel Hill. Despite multiple penalties and turnovers, Utah trailed only 17–14 late in the third quarter. The game changed on a second-and-12 play from the Tar Heels' 32. Eric read the eyes of UNC quarterback Matt Baker, intercepted the pigskin, and raced 37 yards to the end zone to put the Utes up for the first time that afternoon. But the celebration was cut short by a yellow hanky lying back near the line of scrimmage. The interception was nullified by a "roughing the passer" penalty on teammate Casey Evans, who thought he was making a normally aggressive play. As it turned out, the penalty cost Utah the game.

Retaining possession, Baker and the Tar Heels renewed their march down the field and scored to go up 24–14, then added another touchdown late in the fourth quarter to finish off the discouraged Utes. Eric didn't point any fingers, but he took the loss hard. "It was tough, because we were battling," Eric said later. "The game took a huge swing on that play."

Two more heartbreaking losses followed. The Utes, who led

MWC foe Colorado State 14–3 entering the fourth quarter, had three chances from inside the Rams' one-yard line with under a minute to go, but failed to punch home the game-winning score and left Fort Collins with a depressing 21–17 loss.

The following week in Salt Lake City, Utah rolled up 592 yards of total offense against San Diego State but struggled inside the red zone and fell to the Aztecs 28–19. The Utes were suddenly 1–3 in the Mountain West Conference standings and 3–4 over-all. The school that had busted the BCS with an undefeated sea-son the year before was suddenly looking like they'd be lucky to win six games to become bowl-eligible. Discouraged, but willing to face the criticism, Whittingham told the media he was "out-coached" by San Diego State coach Tom Craft and claimed all the blame for the loss and the Utes' three-game slide. He hinted that if the Utes couldn't finish the season strong, he might step aside after one year as head coach. "It's on me," Whittingham said. "I'm clearly the head of this thing, and if I can't get it done, it's on me and I'll find something else to do."

In defense of their coach, Eric and receiver Brent Casteel in-dependently called a postgame sports radio show to defend the coaches and insist that the players were responsible for the team's troubles this season. No one was giving up, Eric said later, but the weight of the losing streak was extremely heavy. "It felt like we were fighting through so much adversity. Things were just not going well. I was tired of losing and tired of nagging injuries," he said, "but we learned a lot from those experiences. They helped build character. I learned what it means to be a leader."

## EDUCATION AND COMMUNITY SERVICE

While dealing with a multitude of challenges on the field, Eric found a measure of peace through service and concern for others off the field. Special education was his major at the University of Utah, and he sought opportunities to spend time with a variety of kids. As a student teacher, he preferred to tutor students one-on-one. He worked for a short time with an eleven-year-old boy named Sutton who had attention deficit disorder. The experience helped Eric understand different methods of working with kids with disabilities. "He was an energetic kid," Eric said. "Once I found out what he liked, he was easy to work with. I got to see up close the different challenges and aspects of teaching in that situation. The kids have feelings, and you feel for them. You try to help. It was great. It's a good feeling, and I hope I helped. That's what I want to do when football is over—teach, coach, and help kids."

Eric's desire to help children went beyond his schoolwork. As his schedule permitted, he went with teammates or by himself to Primary Children's Medical Center on the U's upper campus to bring cheer to the patients. Having learned from his mother's example as a schoolteacher, he befriended several kids and encouraged them to be strong in life's battles. Hearing their stories, sometimes it was difficult for Eric to keep his emotions in check, but these brave children inspired him, and he always walked away uplifted and ready to tackle his own trials. "It put life in perspective and reminded me how blessed and fortunate I am," Eric said. "You've got to do what's right, not take life for granted, and try to make the most of it. I realized so many people wish they could be in my position. You remember that stuff, because it could be gone in an instant."

On one occasion, Eric was invited to spend time at a juvenile correctional facility. After tossing the football with some of the teenage offenders, he shared a message of hope and chasing your dreams. "I tried to help them realize there is a light at the end of the tunnel and you can get there," Eric said. "You can do more with your life. You don't have to follow your friend's path. You can do great things and be accomplished individuals."

When he wasn't tutoring kids or at the hospital, Eric participated in service activities with his LDS student congregation. As a member of the ward activities committee, he helped plan such popular activities as volunteering at the local food bank. These opportunities brought balance to his life and recharged his soul's battery.

Liz Abel, former Utah sports information director, often learned of Eric's activities after the fact, and she suggested that in the future he let her know because it could be a great story in the press. He understood where she was coming from, but he wasn't interested in that kind of publicity. "That kind of stuff doesn't need to be publicized," he said. "Everyone should be doing that kind of stuff. When you do things like that for the publicity, you are doing it for the wrong reasons. To me, it's all about helping the kids and the less fortunate."

## DEFENSIVE SPECIALIST

These meaningful activities provided Eric with perspective during Utah's three-game skid. Fortunately, the Utes' next opponent was UNLV, a team Utah was expected to beat. They did, thanks to a renewed effort and career rushing night of 155 yards and 3 touchdowns by running back Quinton Ganther. The U of U flew away from Las Vegas with a 42–32 victory, and two weeks later in Salt Lake City, they buried the Wyoming Cowboys 43–13. Eric played an important role in the win because Coach Whittingham moved him from safety to cornerback in an effort to slow down the league's leading receiver, Jovon Bouknight. Eric held Bouknight to 4 catches for 43 yards, well below his season average of 105.4 yards per game. Eric also contributed 9 tackles, a sack, 1.5 tackles for loss, and 3 pass breakups. Wyoming coach Joe Glenn complimented Weddle after the game by saying, "He did a good job of taking away our ace."

Eric said the key to slowing Bouknight down was being physical. "I think I got him a little frustrated, because he wasn't able to make plays he usually makes." The experience of covering Bouknight and other elite receivers would help Eric at the end of the season.

The Utes were 5–4 and could become bowl-eligible with a win over New Mexico at Rice-Eccles on a cold, partly cloudy afternoon in mid-November. Despite losing their top receiver, John Madsen, to a broken ankle in the first quarter, Utah played well enough in the first half to lead 27–19 at halftime. The Utes then struggled offensively in the second half, and the Lobos rallied to go ahead 31–27 late in the fourth quarter. With less than two minutes to go, Utah quarterback Brian Johnson attempted to scramble for a do-or-die first down on fourth-and-15 when he was hammered by New Mexico defender Gabriel Fulbright near the Lobo sideline after a gain of 12 yards. Johnson didn't get up. Fulbright was flagged for a personal foul, but Johnson suffered a serious knee injury in the collision and was done for the season. Johnson's seldom-used backup, Brett Ratliff, was able to move the Utes to the Lobo 14, but the game ended when the backup quarterback threw an interception.

Losing Madsen and Johnson were significant losses for Utah, Eric said, considering the team had to defeat their archrivals, the BYU Cougars, in Provo, with a new quarterback and lacking one offensive weapon, to qualify for a bowl game. Few people gave the Utes a chance to win, but no one in the program was about to concede defeat. The team closed practice leading up to the critical contest with BYU to install some new offensive and defensive wrinkles into the game plan. The Utes were inserting Eric at quarterback and punter on certain plays. He had flashbacks to his senior year at Alta Loma as he tried his hand at running the option, throwing passes, and punting rugby-style. "I just wanted to contribute in any way I could," he said.

Defensively, Andersen and Whittingham schemed a new look in hopes of disrupting BYU's pass-oriented offense. If the players saw Andersen move his hands in a juggling motion from the sidelines, it was the signal for as many as nine players to drop into pass coverage, including defensive lineman Steve Fifita. It was an innovation that would help the Utes cause havoc for the Cougars on at least three or four third downs, as well as on the final play of the game.

One final matter was resolved the morning of the BYU game. Spencer Toone, a hard-hitting linebacker from Blackfoot, Idaho, and the U's leading tackler, suffered a broken bone in his hand during the New Mexico game. Despite sharp pain at the slightest touch, he played the rest of the game and was discouraged when X-rays confirmed the break a few days later. He had been battling other minor shoulder and knee injuries all season and wore a bubble cast during practice that helped but was too restrictive. Spencer needed the use of his hand to be able to be effective.

There was no way Toone was going to miss the BYU game, yet when he awoke that Saturday morning at the team hotel, he knew he needed help. The senior approached Eric and Steve Tate, both fellow members of the LDS Church, with a special request. He wanted a priesthood blessing. Eric and Steve, elders in the Church authorized to give blessings, gladly consented.

A short time before the team was scheduled to load the bus for LaVell Edwards Stadium, the three teammates searched the hotel until they found an empty room to use and closed the door behind them. Spencer sat on a chair as Eric and Steve placed their hands on his head. For the first time since his baptism more than a year earlier, Eric participated in a priesthood blessing. Steve, a returned Mormon missionary, listened for the inspiration of the Holy Ghost as he pronounced the words of the blessing. As he spoke, a powerful yet peaceful feeling encircled the players. The prayer was brief. Steve blessed Spencer with health, strength, and a personal reassurance that everything would be fine. It was difficult for the trio to compose their emotions. When Steve finished, Spencer smiled with renewed confidence. He knew everything would work out. "It was a comforting blessing," Toone said. "I knew if I had faith and believed, I could get through it."

"Here we were, hours before kickoff against our bitter rivals, and we are all crying after this incredible experience," Tate said. "We had to find a way to put our mean faces back on."

The spiritual experience left a profound mark on Eric, who often reflects on the emotions he felt in that room. "Spencer was really fragile at that time. Heavenly Father gave him strength and told him he could get through this," Eric said. "It was cool to see a man of his stature be humble enough to ask for help in a time of tension and stress. The main thing I got out of it was to remember to be humble and realize you are not bigger than life. Don't be too stubborn or prideful to ask for help or guidance. Heavenly Father couldn't care less who wins a football game, but he will be there for you when you need him most."

Toone played on. Armed with a small molded cast, a delicate tape job, and gloves, the six-foot-two, 235-pound junior college transfer played like a monster from sideline to sideline, disrupting the Cougars offense. "It hurt, but it was all right," said Toone, who ignored the pain to make eight tackles and help his team become bowl-eligible.

Despite blowing a 24–3 halftime lead, Utah managed to survive BYU's 31-point second-half surge by holding the Cougars scoreless in overtime. Utah quarterback Brett Ratliff, who passed for 240 yards, 4 touchdowns, and rushed for 112 yards and another score in his first collegiate start, found receiver Travis LaTendresse with a 25-yard strike to give the Utes the lead. Then, after holding BYU on first, second, and third down, Andersen made the juggling motion, and the Utes dropped nine players into coverage. The final throw by Cougars quarterback John Beck fluttered to the ground as receiver Michael Reed made an unsuccessful dive to catch it in the back of the end zone. Underdog Utah won, 41–34, much to the dismay of BYU's home crowd of 64,000. A sea of players in red uniforms spilled onto the field to celebrate and soak up the joy of the moment.

Eric turned in a stellar performance. Not only did he limit BYU's standout wide receiver Todd Watkins to 2 catches for 22 yards, he also recorded 5 tackles, held for kicker Dan Beardall on extra points and field goals, punted rugby-style twice for an average of 23 yards, rushed 3 times for 11 yards, and threw one incomplete pass. As a result, Weddle the playmaker had cemented his spot as Utah's designated wildcat back.

Whittingham said the victory over BYU was the sweetest to that point in his coaching career. With a record of 6–5, the Utes were going to a bowl game. They received an invitation to play the 24th-ranked Georgia Tech Yellow Jackets in the Emerald Bowl in San Francisco, California. Tech boasted one of the premiere defenses in the country and ranked among the Atlantic Coast Conference's top offenses statistically.

A week after the BYU win, Weddle was informed he had

been named the Mountain West Conference defensive player of the year. The junior defensive back had thought for sure another student athlete would be honored, considering Utah's struggles during the season. He finished the regular season with 75 tackles, 4 sacks, and 4 interceptions. "I thought it would go to a senior because that's how it usually works," Eric said, "but it's a great honor."

## THE SAN FRANCISCO SHOWDOWN

While Utah was overjoyed to be playing in the Emerald Bowl, the Georgia Tech players were doing their best to act interested. A week before the game, *Atlanta Journal-Constitution* sportswriter Mark Bradley wrote about an incident at a media gathering. Publicist Mike Stamus was interviewing Yellow Jacket players and asked tailback P.J. Daniels what he thought when he learned Tech was bound for the Emerald Bowl, more than 2,000 miles from its campus.

"We got screwed," Daniels said.

"We won't use that part," Stamus said, turning to his cameraman.

In his column a week before the game, Bradley continued, "Is Tech too good for its bowl? Absolutely. You beat two top-10 teams and finish the regular season in the Top 25, and your reward is a 6–5 opponent on a Thursday afternoon in Barry Bonds' bailiwick? . . . The Jackets have become the scourge of the lower-rung bowls. They've won their last two postseason games by the aggregate score of 103–24, and they should hang five or six touchdowns on Utah. And they'll ride the famous trolley and take a tour of Alcatraz and come back with a big trophy and be home well in time to watch the big bowls on TV."

Other players, like GT quarterback Reggie Ball, saw the

situation as an opportunity to play another game. "That's all I wanted," Ball said. "Once I knew we had that, I was satisfied."

Even so, the disgruntled attitudes of the majority of the Yellow Jackets were obvious to the Utah players. "You could just tell they didn't want to be there," Eric said. "When we hung around them during the week, you couldn't see fire in their eyes."

Despite Georgia Tech's overall disappointment, many experts picked the Jackets to win big. This motivated the Utes to win. They also wanted to extend the school's four-game bowl-winning streak to five. "No one's really giving us a chance to win the ball game," said senior running back Quinton Ganther. "But, hey, they've counted us out all year and we're here."

Utah defensive lineman Steve Fifita agreed. "We can redeem ourselves with a win over a quality opponent like this. If we get a win, it proves we're a good team and we were just going through some growing pains."

The matchup between MWC defensive player of the year Eric Weddle and all-American wide receiver Calvin Johnson grabbed many of the pregame headlines. By game time, Eric was sick of reporters' questions and hearing how Johnson was going to have a field day. It was now his personal mission to show the cynics he could shut down Johnson. "I just took the challenge to heart," Eric said. "You want to play with a chip on your shoulder when you take on the top receivers. No one gave me a chance, not only to shut him down, but to even play good against him. It ate at me."

Johnson was widely considered one of the top pass-catchers in the nation. He finished the 2005 regular season with 52 catches for 869 yards and 6 touchdowns to become a unanimous selection on the all-Atlantic Coast Conference team. In 2006, he would go on to win the Fred Biletnikoff Award, given to the country's best receiver, and be selected as the second overall pick by the Detroit Lions in the 2007 NFL draft.

Eric embraced the challenge with extra work in practice and longer film study sessions. Alone in the team room with a pen, spiral notebook, and the remote control, he watched every available tape on Johnson multiple times. There was Johnson, catching 4 passes for 66 yards in the Yellow Jackets' win over 15th-ranked Auburn. He burned North Carolina State for 10 receptions and 130 yards only to drop the game-winning touchdown pass in the final seconds. He caught 6 passes for 89 yards to help Tech win at third-ranked Miami. Johnson also scored touchdowns against Virginia Tech, Georgia, and Wake Forest.

With each play, Eric studied Johnson's pre-snap alignment, the offensive formation, the down-and-distance, and Johnson's pass route, then scribbled copious notes in his tattered notebook. Then he pored over his notes, searching for tendencies and patterns. The more Eric learned, the more he marveled at Johnson's talent and abilities. "He is such a great wide receiver, one of the best," Eric said. "I took the challenge to heart and watched hours of film, looking for anything that would give me an edge."

Eric also had the added advantage of experience. He began the season at strong safety but moved to cornerback for the final three regular-season games because Whittingham wanted him to lock down some of the Mountain West Conference's elite receivers, including Wyoming's Jovon Bouknight, New Mexico's Hank Baskett, and BYU's Todd Watkins.

Against each of those future NFL receivers, Eric focused on playing with sound technique and worked to take away a favorite pass route or tendency from each one. In the upcoming game, Eric wanted to eliminate Johnson's fade route, which is similar to a jump ball in basketball. It's most effective inside the ten-yard line when a quarterback tosses the ball high toward the back corner of the end zone in a spot where only his receiver can leap for it. The fade route is very difficult for a cornerback to defend, especially when matched up against a taller receiver. Despite the degree of difficulty, Eric was confident he could neutralize Johnson and give the Utes a shot to win.

Eric knew he had full support from Coach Whittingham. When asked by the media prior to the game about the Weddle-Johnson showdown, Whittingham remarked, "[Eric] can do it all. He can come up and press you, jam you at the line of scrimmage, and he can play off coverage. I think that's going to be a game within itself. That's going to be a great thing to watch off the ball."

Eric balanced out the mounting pressure by spending time with his wife, as well as other players and their wives. This was the first bowl game since their wedding, and they got a room at the team hotel. In the days leading up to the game, they walked the streets of San Francisco with teammate Tavo Tupola and his wife, Andria; Steve Tate and his wife, Savannah; and Colt Sampson and his wife, CC. They toured Alcatraz, played games, attended team functions and dinners, and even visited children at local hospitals. They would do similar things in 2006 at the Armed Forces Bowl in Texas. Eric was grateful for these moments he could spend with his sweetheart and take his mind off the upcoming game.

Because it was a college football game being played in a professional baseball venue, field conditions were less than ideal. The baseball home of the Giants had some quirky dimensions. The end zone in left field had no warning track, only a padded wall inches from the backline. The right-field wall did little to shield wind gusts off the bay. And after days of rain prior to the game, the recently laid sod was muddy, and the footing was slippery. It was common to see chunks of turf fly off the cleats of players as they ran, cut, and tackled. By kickoff, more than 25,700 fans showed up to see the crimson-clad Utes and the white-and-gold Yellow Jackets on a cloudy, fifty-five-degree afternoon.

Despite playing without quarterback Brian Johnson and top receiver John Madsen, the Utah offense was nearly flawless in the first half. Brett Ratliff, in his second start at quarterback, engineered 3 touchdown drives to put the Utes up 20–0 in the second quarter. All 3 touchdowns came on passes from Ratliff to senior wide receiver Travis LaTendresse.

During one series after the Utes went up 20–0, Utah cornerback Shaun Harper intercepted a Reggie Ball pass. The Utes decided to go for the jugular. Eric came in at quarterback and threw a long pass down field, but Tech defensive back Dennis Davis, one of three Yellow Jacket defenders in the vicinity, picked off the bomb. "I didn't get enough oomph on it," Eric said later. The turnover energized the Tech offense, and they responded with a touchdown of their own as Ball found tight end George Cooper with a 31-yard toss. Shortly before halftime, the Jackets pulled to within 10 points after a 65-yard strike from Ball to Damarius Bilbo set up a short field goal.

Ball wanted to throw to his all-American, but the combined pressure of Utah's defensive front and Eric Weddle's physical, aggressive coverage made connecting with his star receiver difficult. The extra time in the film room paid off as it became easy for Eric to predict Johnson's pass route, and as a result, he covered the towering receiver like a blanket. Eric was also motivated to perform because he had more than fifty family members and friends watching him from the AT&T stands.

Reggie Ball threw in Johnson's direction twice in the first

quarter, completing one pass for 8 yards. In the second quarter, Ball fired seven times to Johnson, connecting once for 11 yards, drawing one pass interference call on Weddle, and missing on the other five. His final two attempts came in the fourth quarter, after the Utes had gone up 38–10. Both attempts fell incomplete. Of 11 passes thrown to Johnson, the receiver dropped two and one was intercepted. Johnson finished the game with 2 receptions for 19 yards. At least one play called for Johnson ended before he got a chance to make a catch. Facing fourth-and-2 from the Utah 24 in the first quarter, Ball dropped back to throw but slipped on the wet grass for an 8-yard loss. Tech coach Chan Gailey said the play was designed to go to Johnson, and "he was going to be wide open, too."

Bill Riley was at the game that day hosting the pre- and post-game shows for the University of Utah radio broadcast. Riley observed that while Eric was sticking to Johnson, a few factors contributed to Weddle's success. First, Riley said, the five-foot-eleven, 195-pound quarterback Ball was simply not a great quarterback. "He was very erratic when throwing the ball," said Riley, now the radio voice of the Utes. "He was probably great at hitting guys when they were wide open, but he was not exactly a guy who could thread the ball into tight coverage. Because Eric had some success early against Johnson, they rarely threw in his direction in the second half."

Second, Riley continued, Johnson's favorite route was the fade, but Tech never got to try it because Utah's defense allowed the Yellow Jackets inside the 20-yard line only once. Georgia Tech reached the Utah 12 with three seconds to go in the first half but elected to kick a field goal. "They took some shots up the sideline at Eric," Riley said, "but Eric's coverage was really good, to the point Johnson never got near the ball."

With Johnson all but neutralized, Georgia Tech was limited offensively. Daniels, the tailback who really didn't want to be there, rushed 20 times for 109 yards. The vaunted Georgia Tech defense never materialized, and the Utes dominated the second half. Ratliff went 30-of-41 for 381 yards and 4 touchdowns, all to LaTendresse, who ended his career with 16 catches for 214 yards. His last touchdown grab in the fourth quarter was the most memorable as he caught a 16-yard pass over the middle and smashed headfirst into a picture of Willie Mays on the left-field wall. He was named the game's offensive MVP.

Another Utah receiver, junior Brian Hernandez, who began his college career at Georgia Tech in 2002, added 8 receptions for 75 yards. Quinton Ganther ran for 120 yards and scored on a 41-yard romp to put a final stamp on the Utes' decisive victory. As the clock ticked down the final seconds, Whittingham received a Gatorade bath. When the game was over, hundreds of Utah fans rushed the field and lifted Ratliff and LaTendresse on their shoulders. *Deseret News* columnist Brad Rock summed up the Utes' victory when he wrote, "They made a Ramblin' Wreck of Georgia Tech."

Some Utah players accused the Yellow Jackets of quitting in the second half. Tech coach Chan Gailey acknowledged the Utes "got us good," but disagreed about his team giving up.

Eric tried to be friendly at the end of the game, but the Tech players just walked away. "I guess that's the way it goes when you're getting pounded like that," he said.

Eric's stat line didn't exactly tell the story of his contribution. He had three rushes for 23 yards; he threw an interception; he made 3 tackles and broke up one pass. As the field goal holder, he ran a fake field goal play for a first down. He also had his name butchered throughout the game by the press box announcer, who called him "WEE-dle," "We-DELL," and "Widdle"—everything but "WED-dle," as he had been known to Utah fans for three years. But for shutting down Johnson, he hoisted the game's defensive MVP trophy, a moment that was proudly applauded by Coach Whittingham.

"They were saying Calvin Johnson is all-this, all-everything, but one-on-one, Weddle's got him," Hernandez said after the game. "We knew we had a shot to win this game because we had what it took to shut down one of their best weapons with Weddle."

Eric was modest amid the praise. "I got the better of the matchup this time," he said. "The game plan worked."

Johnson—later nicknamed "Megatron," after a villain Transformer, by Detroit coaches and fans in the NFL—struggled to explain his limited production after the game but refused to admit Eric shut him down. "We didn't throw the ball," Johnson told *Atlanta Journal-Constitution* writer Mike Knobler, even though Tech had passed 38 times. "I didn't have too many chances to go up against him."

When asked why Georgia Tech's offense struggled, Johnson said, "Everything that went wrong went wrong pretty much interior." When asked whether he meant Tech should have thrown more passes to him, the all-American replied, "I'm not saying that. I'm just saying . . . I'm not even commenting."

When Whittingham heard what Johnson said, he laughed out loud and pounded the table. "Whatever," the coach said. "I know he's a good player, a heck of an NFL player. We had all the respect for him in the world, but Eric handled that assignment."

The victory over Georgia Tech was a delicious end to a tumultuous season. In 2005, Weddle and the Utes experienced the lowest of lows when they lost three straight, then found redemption with a dramatic win over BYU and a decisive victory in the Emerald Bowl. Eric was both happy and realistic about the season. "Seven-and-five is still mediocre by Utah standards," he said, "but it's better than 6–6."

With the experience he had gained and lessons he had learned, Eric Weddle began setting goals to be a better leader, a better teammate, and a better student of the game to help the Utes accomplish more in 2006, his senior year.

## THE BIG COMPROMISE

Eric had maintained his rigorous schedule during his first year of marriage, in addition to commuting each day from Ogden to Salt Lake City, while Chanel drove from Ogden to Logan. When she was on road trips with the USU soccer team, he stayed with teammates in Salt Lake City to save time and fuel. But when he was gone and she was alone in the apartment, at least three days a week, the loneliness troubled her.

Both Eric and Chanel had grown up with a dog at home. Eric's family had a male Labrador retriever, and the Blaquieres had a female golden retriever. To defeat Chanel's loneliness, the couple contemplated the first major decision in their marriage: a male Labrador or a female golden retriever? After some discussion, they compromised: Chanel would select the dog, and Eric would give it a name. They searched online, and Chanel found a female golden retriever for sale in Utah County. One day after practice, Eric drove to Spanish Fork to pick up their new pet. On the way, he stopped at a Walmart and purchased a few necessary items, including a sack of dog food, a bowl, and a few toys. With the puppy sitting on his lap during the entire drive home to Ogden, Eric fell in love with their new pet. He decided to name her Chloe, after a female character he liked on the television series

*Smallville.* The Weddles were so excited that first night that they placed their new family member in a large plastic container in their bedroom. But when the dog whined all night, she was permanently moved to the living room.

It didn't take long for the feeling of parenthood to set in. Each day when Eric and Chanel went their separate directions for the day, they had no way of letting Chloe outside, so they created a confined area for the dog in the kitchen. For several months they came home each evening to unpleasant smells and messes that they had to clean up in their weary state. "We were clearly not ready for children," Chanel admitted.

The Weddles did not appreciate being told how to care for Chloe. When they took her in for immunization shots, a disapproving veterinarian scolded them for not taking Chloe to dog obedience lessons. "Our dog doesn't need obedience school," they vented to each other on the way home. Eventually, Chloe was house-trained and served as a trusted companion for Chanel when Eric was away.

"Having a dog felt like a parent role," Chanel recalled. "'If I can keep this dog alive,' I thought, 'then I'll be able to raise a kid.' Eventually, taking care of the dog became harder than kids because you can't take the dog everywhere you go. But the experience has been a good one."

During that first year of marriage, Eric was able to attend some of Chanel's games in Logan, and she did her best to attend his games. While living in Riverdale, the Weddles were active members of their local LDS congregation. Because of their notoriety, Eric and Chanel were often invited to speak in Church meetings and to youth groups. They also became good friends with another couple in the LDS community, Burk and Staci Potter, and enjoyed some fun activities together.

## LEADERSHIP, MARRIAGE, AND EMERALDS

When Chanel graduated from Utah State in the spring of 2006, the Weddles moved to Sugar House, a community near downtown Salt Lake City, where Eric would do his best to live up to expectations during his senior year at Utah.

# CHAPTER 10

⟶

# THE WIDE WORLD OF WEDDLE

It was on a frigid November night in Colorado Springs, Colorado, that senior Eric Weddle gave one of the quintessential performances of his stellar University of Utah career. A review of the game film, broadcast by The Mountain Network, tells the story play by play.

*First Quarter*

11:50—On third-and-2 from the Utah 35, Weddle, red No. 32, takes the direct snap and spins his way for eight yards and a first down.

9:45—Air Force quarterback Shaun Carney fakes the dive into the line and pitches the pigskin to running back Chad Hall. Weddle bolts up from his safety position to stop Hall after a gain of four.

9:13—On the next play, Weddle and three other Utes gang-tackle AFA tailback Justin Handley.

7:09—Back on offense again, Weddle takes another

third-down snap, fakes the handoff to wide receiver Brent Casteel, and charges forward for 8 more yards and a Utah first down.

6:08—This time quarterback Brett Ratliff hands off to Weddle, who draws defenders before pitching to teammate Daryl Poston for a gain of 3.

4:29—With the ball on the 6, Ratliff tosses left to Weddle, who follows a block by Casteel and dives toward the orange pylon. The referee signals a touchdown. Eric is swarmed by jubilant teammates. He breaks away to hold the extra point for kicker Louie Sakoda. The ball splits the goalposts and Utah leads 7–0.

2:59—Back on defense, Weddle rocks Hall to the turf after an 8-yard run.

*Second Quarter*

10:31—After a few minutes of rest, Weddle wraps up Falcons wide receiver Mark Root after a 21-yard catch.

7:41—Five plays later, Weddle sheds a Falcon block and uses one hand to pull down Hall in the open field, saving a touchdown. The Air Force drive ends when Falcons kicker Zach Sasser shanks a 35-yard FG.

5:41—Eric rushes for gains of 6, 7, and 3 yards on three straight runs. The teams trade punts in the final minutes, and Utah leads at the half 7–0.

*Third Quarter*

13:16—Back in the wildcat formation on third-and-short, Eric catches the snap, fakes to Casteel, and plows ahead for a 5-yard pickup.

7:42—After holding the Falcons on third down, Eric fields his first punt of the night and dodges three Air Force defenders to pick up one yard.

4:07—From his safety position, Weddle attacks Hall and stops him for a minimal gain. Air Force averages 260 yards rushing per game. To this point in the contest, the Utes defense has held the Falcons to 36 yards on the ground. Utah coach Kyle Whittingham smiles because the game plan is working.

1:40—Utah holds once again, and Air Force punts. Eric waves his arm to signal a fair catch and hauls the ball in while surrounded by four Falcons. The third quarter comes to an end with Utah still up 7–0.

*Fourth Quarter*

11:46—Returning to the offensive backfield, Eric fakes another handoff and drives ahead for another 8-yard run. It takes multiple Falcon defenders to bring him down.

10:29—Weddle takes a play off before taking another snap in the shotgun on third-and-short. Weddle runs and spins off one of his offensive linemen, falling forward for 8 more yards.

9:46—Following a 42-yard bomb from Ratliff to receiver Freddie Brown, Eric takes another snap, fakes to Casteel, and uses his shoulder to bulldoze an Air Force linebacker into the end zone for a 4-yard touchdown, his second score of the night. Eric calls Sakoda for the point-after snap. Sakoda drills his 38th consecutive extra point, and Utah leads 14–7.

8:11—Carney drops back and fires a strike down the Air Force sideline, but the pass intended for Hall is incomplete. Running stride-for-stride with Hall is Eric Weddle. Hall complains to the nearest official that he was interfered with but to no avail.

6:38—Hall scampers around the right end for 14 yards and is tackled by Weddle in front of the Air Force sideline. On the next play, AF running back Chad Smith runs left for 6 yards and is drilled by Weddle next to the Utah sideline.

5:34—On second-and-5 from the Utah 7, Weddle and Carney collide near the line of scrimmage. Three plays later, Carney dives into the end zone from inches out. Sasser boots the extra point and the score is tied once again, 14–14. At this point several players on both squads appear exhausted.

2:45—Eric runs behind tight end Colt Sampson for 3 yards. Three plays later, No. 32 surges forward for 7 more yards and another first down. On the sidelines, Sakoda warms his golden toe by kicking the ball into a net.

0:03—The ball comes to rest on the Air Force 20, and Weddle sets Sakoda up for a potential 37-yard game-winning kick. But before Eric can signal for the snap, AFA coach Fisher DeBerry calls two consecutive time-outs in an effort to ice Sakoda. It doesn't work. Lining up a third time, Weddle calls for the snap, puts the ball down, and Sakoda's kick soars through the uprights. The Utes win, 17–14.

Postgame—As officials confirm the kick is good, Weddle and other teammates surround Sakoda for a group hug. On the Utah sideline, Whittingham pumps his arms triumphantly. Across the field, DeBerry throws his hat in disgust and yells something at the nearest official. Exhausted, Weddle shakes hands with several Air Force players and DeBerry. Eventually the Utes gather in the corner of the end zone, where Eric leads his team in a helmet-pumping version of "Utah Man."

Playing running back and safety, two of the most physical positions on the field, as well as special teams, Eric finished the frosty night with 8 tackles, 12 carries for 73 yards, and 2 touchdowns. He helped the Utah defense hold the Air Force rushing attack to 116 yards, well under their 260-yard per game average. More impressive, perhaps, was the fact that he was on the field for 90, or two-thirds, of the game's 136 total plays. Eric participated in all 63 defensive snaps, ran a season-high 14 plays on offense, held for all 3 kicks—including the game-winning field goal—and was on the field for 6 punt or kick returns and all 4 of the Falcons' field goal attempts and extra points. DeBerry was impressed.

"I told him after the game, 'They're cheating you, son,'" DeBerry said. "'They ought to be giving you two scholarships.'"

Kyle Gunther, the Utes starting center in 2006, said Utah's coaches argued over where to play Weddle during the Air Force game. "The offensive coaches wanted to give him ten carries a quarter. The defensive coaches wanted to save him for defense. He was also playing special teams. The guy never left the field," the sports talk radio show host said. "We needed him on offense or we weren't going to win. We had two counter plays we literally ran all year long. Our starting running back would get the ball and get tackled for a loss. Eric would run the ball and gain seven yards. He had great vision. I think he was durable enough to have a hundred tackles on defense and a thousand yards rushing if they had let him, because no one could stop him. No doubt about it, he was the best running back on our roster in 2006."

Utah quarterback Brett Ratliff said that when Eric touched the ball, good things happened. "He's the guy we feel like we need to get the ball to. Any situation, put Eric in," Ratliff said after the game. "When he's doing that well, it's hard not to get him the ball. It's a joy watching him play defense, watching how well he reads offenses and makes big plays. But it's nice to have him come over to the offensive side and make plays for us, too. Even on special teams, he does it all. We have him everywhere."

## MR. EVERYTHING

Only a handful of college football players have played both ways in the last twenty years, most of them at wide receiver and cornerback, such as Michigan's Charles Woodson (1995–97), Georgia's Champ Bailey (1996–98), and Ohio State's Chris Gamble (2001–03). Stanford's Owen Marecic started at fullback and middle linebacker for the Cardinals in 2009 and 2010. Why do so few go both ways these days? A September 2010 *Sports Illustrated* article featuring Marecic states that "today's game is far more physical and infinitely more complex than it was even 20 years ago, and because of NCAA-mandated time limits on practice, there is far less time to absorb it all."

Eric was one of those rare throwback players with the capability and willingness to do anything his coaches asked of him. For the University of Utah in 2006, Eric was Superman in a crimson uniform. The versatile Mr. Weddle could play any position in the defensive backfield. He lined up at quarterback to move the chains on third down, score touchdowns, milk the clock, and execute trick plays. He returned punts and held for the kicker on extra points and field goals. When a play needed to be made, the team looked to Eric. "I loved the ball in his hands," Coach Whittingham said. "When the ball was in his hands, he made good things happen. In this day and age, it's very rare that someone plays both ways. It takes a very special athlete to do that. Needless to say, he had the skills to get it done. He had endurance and stamina. He was exceptionally tough, mentally and physically. We wanted to maximize his abilities."

Going into his senior year, Eric had started thirty-two of thirty-three games in the secondary, and he was the undisputed leader of the defense. His teammates and coaches admired his professional demeanor and approach. "He's the team leader, and he has accepted that role," Gary Andersen recalled. "He had great athletic ability, unbelievable instincts. His ability to prepare for whatever he was doing was unlike any kid I had ever been around. I wasn't willing to give up Eric Weddle for very many minutes in practice, but there is absolutely no question we wouldn't have had the success we had that year without Eric."

As he had done many times since Pop Warner and Little League, Eric embraced every opportunity with confidence and enthusiasm. He was happy to carry the load. "It's not anything where there's more pressure on me. It's not anything that's going to make life any harder. It's just more things to do and just makes my life a lot more fun," he said that fall. "I just want to win. My teammates know that's what I'm all about. If we win a championship, then I've succeeded."

There were many moments from Eric's senior year that demonstrated his value to the Utes.

- After hearing a radio interview in which Northern Arizona wide receiver Alex Watson called the Utah secondary "a suspect group," Eric limited the Lumberjack speedster to three catches for 19 yards in a lopsided Utah victory, 45–7.

- As part of a 48–0 blowout at Utah State, Weddle didn't allow USU's top receiver, Otis Nelson, a single catch.

- In one of his greatest displays as a Ute, Eric intercepted 3 passes, returned 2 for touchdowns, and rushed for a score to lead Utah to a 38–7 win at San Diego State. When SDSU wide receiver Brett Swain beat Eric for a touchdown catch early in the first quarter, Eric took it personally. On the Utes' next possession, Eric scored on a 2-yard dive. Thirty-two seconds later, Weddle intercepted a pass and zigzagged 30 yards for another touchdown. In the fourth quarter, he tied Erroll Tucker's twenty-one-year-old school record for 2 touchdown interception returns in a single game. Eric had a shot at a fourth interception on a Hail Mary pass before the half, but, following Whittingham's instructions, he just knocked the ball down as time expired. As if he needed to do more, Eric also held Aztec receiver Brian Spinks to one reception for 17 yards. The next day Weddle was named the Walter Camp Football Foundation national defensive player of the week. Performing that way in southern California, with many friends and family watching, made the memory special for Eric. "Oh, man, that is one game I will remember for the rest of my life," he said.

- In a disappointing 36–3 home loss to Boise State, Eric was a bright spot with two interceptions and six tackles.

- Many still marvel when considering a play Eric made in Utah's 20–7 victory over TCU. With the Horned Frogs trailing 17–7 in the fourth quarter at Rice-Eccles, TCU quarterback Marcus Jackson fired a quick pass to running back Lonta Hobbs. As Hobbs caught the ball, Eric almost simultaneously attacked and somehow stripped the pigskin from Hobbs's hands before the two players hit the turf. It was clearly a turnover, but the play happened so fast and so cleanly that game officials in the press box weren't sure whether to credit Weddle with a forced fumble and recovery or an interception. It was eventually ruled an interception. "I have never seen anything like that. Only a player like Weddle could have made a play like that," said teammate Steve Tate. "He's a ball magnet."

- Eric completed the first pass of his career in a 35–22 win at home over Colorado State. On the last play of the first quarter, Eric found teammate Brent Casteel with a 25-yard pass that led to a 6-yard touchdown run by Eric.

Off the field, Eric was the face of the team. Even though the university couldn't print his name on the back, the school began selling No. 32 football jerseys in the campus bookstore and other merchandise locations. Chanel remembers one fan creating a T-shirt that said, "Where's Weddle?" and highlighted all the different positions he played. He was also invited to be part of a promotional television commercial for the school. As part of the commercial, Eric was asked to remove his shirt and flex.

Teammate Kyle Gunther said Eric's teammates teased him because the producers had to spray-paint abs on the senior safety.

Eric was popular with the media. Almost every day after practice, an official from the athletic department handed Eric a cell phone for interviews with radio stations, newspapers, and magazines all over the country. One sportswriter, Michael C. Lewis of the *Salt Lake Tribune,* recalled seeing Eric do a phone interview while he played catch with teammate Casey Evans. "He never dropped the ball, of course," Lewis said. Members of the press were drawn to Weddle for his candor, sense of humor, and down-to-earth personality. They respected him because he didn't dodge hard questions or duck out the back door after a tough loss. "A lot of players give you coach-speak. He was a straight shooter who never sugarcoated anything. He knew his place. He also had tact," said Bill Riley, the radio voice of the Utes. "You enjoyed talking to him because you knew you'd get the straight story."

Former Utah sports information director Liz Abel appreciated Eric's polite manner and willingness to do any interview anytime, anywhere. "We nominated him for a bunch of awards, and those things take a lot of time," Abel said. "I told him there are a ton of good players, and for things to work out, he had to be accessible for anything—phone, e-mail, meeting people, etc.—and I was going to really push him to go the extra mile, stay after practice, speak to everyone, from the student newspaper to *The New York Times.* He was really appreciative, and he did it all in a team way. He was not a selfish, 'me-me-me' guy. He understood that in being promoted himself, he was helping to promote our whole program. He was willing to be the poster boy, and not everyone is."

Teammates and coaches also respected Eric for the time he spent preparing for each opponent, a skill that has helped him succeed in the NFL. Weddle was notorious for analyzing opponents on film for hours, uncovering their tendencies and applying what he learned on the field. Eric became so proficient at understanding the other team's plays that he would scold the scout team for not running a play properly. "He would say, 'They don't do that.' He would get upset," said former teammate Morgan Scalley, now a Utah assistant coach. "It was almost as if he was bored at practice because he knew what was going on while the other guys were still learning."

Being bored at practice occasionally led Eric to butt heads with his head coach, but it wasn't because he was disinterested. "A couple of times I turned around and he was texting or had a newspaper in his hand," Whittingham said, "so I got after him a few times, but it was few and far between. He had such an aptitude for the game of football, a level few players reach. He would absorb things so quickly and so completely that oftentimes we were covering stuff he didn't need to cover. Eric could look at a formation and tell you what was coming before the ball was snapped. He got bored with the same technique and fundamentals because he had them down pat, so we had a few run-ins."

Andersen agreed. "Some players can look at game film and it's like they are watching cartoons. Others pick up a few things," Andersen said. "The difference for Eric was he could study one single person and find all the tendencies and scheme off it. As simple as that sounds, that is very unique for an individual in college football. He saw things I didn't see. He would make a tremendous coach someday."

As a leader, Eric was admired for his poise amid his many responsibilities, but he wasn't the vocal cheerleader type. "You never saw him get stressed out, worried, or ruffled," Scalley said. "He was always up for the challenge. If someone made a play on him, he was quick to forget it and come back the next play. He had a confidence about him that few players have."

Eric's fearless approach made a strong impression on sophomore Louie Sakoda, a walk-on kicker who eventually earned consensus all-American honors. When Sakoda took over the field-goal-kicking duties in 2006, he learned quickly he could trust Eric as his holder. Eric didn't have to say anything to earn Sakoda's trust—it was what he didn't say that made the difference, Sakoda said. "Every holder looks back and gives the kicker a nod to see if he is ready and the kicker nods back. Eric always had a comfortable, confident swagger about himself that carried over to me. Even if it was a bad snap, I knew the ball would be there. Even after he had sprinted a hundred yards for a pick-6, and was out of breath, exhausted, and shaking. Every single time it was perfect," Sakoda said. "I couldn't ask for a better holder. I attribute a lot of my success to him. He made kicking something I never had to think about."

Having been a holder in high school, doing it in college came naturally for Eric. He takes pride in the fact that he has never botched a snap. "I loved the pressure of being the holder, knowing either you get the job done or you fail," Eric said. "People don't congratulate you for getting the ball down. It's expected. I love the chance to have everything in my hands, and it's another opportunity to be in the game."

## "I NEVER WANTED TO LET MY TEAMMATES DOWN"

Eric's teammates relied on his leadership to recover from painful back-to-back losses in the latter part of October. After a respectable win over TCU, the Utes defense spotted the University of Wyoming 24 points and went on to suffer defeat, 31–15, in front of almost 21,000 fans in Laramie, Wyoming. Utah's defense played better in the second half. Eric returned a fumble 35 yards for a touchdown, but the offense mustered only 144 yards total offense and allowed 6 quarterback sacks. Even when the Utes knew what the Cowboys were going to do, they couldn't stop it. Eric described his performance as "subpar."

Utah tried to fix their mistakes in Albuquerque, New Mexico, the following week, but problems persisted. The Utes jumped out to a 24–3 lead, only to see New Mexico come back for a 34–31 victory. Andersen said the Lobos won because they had an effective game plan for attacking Utah's man-to-man coverage. New Mexico used crossing patterns that made it difficult for Eric to stay with the Lobos' speedy wide receivers. Two significant plays—touchdown passes of 40 and 42 yards from UNM redshirt freshman quarterback Donovan Porterie to wide receiver Marcus Smith in the second and third quarters—changed the momentum of the game. The defense gave up 350 yards passing and 3 touchdowns to Porterie. "Teams would gear their offense to me. New Mexico had the perfect plan," Eric said. "I would always press [a defensive tactic for playing close to the receiver at the line of scrimmage] and watch the underneath routes. They [UNM] would send someone to pick me or they would run away from me. In the first half, our plan worked. They adjusted at the half and I couldn't stay with them in the second half." New Mexico sealed the victory with a one-yard touchdown plunge by running back Martelius Epps with 2:09 remaining. Utah failed to respond and fell to 4–4 on the season.

In the locker room after the New Mexico loss, Weddle remained in the showers longer than usual, replaying the game. He was one of the last to get dressed. With his emotions still raw from a disappointing defeat, he addressed the team.

"He was in tears, apologizing to the team," Tate said. "By no means was it all his fault. We all made bad plays. But we learned something about Eric that day. Everyone can be successful and deal with the highs of the game. But it's how you deal with the lows of the game that makes you a great player. Eric stood up, and we followed. How he handled it was characteristic of the guy he is. He took us on his shoulders and said it would never happen again. He found the positives, and we rallied behind him to finish the season strong."

Eric's accountability impressed his defensive coordinator. "Rather than ducking his head and running away, he took responsibility and learned from it," Andersen said.

"Not one of my fonder college memories," Eric said. "It was hard to deal with because I never wanted to let my teammates down. I wanted to learn from it."

Casey Evans, Eric's roommate when the team traveled, said the Wyoming and New Mexico losses were both turning points in the season. "We got torched. You never saw Weddle get beat like he did in those two games. He was in a grumpy mood, and the losses made it worse," Evans said. "But you could trust him to bounce back and learn from it. It was a wake-up call."

Whittingham said the New Mexico loss was as low as he ever saw Weddle. "But I learned again what I already knew, that he is the consummate competitor and he would bounce back. He would finish the season strong. He came back harder than ever before."

Once again, Eric found perspective and inspiration off the field by getting to know Ryker Fox, a courageous six-year-old Salt Lake City boy who was slowly dying of an inoperable brain tumor. Football was Ryker's favorite sport, and he dreamed of one day playing in the pros. When Coach Whittingham heard Ryker's story and learned he was a Utah fan, the boy was invited to spend some time with the team. The players adopted Ryker as their twelfth man, gave him a jersey, and extended an open invitation to attend practices and games. When Ryker became acquainted with the team that fall, doctors predicted he had less than a month to live, but he surpassed their expectations. At one point during the 2006 season, Ryker passed out black wristbands with his name to the players and coaches. Those black bands meant a lot to Eric, and the senior captain wore them everywhere with pride. He said they were a motivating reminder of Ryker and the real problems true heroes face every day. When Utah defeated Tulsa in the Armed Forces Bowl at the end of the season, a group of Utes carried Ryker off the field on their shoulders.

When Ryker died in February 2007, two months after his seventh birthday, the team created an award in Ryker's honor. At the end of each season, the Ryker Fox Award is given to a player who has overcome adversity, including injury, personal tragedy, or any other hardships. The recipient must also demonstrate overall toughness, just like Ryker. "He was an inspiration to the team," said Jeff Rudy, Utah's director of football operations.

Several years later, Eric and others still wear Ryker's wristbands. "I still support him," Eric said. "I have never taken them off for anything."

## THE COUPLES

While Eric was in the middle of his senior year, Chanel was working for the state of Utah as a social worker. The young couple, with their dog, rented a small home in Sugar House and regularly participated in their LDS meetings and activities. The Weddles also continued to do something they had started in San Francisco.

Each Monday night from August to November was couples' night. Eric and Chanel, together with a few other young couples, took turns hosting small gatherings. The group usually included tight end Colt Sampson and his wife, CC, offensive lineman Tavo Tupola and his wife, Andria, and kicker Dan Beardall and his wife, Tawni. At each gathering, someone shared an inspiring or spiritual thought, and there were refreshments and a fun activity. Going out to dinner was a popular choice, and Eric especially enjoyed bowling night because he and Chanel often won. When the men were with the football team, the women organized a girls' night. The Weddles always felt bolstered and uplifted by these Monday night activities.

"It was so fun to share experiences with each other," Eric said. "I always came away feeling strengthened."

## WEDDLE'S METTLE

The most endearing moment of Eric's college career came after his most devastating defeat.

Utah emerged from the fog of back-to-back losses to Wyoming and New Mexico to win their next three games. The Utes thumped UNLV 45–23, topped Colorado State 35–22, and escaped from Colorado Springs with a 17–14 victory over Air Force. The three-game winning streak provided the 7–4 Utes with momentum going into their final home game against instate rival BYU. Considering the adversity Utah had experienced, a fifth straight win over the Mountain West Conference champion Cougars, who were 9–2, would provide a perfect end to the regular season. The contest would also be Eric's final home game in Rice-Eccles Stadium. The senior captain couldn't believe how fast four years had flown by. He couldn't fathom going out with a loss to the Cougars on senior day.

For BYU quarterback John Beck and his team, a win at Utah would mean redemption. The Cougars had dropped four straight games to the Utes. The previous two losses still haunted Beck.

The 2004 game in Salt Lake City ended in a 52–21 blowout. After then-coach Gary Crowton addressed the Cougars in the visiting locker room, Beck quietly returned to the field to take a mental picture of Utah's fans and players celebrating their un-defeated season. "Before I left BYU, I wanted to have a moment like that for our team," he said. But when Utah came to Provo in 2005, without their starting quarterback and top receiver, and stole another victory in overtime, Beck realized he had only one more shot to experience the feeling of beating Utah.

The highly anticipated matchup at Rice-Eccles unfolded like a classic battle of street ball between rival neighborhoods. "I had my guys and he had his guys and everybody was going at it. The game had that feel," Beck said. "I knew I was playing against someone who was a very good leader. After three years we knew each other well enough because we had watched each other so many times, and there was a mutual respect for each other. There was nothing that was going to take us out of that game."

BYU jumped out to a 14–0 lead in the first quarter, and Utah countered with 24 points in the second and third. As the Cougars rallied back in the fourth quarter, Beck and Weddle con-versed a few times between plays. After Beck completed a pass to freshman wide receiver McKay Jacobsen, Weddle told the BYU quarterback, "Hey, quit throwing perfect passes. We don't like it."

With 13:15 to go in the game, Beck took the snap and floated a 4-yard fade to Jonny Harline, who was being covered by Weddle. Both players leaped for the pigskin and touched leather at its highest point, similar to a jump ball in basketball. But Harline was able to tip the ball to himself and secure it with his right hand before both players hit the turf. Harline's catch is immortalized in a large framed picture hanging outside the BYU coaches' offices. The ruling on the field was a touchdown, despite Weddle's protests.

"After the play, Eric and I were standing near one another. He turned and said, 'John, there is no way he caught that in bounds,'" Beck said.

"Dude, I'm telling you, Eric, he caught it. I just watched the replay on the board—watch, they're going to show it again," Beck replied.

While the replay booth reviewed the play, there was red No. 32 and white No. 12, standing together, squinting and studying the play on the south end zone screen. Even after he saw it, Eric wasn't convinced. "There is no way he got it in bounds. He had to have landed out," Weddle said.

"We just watched it. He was in," Beck said again.

When BYU was awarded six points, the ultra-competitive Weddle could only fume as the game continued.

The Cougars scored a second fourth-quarter touchdown with 3:23 to play when Beck found his other tight end, Daniel Coats, on a 2-yard touchdown pass. The Utah offense responded with a 13-play, 90-yard drive, including a fourth-down conversion, which ended with a thrilling 19-yard screen pass from Ratliff to speedy receiver Brent Casteel. With Weddle's hold and Sakoda's extra point, the Utes led 31–27, and more than 45,000 fans were on their feet, sensing a fifth-straight Utah victory in the "Holy War," a term coined by fans to represent the intense rivalry between these Utah-based colleges.

But 1:09 still remained on the clock, and Beck was optimistic. "When the game came down to the wire and Utah scored to go ahead, I couldn't believe it. We had played so well. We worked so hard," the quarterback said. "I made the decision that we were going to win. I had this calm, it-is-going-to-happen feeling."

With the late afternoon sun setting on Rice-Eccles Stadium and Beck's college career, the Cougar quarterback orchestrated a 64-yard drive in the final minute to set BYU up with third-and-10 on the Utah 11 with 3.2 seconds remaining. The Cougars called time-out, and offensive coordinator Robert Anae called "59," giving Beck the primary option of throwing another fade to Harline on the right side of the end zone.

Taking a deep breath, Beck took the snap and began to improvise. The fade wasn't an option because Utah's defense dropped eight players into zone coverage. He began to scramble. Harline followed the play initially, but recognizing the defense, he galloped to the other side of the end zone, covering some 40 yards. With the clock showing 0:00, Beck scrambled to his right in search of an open receiver, and the defense followed, leaving Harline all alone on the left side of the field. Beck saw him out of the corner of his eye and launched a pass across his body. The ball came to rest in Harline's arms as he slid to his knees. BYU 33, Utah 31. The BYU sideline erupted as players stormed the field. Utah fans were stunned into silence. Beck's emotions overflowed.

While Beck was swarmed by teammates, losing to BYU in his final home game was a bitter pill for Eric to swallow. Once again, Eric had rarely come off the field during the game. He had nine tackles, rushed for 25 yards, and even threw an 18-yard touchdown pass in the second quarter. On the game's epic final play, he was on the opposite side of the end zone when Harline caught the ball. In the blink of an eye, the game was suddenly over and Utah had lost. "I didn't get over that loss for weeks," Eric said. Even thinking about it now is still upsetting to him.

But he acknowledged the game was a classic. Both teams made comebacks and showed a lot of character. Weddle admired Beck, quietly observing the way the BYU quarterback had handled pressure and intense scrutiny over his career. Eric had also been taught by his father to always respect your opponent and play with sportsmanship. "You always congratulate your opponent and never make excuses for a loss," Eric said, recalling his father's words. Despite his personal feelings, Weddle located the quarterback and offered congratulations. Weddle put his arm around Beck's shoulder as they walked a short distance together. "For whatever reason, I felt it in me to go up to him and say, 'Hey, man, I feel horrible right now, but I am happy for you,'" Eric said. "Obviously I would go back and win that game a thousand times, but it was *his* shining moment. I can appreciate and respect a guy who puts it all on the line and does whatever he can to help his team win. I see myself as that guy. . . . Sometimes you've got to be the bigger man."

While Beck's recollection of what Weddle said at that moment differs slightly (he recalls Weddle saying something such as, "That was awesome—an amazing game. A lot of people are going to remember this one—great job"), the classy gesture left a deep impression on Beck. "I have been in games like that. To go down to the wire and lose, you know he was sick inside. Not everybody has character like that," said Beck, who has since suited up for the Miami Dolphins, Baltimore Ravens, Washington Redskins, and Houston Texans. "People don't understand how much high-caliber athletes invest to get those wins, and when it doesn't happen, it hurts. He walked up at a moment when it hurt and was a person of high character. That is the mark of a champion on and off the field. To be honest, if I had lost that game, I don't know if I would have walked up to say, 'Great job.'"

The two players talked about one other thing in their brief exchange—fishing. A mutual friend had tried to set up a fishing trip for the trio, but it didn't feel appropriate to go until the season was over. "On TV, when I had my arm on his shoulder, you can see me smile at him. That's when I said, 'I guess we can go fishing now,'" Beck said.

Weddle agreed. "Yeah, we'll have to do that."

Chad Lewis, a former BYU and NFL pro-bowl tight end with the Philadelphia Eagles, later said the exchange between Weddle and Beck set a remarkable example of sportsmanship for every athlete in Utah. "It was incredible," Lewis said. "For me personally, and for all the players at BYU and Utah, Eric set a standard of class that was very impressive."

Out of that unique moment emerged a lifelong friendship. The men have homes fifteen minutes from each other outside of San Diego. They make it a priority to get together from time to time for fishing or a barbecue at a beach house. On multiple occasions, John has invited Eric to play in his charity golf tournament. Beck admits that Weddle is the better golfer, but the Cougar is better at catching fish. Of course football is a favorite topic. "He's kind of a nerd in a sense, always joking around," Weddle said. "When we get together it's a good time."

"It's funny," Beck said. "Neither of us knew the other until the rivalry. Neither of us is from Utah. But our paths crossed, and now we live by each other. It's been interesting to see how it has all played out since then."

## ONE FINAL PICK

Following the BYU game, Weddle was flooded with multiple honors and accolades. For the second year in a row, he was named the Mountain West Conference defensive player of the year. He was also named a consensus all-American.

With a record of 7–5, Utah was invited to play the Tulsa Golden Hurricane in the Armed Forces Bowl in Fort Worth,

Texas. With Weddle making plays on both sides of the ball, the Utes led from the start and won comfortably 25–13. Once again, Eric showed why he was considered the most versatile player in the nation. He recorded six tackles, half a sack, a fumble recovery, an interception while rushing for 56 yards, and a touchdown. He also held the ball perfectly while Sakoda booted 4 field goals to earn MVP honors. With the victory, Utah also extended its bowl win streak to six in a row, at that time the second longest in the country.

The Utah victory was secured on one final drive that was classic Weddle. Midway through the fourth quarter, with Utah up 19–13, the Utes milked the clock by handing off to Eric. Weddle left and Weddle right, he carried the ball seven times for 34 yards, including a 4-yard touchdown that put the game out of reach. As he crossed the goal line, he triumphantly raised the ball over his head.

"Our team needed a running game. I was happy, knowing the coaches trusted me enough on that final drive to get the job done," Eric said.

Eric probably could have scored a second touchdown on the final play of the Armed Forces Bowl when he picked off a pass by Tulsa quarterback Paul Smith with nothing but green grass in front of him, but he didn't. After 10 yards, he slowed down and took a knee to end the game. Knowing they had the win was enough. "I should have batted it down, but I was like, 'Aw, I might as well catch it.' But out of respect, I took a knee. The coaches harp on that—to be classy and show respect to your opponent—and that's how I've been my whole career. I didn't want to do anything other than that," Weddle said.

It's safe to say Utah would not have achieved its 8–5 record that season without the remarkable efforts of its senior captain. Among his most significant contributions, Weddle started all thirteen games and played virtually every position; he rushed

Eric and his father, Steve, in the
hospital after Eric was born.

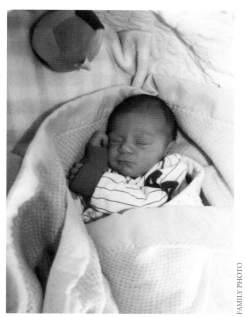

Eric as a newborn.

Eric, age 3, and his big sister, Kathleen,
during a family vacation.

Eric, age 4, dresses up as an Army
soldier for Halloween.

Eric and his father, Steve, return from a successful fishing trip.

Eric, age 5, played for the Astros in
his first year of T-ball. Steve was one of
Eric's Little League coaches.

Eric, age 10, played for the Wolverines
in his second season of Pop Warner football.
He wore No. 22, after his favorite NFL
player, Emmitt Smith.

Eric, age 10, and his dog, Keisha, after a pheasant hunt in Norco, California.

During a game in his second season of Pop Warner football,
Eric takes a handoff and follows his blockers.

Eric played on the varsity basketball team
as a junior at Alta Loma High School.

Chanel visiting Eric's house in
2001 to meet his sister and grandparents
for the first time.

During a baseball game toward the
end of his junior year, Eric was hit in
the left eye with a fastball, an injury
that led him to give up baseball.

Eric escorted his future wife, Chanel,
to the school prom in May 2002.
He was a junior; she was a senior.

Although the team didn't advance deep into the state playoffs, Eric's senior season on the football team was his most memorable.

It was during Eric's senior year at Alta Loma that he began to play multiple positions.

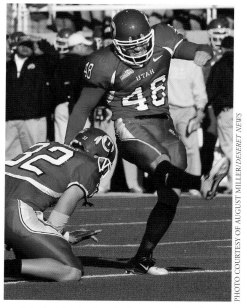

Eric tackles an Air Force ball carrier during Utah's memorable 45–43 triple overtime win over the Falcons on November 1, 2003.

Eric holds the football as Dan Beardall kicks the extra point in Utah's 43–13 victory over Wyoming in 2005.

Parents Debbie and Steve, sister Kathleen, with Eric and Chanel after
a November 2004 Utah victory at Rice-Eccles Stadium.

Eric and his grandparents Jean and Norm Weddle after a 2004 Utah game.

Eric and teammates celebrate an interception against Colorado State in 2004.

Eric knocks away a pass intended for Pittsburgh's Greg Lee during the 2005 Fiesta Bowl in Tempe, Arizona.

Eric intercepts a pass in front of Air Force receiver Jason Brown during a game at Rice-Eccles Stadium in 2005.

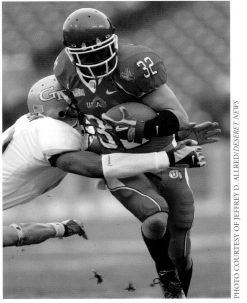

Utah head coach Kyle Whittingham congratulates Eric following Utah's 41–34 overtime victory over BYU in Provo in 2005.

Eric runs the ball against Georgia Tech's David Sanborn during the 2005 Emerald Bowl in San Francisco.

Eric and Chanel were married in the LDS San Diego California Temple in July 2005.

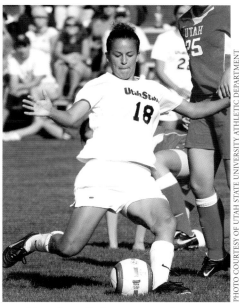

Chanel excelled as a soccer player in high school and at Utah State University from 2002 to 2005.

Newlyweds Eric and Chanel after a 2005 game. Chanel came straight to Salt Lake City after playing in a USU soccer game.

Members of the Weddle and Robles families, along with close friends, gather in San Francisco to support Eric and the Utah Utes prior to the 2005 Emerald Bowl.

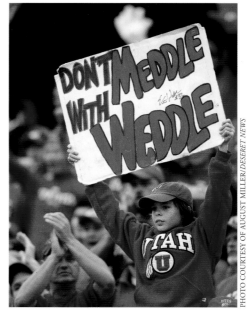

Eric intercepts the pass against TCU in 2006.

A young Utah fan holds up his Weddle sign in 2006.

Eric catches a pass during practice for the Senior Bowl in Mobile, Alabama, in January 2007.

Eric signing his contract with his agent, David Canter.

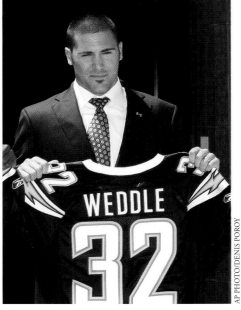

Eric holds up his new San Diego jersey before a press conference at the Chargers facility in San Diego in 2007.

Debbie and Steve pause the game to celebrate Eric's one-handed interception of Peyton Manning's pass in San Diego's 2007 AFC Divisional playoff 28–24 win over Indianapolis.

Eric's parents, Steve and Debbie Weddle (left), and Chanel's parents, Sonya and Ron Blaquiere (right), join their children on the day of granddaughter Brooklyn's blessing in March 2008.

Parents Eric and Chanel celebrate daughter Brooklyn's second
birthday with a pony ride in the backyard of their Escondido,
California, home. Gaige, the couple's son, is 6 months old.

Eric reads to children in his mother's kindergarten class at
Payne Elementary School in El Monte, California, in 2008.

Eric celebrates an interception
return for a touchdown against the
Miami Dolphins in 2009.

Eric prepares to tackle St. Louis
running back Steven Jackson during
a 2010 game in St. Louis.

Eric and his Camaro, "Black Beauty,"
in June 2010.

The first Weddle family photo after
daughter Silver's birth, 2011: Gaige, Eric,
Brooklyn, Silver, and Chanel.

Eric reaches up to say hello to daughter Brooklyn and son, Gaige,
following a 2011 game against the Buffalo Bills in San Diego.

Eric holds baby daughter Silver while studying his game notes in his southern California home in early 2012.

Suiting up in a San Diego Chargers uniform, Gaige Weddle prepares to watch his father, Eric, play in a 2012 game.

The Weddle family celebrates Halloween at the local pumpkin patch in 2012.

Eric hugs his son, Gaige, at the NFL luau, one of several events leading up to the 2012 Pro Bowl in Hawaii.

44 times for 203 yards and 5 touchdowns; he completed 2-of-4 passes for 43 yards, including a score; he led the MWC with 7 interceptions, including 2 returned for touchdowns; he deflected 2 passes, recorded 64 tackles, caused a fumble and recovered 3 others, including one for a touchdown; and he returned 8 punts for 44 yards. Eric Weddle is also the only player in school and MWC history to register touchdowns each in passing, rushing, interceptions, and fumble recovery in one season. Not bad for a one-star recruit who was offered a single scholarship.

Weddle's illustrious college career had come full circle. After getting burned deep in his first action as a freshman against Utah State, Eric walked away with an interception in a bowl victory. And he had done it with class.

## THE GREAT ONE

On the Monday after Utah's loss to BYU, *Deseret News* columnist Doug Robinson published a letter to Heisman trophy voters under the headline, "Why not give Heisman to Utah's Eric Weddle?"

There was no clear-cut winner that year, but experts predicted Ohio State quarterback Troy Smith would win the award, and he eventually did. But Robinson's thesis was this: "Instead of giving the trophy to the best running back or quarterback, why not break tradition and give it to the BEST FOOTBALL PLAYER? Why not give the Heisman Trophy to Eric Weddle?" he wrote. "Weddle is the best all-around football player in the nation, period. He is a gridiron sensation in the West. He gets more ink than Tom [Cruise] and Katie [Holmes]. When is the last time you heard fans chanting a defensive back's name during a game? . . . Why not give the trophy to a guy who plays full-time cornerback/safety and part-time quarterback, punt returner and holder for field goals and extra points?"

Robinson quoted former Wyoming coach Joe Glenn, who said of Weddle, "He should win the Heisman Trophy. I sincerely mean that." The columnist went on to say, "The only people who spend more time on the field than Weddle each Saturday are the referees."

So where does Weddle rank among the all-time Utah greats?

Only one defensive back in Utah history has been named a consensus all-American—Eric Weddle. Bruce Woodbury, who worked in the Utah athletic department for more than 35 years, recalls many great defensive backs who have worn the Utah feather and drum but were not consensus all-Americans. Larry Wilson starred for the Utes in 1959 and went on to a career in the NFL. Norm Thompson was a Utah all-conference safety in 1969. Jeff Griffin was a second-team all-American in the late 1970s who also played in the NFL. Erroll Tucker was an all-American return specialist who played defensive back. And Eric's former teammate Morgan Scalley was a second-team all-American. Harold Lusk (1993–1996) and Andre Dyson (1997–2000) also earned all-conference honors.

"It's pretty tough to say any of them was better than Eric," Woodbury said. "He might be the best ever. I think he is. He was something."

Coach Kyle Whittingham has said Eric might be the best all-around player to wear a Ute uniform. Considering the long list of Utah players in the NFL, the statement carries some weight. "Our secondary was built around one of the best players in the country. He was capable of playing multiple positions," Whittingham said. "Eric will go down as one of the best safeties to ever play at Utah."

"He could have started at any school in America and had a

great career," said Urban Meyer, now the head coach at Ohio State.

Eric saw action in forty-eight games and started forty-five in four years. Weddle's 18 career interceptions place him at second all-time, behind 19 by Lusk. He had 277 tackles and sacked 10 quarterbacks. He also scored 10 touchdowns.

As impressive as his career numbers were, Eric wondered if they were good enough to get him a shot in the National Football League. How would league general managers evaluate him? Which teams might be interested?

The answer would almost seem too good to be true.

# CHAPTER 11

⟍

# AGENTS AND PHONE CALLS

D avid Canter had known it was a possibility, but he still wasn't prepared for it emotionally. He felt like he had just lost a dear friend. "We just lost the most important player I have ever recruited," said the sports agent, breaking the bad news to his wife.

The date was Thursday, December 21, 2006, one day before Canter and his wife had planned to fly to Fort Worth, Texas, to watch the University of Utah take on the University of Tulsa in the Armed Forces Bowl. Afterward, David hoped to add Ute captain Eric Weddle to his list of clients.

Sitting on his kitchen countertop at the couple's Florida home, tears flowed as the sports agent recounted the phone conversation he had just had with Eric, a potential client who had become more like a brother in recent months. Eric's first words captured David's full attention.

"Hey, listen, we have always been honest with each other," Eric said. "I want to be honest with you."

Oh, no, Canter thought, it is never good when a player begins that way. The agent already knew where this was going.

"We've been talking here with my wife, dad, and mom. You know how I feel about you," Weddle continued, "But there is another agency they want me to go with."

David could sense reluctance in Eric's voice, yet the Utah all-American was delivering the equivalent of a Dear John letter. "It was upsetting him, and, obviously, as an agent you take some comfort in that," David said years later. "But it doesn't pay your mortgage. You don't get any money for finishing as the player's second choice."

And so the call ended rather quickly. Still seated on the kitchen countertop, Canter continued to weep. Eric had been his number one target that year. When Canter had first learned about Weddle, he had his doubts. Why would a married, converted Latter-day Saint from southern California sign with a Jewish sports agent in Florida? But David was pleasantly surprised to learn that Eric was interested. They had met for the first time early in 2006 when Eric and Chanel traveled to Las Vegas for a Rascal Flatts concert. After introductions, David and Eric spoke for about five minutes, and in the weeks and months that followed, they developed a professional relationship via text messaging. They became so well acquainted that before long David was openly telling other recruits that Weddle was his top priority. "If I get Eric Weddle, I'm not going to sign another safety," Canter had said. He had a good feeling about Eric.

"I've had multiple top-10 picks," Canter said later. "But something told me Eric isn't just a client, he's a brother for life. There was incredible symmetry in our lives. We even share the same birthday."

Where was that good feeling now? Drying his eyes, David

remembered the trip to Texas. "Screw it," he thought. "We don't need to go to Dallas now." Attempting to accept his fate and move on, he retreated to his office, logged on to his computer and cancelled the plane tickets. Four hours later, he would regret that emotional decision.

Meanwhile, in Texas, Eric second-guessed the Dear John phone call he had just made to Florida.

In the past few months Weddle had sat through interviews with several agents but he always felt most comfortable with David. He met David through one of Canter's former associates. Weddle liked Canter for several reasons. First, he and David hit it off from the start and thought a lot alike. Second, Canter was always quick to respond to questions with a phone call or text message. Third, he wasn't afraid to tell Eric his honest opinion. "He was up-front and real. He told me the positives and the negatives and didn't sugarcoat things." Fourth, Canter represented fewer than twenty players at the time, and Eric liked David's style of giving each client the same amount of time, energy, and respect. Eric also admired Canter's work ethic. He felt he could trust him. "He wasn't dealing with a hundred other guys. I didn't want to play second fiddle to someone else. I knew he would outwork any other agent to help me get what I needed," Eric said. "He was a guy who was going to be there for me when I am done playing. I knew he would still be a brother at age sixty."

Although Canter was fairly young, less than two weeks from his thirty-fourth birthday, Eric knew the sports agent had started from nothing and had overcome a lot of personal adversity. After David played football for the Division III national champion Ithaca College Bombers in New York, he worked for the Florida Marlins during the strike-shortened 1994 season as a game day operations intern. With the Marlins, David observed the daily operations of the professional sports business and grew to dislike how owners treated their ball players. Someone needed to represent the athletes and protect their interests. He had found his calling in life.

David enrolled at the University of Miami law school. One day during his second semester in 1996, he realized he had a broken taillight and pulled over to a Shell gas station in Coconut Grove, Florida. As he fixed the problem, David saw Miami Dolphins wide receiver Lamar Thomas stroll out of the gas station. Seeing an opportunity, Canter approached Thomas, introduced himself and asked if he could speak to him about the agency business. They spoke for more than twenty minutes. That chance encounter led David to engineer marketing and endorsement deals for Thomas and to handle marketing for ten other Dolphin players.

He became certified as an NFL Players Association contract advisor in 1997 and began recruiting clients. He started an agency called Total Entertainers and Athlete Management with two partners who were in the financial services industry, and he signed three Florida Gators in 1998. His first draft pick was Tony George, a defensive back who went in the third round to the New England Patriots.

At the height of his business three years later, Canter shared seventy clients with partner Steve Weinberg. Canter claims, however, that when Weinberg was sanctioned by the NFLPA that year, his partner smeared Canter's name with clients and many dumped him for other agents. The defections cost Canter millions. Still determined, David spent the next three years starting a new agency, DEC Management, Inc. When David began recruiting Eric in 2006, he represented approximately twenty-five players, including Carolina running back Stephen Davis and Troy Williamson, then a wide receiver with the Minnesota Vikings.

As impressed as Eric was with David, he also valued the opinions of his wife and parents, and they favored a different agent. They were wary of Canter's past and felt more of a connection with the other agent. The four engaged in a serious discussion in a Dallas hotel room. Eric considered carefully everything his loved ones said. He prayed about the matter. Then he called David with the bad news.

Almost four hours after that call, a remorseful feeling led Eric to realize he had made a mistake. Resolved to repair the damage, he told his wife and parents he respected their opinions, but David was the best man for the job. "'This is who I am going to take,' I said, and they said, 'All right,'" Eric recalled. He picked up his cell phone and dialed David's number. This decision would prove to be monumental.

His emotions were still pretty raw, but David was doing better now. He was back in the kitchen helping his wife make dinner when the telephone rang. He glanced at the caller ID and did a double take when he saw the name "Eric Weddle." He hesitated only a moment before taking the call.

"Hey, is it okay if I put you on speaker phone?" Eric asked.

What? David thought. This kid just told me he isn't hiring me, and now he's going to embarrass me in front of his wife and parents?

"Listen, I just wanted to say this with my mom and dad present," Eric began. "They understand what kind of human being I am. They understand all the decisions that I've made in my life. They trust me one hundred percent. I told them I wouldn't feel right not hiring you, and so we wanted to say, 'Congratulations, you are my agent.'"

Another overwhelming flood of emotion swept over David, and he almost dropped the phone. Once again, he broke down in tears, as did his wife. "I am man enough to admit it," David said. "It meant that much to me."

There was another reason to cry. Rebooking his cancelled plane tickets to Dallas cost an extra $1,400 and included connecting flights, something he and his wife detested. "Obviously I should have waited," Canter said later.

Despite Eric's phone call, David's emotional roller coaster ride wasn't over quite yet. After Eric and the Utes defeated Tulsa in the Armed Forces Bowl, Eric, Chanel, Steve, and Debbie met with the Canters. Having seen other agents mulling around the stadium talking to other players, David felt an urgency to sign his new star to an actual contract. But when the agent pulled out his representative agreement, Eric declined to sign. "Eric said, 'No, I'm not going to sign with you right now,'" David recalled. "'I'm going home to enjoy my post-football vacation and let it all sink in. I will sign with you when I land in Florida in a couple of days.'"

Canter had no idea what to think at this point. He tried not to imagine the worst, but in a cutthroat business where players have so many clamoring for their attention, and having been burned before, David figured Eric would end up going in a different direction. "I was thinking about all the other agencies that were going to call and text Eric, bad-mouthing me. I'm not going to be hired," David said. "Sure enough, Eric starts forwarding text messages from other agencies he had already turned down. To this day, I'm absolutely shocked, truly, at how my competitors treated Eric. For several months they said what a great person he is and how they trusted he would make a great decision. Then he tells them he is going to hire me, and the hate, lies, and venom that was spewed from them was magnificent, in a bad way."

True to his word, however, Eric stepped off a plane in Florida four days later and officially signed with David and DEC Management, Inc. Eric was ready to get to work. David breathed a sigh of relief.

As of 2012, more than eighty percent of David's sixteen NFL clients have come to him because of Eric Weddle. "Honestly, I am probably not in business if I don't represent Eric Weddle," David said. "I owe this guy my life." Among his clients are several former University of Utah players, as well as several San Diego Chargers, who hired Canter after observing his work with Eric. "He is just a special human being," Canter said of Weddle. "This is not an easy business, but when you have a client like Eric, you realize why you are in it. The roller coaster, the insanity and the bad times, which often outweigh the good, are worth it because of someone like Eric."

## PREPARING FOR THE NFL DRAFT

After the holidays, Eric said farewell to Chanel for several weeks and departed for Miami. For the first time in their marriage, they would be apart for an extended period of time while he trained for the 2007 NFL draft.

"It was difficult. She flew out a few times to see me, but we agreed this was a time for me to concentrate on making my dream career a reality," Eric said.

David offered to give the Weddles a loan so Chanel could move to Florida to be with Eric, but they reached a mutual decision for Chanel to remain in Utah with the couple's dog.

"For starters, I didn't want to go into debt," Chanel said. "Second, Eric needed to focus, and, third, it was not like we were going to be able to spend time together if I was there. Fourth, I think I would have been bored out of my mind. So it was for the best for me to stay in Utah."

She laughs now at the memory of all their friends constantly asking, especially at church each week, how Eric was doing. "I would get so frustrated. Why does everyone always ask about Eric and not about how I am doing?"

For Eric, the next four months consisted of peanut butter-chocolate breakfast shakes, lifting weights, defensive back drills, interviews with media, coaches, and scouts, and an occasional phone call home to Chanel. Beginning in January, Eric and a group of David's new players lived in a five-bedroom house and maintained a strenuous workout schedule.

Three weeks after landing in Florida, Eric was among one hundred draft prospects invited to participate in the Senior Bowl in Mobile, Alabama. This was his first major exposure to the national media as an individual. Weddle was assigned to the North squad under the direction of then-Tampa Bay Buccaneers head coach Jon Gruden and his staff. The Senior Bowl featured the country's best professional football prospects and was attended by more than seven hundred NFL coaches, scouts, and other front office personnel. Eric approached the event as just another game, spoke to coaches and the press as if he were in a job interview, and tried to have fun. He was asked at least a thousand times if he would rather play safety or cornerback. Whatever the team needed, he was comfortable in either position, Eric repeated again and again.

Because there were fifty players on the roster, Eric saw limited action in the all-star game and had only one tackle, but he left a positive impression on coaches and general managers. A short article on SI.com indicated that Eric's draft stock rose as a result of his participation in the event. "The versatile defensive back started making a lot of plays on the ball [during the week]. Truly a hardworking player, he broke up several passes and was consistently around the action," wrote SI writer Tony Pauline.

"When teams saw him at ground level, saw him do the same things he did in college against the other top seniors in the country, the list of doubters was cut in half," David said. "He was really impressive on the field, his personality was impressive—but he wasn't fast enough."

Eric's next stop was Indianapolis, Indiana, for the NFL scouting combine in late February. Going into the combine, Eric was projected as a third- or fourth-round pick. He had many strengths: he displayed intelligence and instincts; he was capable of playing various positions; he was an aggressive open-field tackler and hitter; and he was effective in man coverage. He lacked a few inches of height, however, and the blazing speed of a cornerback, and was said to have a weak power base.

When it was Eric's turn to run, he recorded a time of 4.48 seconds, which bumped him up to a possible second-round pick. "Everyone thought I was slow, but interest increased when a lot of teams realized how fast I was," Eric said.

Eric's turn in the NFL combine happened to fall on February 25, Chanel's twenty-fifth birthday. Instead of shopping, eating cake, and celebrating her life, Chanel was glued to the couple's twenty-five-inch television back in their Utah home. "It was stressful. League coaches and scouts were going to judge him and base their evaluations on everything he did," she said. "Everything was riding on his performance, and I could tell he gave it all he had. I was proud of him."

In mid-March, Eric showed up at the Spence Eccles Field House for the University of Utah's "Pro Day." At that point, he had solidified himself as a second- or third-round selection but didn't want to leave any doubts in anyone's mind. The smaller setting also allowed for more one-on-one interaction with coaches and scouts. "I wanted to put myself in the best position possible," Eric said. The stressful combine was over, so he enjoyed being back with former teammates. "I had fun cheering them on," he said.

Early in April, Weddle was invited to "trip" with the Baltimore Ravens and San Diego Chargers. He toured their facilities and met with front office personnel, coordinators, and position coaches. They discussed Xs and Os in depth and analyzed every aspect of Eric's life. When Eric was at the Chargers facility, he walked out on the field to find members of the team and head coach Norv Turner. Eric introduced himself to the coach, and they spoke for a few minutes. As Eric observed the defensive backs, Turner pulled him back and said, "I got this feeling we are going to trade up and get you."

Yeah, right, whatever, Eric thought before flying back to Salt Lake City. "I didn't think anything of it." Of course, playing for the Chargers was his preferred choice. But realistically, it was an unlikely scenario. Eric was projected to go somewhere in the middle of the second round, and many teams picking ahead of San Diego told Canter they would take the Utah all-American if he were available.

As a kid, Eric idolized Emmitt Smith and the Dallas Cowboys, but America's team had very little interest in Weddle. "The Cowboys said he wasn't big enough and wouldn't take him, even if he was available in the third or fourth round," Canter said.

When Eric heard this, any and all love for the Cowboys vanished, replaced by determination to once again prove his worth. "It hurt for a second, then I instantly hated them. All the memories, cheering for them, pretending to be Emmitt, everything I loved about them—instantly erased. I got rid of any Dallas gear I had," Eric said. "They didn't like me? I wasn't good enough? You think someone else is better? Fine, I will show you."

One unidentified NFL scout told CBSsports.com that Weddle reminded him of former St. Louis safety Cory Chavous. "I consider Chavous to be the most instinctive safety in the league," the scout said. "Like Chavous, Weddle gets maximum use of his athletic ability, combined with great ball reaction skills. Both are not the strongest or fastest at their respective positions, but both offer intelligence, instinctiveness, and a strong desire to make the play." The scout also predicted Weddle had pro-bowl potential.

As the April 28 draft loomed, CBSsportsline.com senior writer Clark Judge wrote that LSU's LaRon Landry was the best safety in the draft, but "the most intriguing one is Eric Weddle." Judge described Weddle's flexibility in playing various positions and stated, "While it doesn't make him unique, it does make him extraordinary—especially in an age of specialization where some guys make it as situational pass rushers. It also makes him attractive to NFL clubs looking to fill a roster spot with someone who can play more than one position."

One unidentified NFC scout told Judge, "I love this guy. If you got him in the second round and didn't wind up with another safety, your draft would be a success."

"Anyone who takes him in the second round of this draft will have themselves a steal," said another scout.

Judge wrote that Weddle reminded him of another all-purpose defender who turned heads at the 2000 combine. This player was listed as a linebacker but played safety, tight end, wide receiver, and returned kicks. Judge was referring to New Mexico's Brian Urlacher, who went on to become an all-pro linebacker for the Chicago Bears. "This guy's no Urlacher," another scout said of Weddle, "but he can do so many things you can't ignore him."

Judge concluded by saying he'd want Eric Weddle on his football team. "He's energetic. He's productive. He's determined. . . . That won't put him in LaRon Landry's zip code April 28, but it should keep him in the NFL for years."

A predraft evaluation of Weddle by ESPN.com's Scouts Inc. summarized: "Weddle gets the most out of his physical tools, and he is one of the most versatile prospects in the 2007 class. He has experience at every position in the defensive backfield and every offensive skill position, while also performing as the return specialist and holder. However, in order to emerge as a starter at the next level, he must overcome a lack of ideal size and natural fluidity. Regardless, Weddle is the type of player that coaches love having on their team, and he should find a way to contribute in several areas."

David got Eric one endorsement before the draft. He was offered a small deal with Under Armour sports gear and even got to be in a commercial. As part of the commercial shoot, Eric and Chanel were flown first class to Dallas to meet Under Armour founder Kevin Plank. "It was our first and only time flying first class," Chanel said. "They served us these freshly baked cookies that were so good."

While in Dallas, they met San Diego wide receiver Vincent Jackson, a future teammate. Eric mentioned he had just "tripped" to the Chargers, got the big tour, met several front office personnel, and hoped that was a good sign. Jackson told the Weddles he would love to see Eric in San Diego powder blue, but it was not very likely. "He said you never get drafted by teams that invite you for a visit," Chanel said. "So we thought San Diego was out of the picture."

## THE DREAM SCENARIO

The eve of the 2007 NFL draft was reserved for close family and friends—and a camera crew from the Mountain West Sports Network. Eric and Chanel agreed to let the small crew into their inner circle to document his draft experience.

The Weddle family draft party officially kicked off on April 27 with a private dinner at the Cask 'n Cleaver Steakhouse in Rancho Cucamonga, California, at 7:00 p.m. Among those invited were Eric's close friends from high school, the Canters, and members of Eric's and Chanel's immediate and extended families. Amid the laughter and mouthwatering steak, Eric tapped his glass to get everyone's attention. He assured everyone he had not prepared a speech but just wanted to express his gratitude for all the love and support he had felt throughout his life. "I love everyone and am thankful to have everyone here," Eric said on that memorable occasion. His remarks were answered by a light applause.

Before the gathering dispersed, photos were taken, and everyone speculated as to Eric's draft destination. David pointed out that he was wearing Baltimore Ravens purple for a reason, and in the morning he intended to wear San Diego Chargers blue. That announcement was received with more laughter and shouts of approval. When the party broke up three hours later, most returned to the Weddle home to watch NBA basketball and shoot some pool. Sporting shades and a freshly shaved head, Eric told the film crew, "We're going to have some fun. It's the last night, we're together, and hopefully good things are going to happen. I'm out."

The morning of the big day found the Weddle men at the Sierra Lakes Golf Club in nearby Fontana, where Eric, his father, and Uncle Larry played eighteen holes in three hours. Eric shot a 73, his best score ever. The Mountain West camera crew also tagged along. Not only did Eric relish the opportunity to bond with his father and uncle, but he also wanted to fill the morning with activities to take his mind off the upcoming draft.

By 11:00 a.m. on Saturday, everyone was back at Weddle headquarters in Alta Loma, and the draft party was under way. While Debbie and her sister prepared a family favorite, easy enchilada casserole, and spread out a buffet of fried chicken, salads, and desserts, family and friends played pool in the garage or socialized wherever they could find a seat. Every television in the house was locked on to ESPN as teams made their selections. After a game of pool, Eric and others moved out to the street to toss the pigskin. When it was time for a change, he transferred to the living room to entertain everyone with tricks he had taught Chloe. Then Eric groaned as he realized only two hours had passed and the draft was just seventeen picks old.

The most notable thing to Eric as he watched NFL commissioner Roger Goodell repeatedly step to the podium was the selection of safeties. LSU's LaRon Landry was the first safety to go at number six to the Washington Redskins. "The faster they go, the quicker I'll be picked," Eric said. The Tennessee Titans picked University of Texas safety Michael Griffin with the nineteenth pick. With the twenty-first pick, the Jacksonville Jaguars opted for Florida's Reggie Nelson. When Brandon Meriweather, University of Miami, was taken by New England with the twenty-fourth pick, Eric hoped his turn was coming soon, although he was prepared to wait. It was about 1:30 p.m.

Almost four hours later, around 5:00 p.m., the Chicago Bears were on the clock as Eric was sitting in the family La-Z-Boy. He was surprised when his cell phone finally rang. Curiously, he noticed San Diego's 858 area code on his phone. He answered and realized he was on the line with Chargers general manager

A. J. Smith. Everyone in the room leaned in to listen. When they heard Eric say, "You know I am going to come in there and go to work. I won't let you down, sir," the euphoria was uncorked. People began jumping up and down, screaming and crying. The cheers became so loud that Eric had to step outside to hear the call. The Mountain West cameras were rolling and didn't miss a thing.

Moments later, Eric addressed his new coach, Norv Turner. "How you doing, Coach? Yes, Coach, I am ready to work. I am ready to roll," Eric said again. "Yeah, whatever you need me to do, I'll be down there." A few minutes later, Eric's name flashed across the screen as the thirty-seventh overall pick, making his selection official. The group celebrated with another boisterous ovation. The party spilled into the backyard as loved ones rejoiced. How sweet it was. As Eric paced back and forth with the phone at his ear, Steve wiped away tears and ordered someone to grab his Chargers hat for Eric. Continuing his marathon call, Eric conversed with several people in San Diego's organization. When he finally hung up, "Wow," was all Eric could say. His childhood dream had come true.

"I remember Chicago was on the clock, then it flashed and said San Diego was on the clock. Then they called me and it clicked as to what was going on. It was one of the craziest, coolest moments of my life," Eric said. "I was speechless. Chanel gave me a big hug and said, 'We did it, babe!'"

To everyone's surprise, the Chargers engineered with the Chicago Bears one of the biggest trades of the entire draft. San Diego gave the Bears four draft picks—number 62, number 93, and number 167 in 2007, as well as a third-round pick in 2008—in order for San Diego to move up in the second round and take the 5-foot-11 safety.

"At first I wondered if they were telling me they might take me with the sixty-second pick," Eric told his friends. "Then when I turned and saw the Chargers had traded, I was like, hold on, what's up? They told me, 'We're giving up a lot of players for you.' I said, 'All right, let's go to work.'"

The trade immediately became a topic of discussion among ESPN's talking heads: "Did the Chargers give up too much for Eric Weddle?"

"That's an awful lot to give up. . . . They're telling us they don't need all those other draft picks [because of the talent already on the roster]," said ESPN's draft expert Mel Kiper.

"Far be it from me to criticize people who have had success in the draft like A. J. Smith and Buddy Nix, but it seems like a heavy, heavy price," added ESPN's Chris Mortensen.

NFL Network's Mike Maycock disagreed. "He will upgrade them athletically in the middle of the field," the analyst said. "I like this kid a lot. He's an instinctive kid with a nose for the ball."

Canter also defended the Chargers. "Eric is two or three players in and of himself," the agent said. "The Chargers probably think they stole him."

Coming off a 14–2 season, Coach Turner told ESPN that getting Eric was a priority. He praised Eric for his confidence and intelligence. "Eric was obviously a guy we wanted to have here. He's an outstanding football player. The great thing about Eric is he can have an impact right away. He has a knack. Some guys have it and some guys don't."

Nix, then San Diego's assistant general manager, said the Chargers needed a good safety. "He was high on our list from the start. We're not worried about what we gave up; we're thinking about what we got."

A short time after Eric ended his conversation with the

Chargers, he received a congratulatory call from his former college coach, Kyle Whittingham. Eric, still in a state of unbelief, thanked Whittingham for everything.

"Boy, he was fired up," Whittingham said. "I told him that the things we have been talking about for the last five years have come to fruition, that he made it and has his shot at the big time. I told him he deserved it and to make the most of this opportunity. There was no doubt in my mind that he would."

Another round of applause came when, thirty minutes later, three picks after Weddle, Eric's friend, BYU quarterback John Beck, was selected by the Miami Dolphins. Another local product, Boise State defensive back Gerald Alexander of Eric's former rival Rancho Cucamonga High, was taken by Detroit with the sixty-second overall pick in the second round.

Debbie filled glasses with chilled champagne or nonalcoholic Martinelli's sparkling cider. With dozens standing around him in the backyard, Steve Weddle made a toast to three of the happiest moments in his life: first, when he married Debbie; second, the birth of his children; and third, Eric's selection by the Chargers. "This is one of my happiest moments with you, son," Steve said. "Only certain people achieve this in their lives, and for you to do this is unbelievable. I am so proud of you."

After the big news, Sonya Blaquiere found a quiet spot in the Weddles' backyard and said a prayer of gratitude. "I am terrified of flying," she said. "We were sure he was going to be drafted some place where we would have to travel a long distance to see them. When it happened, I started bawling. I was so grateful and got on my hands and knees. Eric and Chanel's coming to San Diego was the best-case scenario. She is my only daughter, and we are so close. I felt nothing but gratitude to the Lord."

The next morning, Eric put on a suit and tie and drove with

Chanel to San Diego for a press conference that included a slew of media interviews and introductions. It took a few days for his new reality to sink in. Eric marveled that, of thirty-two possible destinations, he would get to play an hour and a half from his family and friends. "It was an unreal experience for San Diego to pick me at the time they picked me," Eric said. "For them to trade up shows what they think of me as a football player and a person. When I go down to San Diego, I'm not just playing for myself. I'm playing for all those who have stood behind me for the last twenty-two years."

April 28, 2007, was a day that changed Eric and Chanel's lives. Within a month they would also find out they were expecting their first child. An exciting new life was about to begin.

## CHAPTER 12

# *THE ROOKIE*

Eric Weddle was nervous his first day as a San Diego Charger, but it wasn't obvious to others. Kevin Acee, a sports columnist who covers the Chargers for the San Diego *Union-Tribune,* said Weddle "worked the room as well as any politician during an afternoon media gathering at Chargers Park in which the team's top three draft picks were introduced." Eric even spent a few minutes conversing with San Diego's Pro Bowl quarterback Philip Rivers as if they were old buddies. Acee said Weddle displayed easiness and familiarity uncommon among players drafted just a day before. Everyone from the media to the team seemed impressed by the new guy.

"He was well spoken, sincere, and passionate. He wasn't just talking—he believed in what he was saying. Right away you knew he was going to be one of those guys," Acee recalled. "They liked his character. They knew they wouldn't be getting [troublesome] calls at three a.m. about Eric. He is definitely a stand-up guy."

"He impresses you with his confidence," said Buddy Nix,

then San Diego's assistant general manager. "He thinks he's going to make every play. Look at Troy Polamalu, John Lynch, Rodney [Harrison]. Rodney wasn't fast. But those guys have a knack. He has that."

Eric opened his remarks to the media that April day by thanking San Diego owner Dean Spanos, general manager A. J. Smith, and head coach Norv Turner for taking a chance on him. Eric also addressed claims that the Chargers gave up too much—four draft picks—for him by summarizing his improbable journey to the NFL: "I don't really care what those analysts think. I know [the Chargers] believe in me. If they didn't they wouldn't have got me where they got me. I just have to go prove them right. . . . I've been doubted my whole life, whether it was in Pop Warner, high school, or college. People say I'm not big enough, fast enough, strong enough. But I just go out and play."

Eric showed his commitment to his new team by arriving an hour early to every off-season workout. Practices started at 8:00 a.m., but from June until August, Eric left his Escondido home at 6:30 a.m. in his trusty Honda Accord to beat traffic on Interstate 15 and arrive at the Chargers complex by 7:00.

Overwrought with nervous energy and worried that he hadn't been getting enough exercise, Eric went for a midnight three-mile run two days before minicamp. He knew the workout would make his muscles sore, but it didn't matter. He was about to fulfill his childhood dream of playing in the NFL and competing against some of the greatest football players in the world, and he wanted to feel physically ready. Eric also wondered how he might be received by his teammates. He desperately wanted to earn their respect.

It wasn't until he got back to the football field that Eric started to feel comfortable.

## THE PLAYERS

One of his first assignments in training camp was defending Antonio Gates, a Kent State basketball star turned all-pro tight end. "He was the best tight end in the game, and we would go one-on-one," Eric said. "He would catch one, then I would break one up. He gave me some great tips and observations early on by explaining how opponents played him. It helped me a lot. It gave me confidence that if I could battle against a guy like Gates in practice, I would be fine as a rookie."

As training camp unfolded and the season progressed, Eric's work ethic and easy demeanor helped him gradually earn the respect of his teammates. Steve Gregory, an undrafted free agent who had played college ball at Syracuse, was a second-year strong safety in 2007. Besides playing the same position, Gregory and Weddle discovered they both liked golf. Eventually the two safeties would hang out off the field and become road trip roommates. Gregory was also fond of reminding Eric of one of Eric's early rookie moments when the defensive backs were participating in a drill. "We had all these fans watching us, and Eric was trying to be a hot shot. He was backpedaling, and he tripped and hit the turf," Gregory said. "It was one of those not-so-athletic moments that we all have, but I like to give him a hard time about it." Five years later, Gregory would ask Eric to be the best man at his wedding.

On the practice field in San Diego, Eric met and observed several teammates who were lifelong students and masters of the game of football. Going into his third season, outside linebacker Shawne Merriman's ferocious pass rush intimidated opposing linemen and quarterbacks, and fans loved his "lights out" sack dance. Merriman was one of the team's defensive leaders in 2007. "A lot of players rallied behind and looked up to him," Eric said. "He was passionate, energetic, and relentless. He was a great player."

Ryon Bingham, a defensive lineman from Nebraska, was the only other Latter-day Saint on the team. Bingham grew up in the Salt Lake City area and played high school football at Alta with Dave Revill, Eric's former Utah teammate. As Eric and Ryon became acquainted, their wives did, too. When the Chargers played the New Orleans Saints in London, England, during the 2008 season, Ryon's wife, Danie, and Chanel toured the city together while their husbands practiced for the game. In the years that followed, the two families hosted barbecues in their backyards, played at the beach together, and took the kids to Disneyland together.

Weddle also grew to appreciate the advice and friendship of two San Diego defensive veterans, cornerback Quentin Jammer and defensive end Shaun Phillips. Jammer was one of the best corners in Texas Longhorn history before being selected by the Chargers in the first round of the 2002 draft. Jammer knew the tricks of covering the NFL's top receivers, and he helped Eric understand defensive schemes from the secondary. Phillips, who sacked quarterbacks for Purdue before coming to San Diego in 2004, offered more general advice. They talked about everything from the game to the business of football. Eric came to view Jammer and Phillips like big brothers.

"I gravitated toward these guys because they were veterans of the league and they played at a high level," Eric said. "'Jam' was more quiet, and 'S.P.' and I have similar personalities. I watched the way they worked at their positions, and they helped me adjust and feel more comfortable, which really helped me as a rookie. You realize they brought you in to take someone's job, which doesn't sit well with most guys. So it means a lot to a rookie when an older guy will come over and say, 'Hey, this is how it is—I am here for you, whatever you need,' and give you tips. It means a lot when you are a young guy."

Eric and his fellow rookies were also spared from much of the hazing and initiations that have befallen some players entering the NFL. The most notable thing Eric had to endure was singing a capella in an evening meeting with the team, coaches, and trainers. The objective was not to get booed off the podium. Eric loves R&B music, so he busted out one of his favorite Usher songs, "Nice and Slow," with dance moves.

"It wasn't so bad," Eric said. "By the second verse, the whole team was singing with me. I don't think they expected that from a white guy, but it was fun. I love to sing even though I am terrible at it. Now any time guys get up there and try to sing, I try to sing with them."

## TWO STARS

Philip Rivers was one of three star quarterbacks taken in the first round of the 2004 NFL draft, along with Eli Manning and Ben Roethlisberger. San Diego had the overall first pick in the draft and wanted Manning, but Manning said he would not sign with the Chargers. San Diego adjusted by negotiating a trade with the New York Giants to get Rivers, a player that then-head coach Marty Schottenheimer had coached in the senior bowl. When Chargers quarterback Drew Brees signed with New Orleans after the 2005 season, Rivers became the starter. As of the 2012 season, Rivers has thrown for more than 27,000 yards, 189 touchdowns, and earned four pro bowl invitations.

Eric was impressed when the star quarterback spoke with him as if he were just one of the guys. Eric admired not only Rivers's work ethic and competitive personality but also his devotion to family and his Christian faith. "He is one of those guys who gets along with everyone. He likes to talk trash, but it's all in good fun," Eric said. "He's the starting quarterback, but he knows everyone's name and always says hello.

"With Philip, we always talk about our families. He is a devoted father and husband, and I admire that about him. He has always been friendly and easy to talk to."

From his first days with the Chargers, Eric took an immediate liking to San Diego's star running back LaDainian Tomlinson. Eric was well aware of Tomlinson's long list of accomplishments in college and the NFL. After winning the Doak Walker Award as the nation's best running back at TCU, "L.T." was taken by the Chargers with the fifth overall pick in the 2001 draft. By the time Eric joined the team in 2007, Tomlinson had already played in four pro bowls and won the league rushing title in 2006. L.T. had heart and was durable.

Tomlinson sought Weddle out and introduced himself. Then he bragged about the times his alma mater, TCU, had defeated the University of Utah. Eric embraced the teasing and friendly banter. "He was nice, very approachable, and down-to-earth. He was a guy I looked up to, and he helped me a lot that first year," Eric said.

Following one practice session in training camp, many were upset with Eric for smashing a teammate when he ran a pass route across the middle of the field. Eric said Tomlinson came to him later that day and told him not to worry about it.

"Practice how you play," Tomlinson told Weddle. "[Former Chargers safety] Rodney Harrison practiced like that, and people respected him for it. It's part of the game. You got to be yourself and don't let people talk you down. You got to do what you got to do to be the best you can be."

Eric took the veteran's advice to heart. He appreciated that a player of Tomlinson's stature would go out of his way for a rookie.

Each Tuesday that season, the team's weekly day off, Weddle, Gregory, and Jammer always tried to work in a few hours of golf. When the Chargers started a winning streak late in the 2009 season that extended into the playoffs, the trio superstitiously continued their golfing tradition and invited Tomlinson to join them. Weddle and Tomlinson became good friends after that, which made it difficult for Eric in 2010 when L.T. left the Chargers and signed with the New York Jets.

"I was around him for three years," Eric said. "He was a great teammate and a great person."

## MISSIONARY MOMENT

In getting to know Eric, his teammates occasionally asked him about his religious beliefs. Bingham remembers one occasion when he, Weddle, Tomlinson, Merriman, and Gates were all seated around a table having lunch in between practice sessions. Someone said to Eric, "So you're Mormon, right?" Among various topics, his teammates began asking why Mormons don't drink, have premarital sex, or go to strip clubs. "And who is Joseph Smith?" one wanted to know.

"Some of the guys brought up stories they had heard and were joking around about the LDS Church," Bingham said. "Eric stood strong. He clarified the misconceptions and told them what we believe. I was impressed with the way he presented himself. It's not always easy to defend your religion to your friends, especially being a rookie and talking to people you look up to, like the stars of the team. They think it's a joke sometimes, and you can imagine there have been several occasions like that. But Eric responded in such a way that it inspired them to want to know more. I remember them saying, 'Oh, that's cool.'"

"I don't want to push my beliefs on my teammates," Eric said, "but I also don't want to be pushed around and made fun of, so it helped when I explained things and answered their questions. Answering questions about the Church is something I've become used to because the majority of my family and friends aren't Latter-day Saints."

It wouldn't be the last time Eric addressed religious questions from teammates. "In my profession you've got to have guys trust you," he said. "You've got to build rapport. If they get the idea that I am looking down on them, it's not a good feeling, so I don't really come out and say this is what I believe. But if they ask questions, I will answer and go with it. The most commonly asked questions center around if we really believe in Jesus Christ and why I wear [temple garments]."

## THE COACHES

Former San Diego head football coach Norv Turner was criticized for practically everything during his tenure with the Chargers. Among the list of complaints are slow starts to the season, poor play calling, coaching philosophies, and failing to win in the playoffs after regular-season success. In a one-on-one interview with Acee in 2009, Turner was asked if he was familiar with the websites "nomorenorv.com and firenorv.net."

"I know they're there, but I haven't had my kids teach me how to log on to them," Turner said.

Although Turner was fired after the 2012 season, Eric respected the man. Weddle described the longtime NFL coach as an "intense, diligent, and extremely hardworking head coach who cares about his players and wants to win more than anyone out there."

Yet with Turner, Eric understood he wouldn't share the same tight-knit relationship he had with Kyle Whittingham at Utah. Eric could talk with Whittingham about football and the state of the Utah program, as well as relationships and religion. His relationship with Norv was much less personal. Part of that is simply the nature of NFL football.

"In high school and college, you are still being guided and driven," Eric said. "In college, Coach needs to know if you're going to class, if you're getting good grades, and that you're not getting tickets or stealing. In the NFL, you're an adult. They aren't going to teach you how to be a man. It's about producing wins, coming to work every day, and getting the job done. Coaches are different from each other because they have different priorities. Norv worked hard to put us in a position to win games. He cared for us like his own kids. The credit goes to the players when good things happen, and anything bad is on the coach. He expected us to be motivated. He always schemed how we could attack the next opponent."

Eric had limited one-on-one interaction with Turner. When the two did talk, it was all about football. The coach would offer quick pointers or personal observations about the opposing team's offense. Turner also wanted to know when Eric was going to intercept another pass.

"He was a father figure," Eric continued. "He treated you like a man. He wasn't a yell-at-you, rah-rah guy. He didn't degrade you the way others might, but he still expected and demanded a lot. He was a passionate coach who wanted the best for you, and I could respect and play for a guy like that."

Turner did have a humorous side. At one point players

invented a soft birdcall for when Turner was approaching and a player was dozing off or not paying attention in team meetings. It didn't take long for the coach to catch on to the game, and as soon as the players realized that, they started exaggerating the bird sounds when he entered the room.

Two other coaches on the staff influenced Eric during his first year. Ted Cottrell was the defensive coordinator, and Bill Bradley was the defensive backs coach for the 2007 season. Eric learned a lot from both men, but especially from Bradley, who had played college ball at the University of Texas in the 1960s then played for the Philadelphia Eagles and the St. Louis Cardinals in the 1970s. Bradley reached the coaching ranks of the NFL in the 1990s, where he was the defensive backs coach for the Buffalo Bills, New York Jets, and San Diego. He was also the defensive coordinator for the Baylor Bears for three seasons.

When Eric "tripped" out to San Diego before the draft, he spent significant time with Bradley, including a drive to the beach and the coach's home. "They really hit it off," Chanel said. Bradley's daughter has even worked as a part-time nanny for the Weddles. Eric respected Bradley's old-school player's coach approach.

"I learned a lot from him about reading the quarterback and playing the ball," Eric said. "He kept things simple and always preached that the quarterback will take you where the ball is going. Bradley believed in me and was one of my biggest supporters. He always had my back."

## THE CHALLENGES

The jump from college to the NFL can be a shock for some players. There's the grind of the longer season, learning new assignments, and—especially in Eric's case—adjusting to limited playing time. As the season got under way, Eric did his best to adjust to the daily rigors and routines of NFL life. As a senior at Utah, he had been a full-time student who practiced three or four hours a day, five days a week, and played twelve games in a season (thirteen with a bowl game). As a rookie in the NFL, Eric worked more than ten hours a day, six days a week, attending meetings, participating in workouts, practicing, and studying film. Including the preseason, the regular season, and the play-offs, he played in twenty-three games.

In addition to the increased physical toll, Eric realized professional football was a full-time job. And in this job, players either knew their assignments on the field or they quickly found other work. "For me, adjusting to the NFL was not so much about the speed of the game, but knowing the defensive scheme," Eric said. "When I didn't know what I was doing, I made incorrect reads, missed tackles, and was caught out of position. As a young player, you may get only one or two chances in a game, and you have to make the most of them. You can't make mistakes in the NFL like you can in college. You definitely have to raise your level of play, and that was something I had to deal with."

After being the University of Utah's jack-of-all-trades and never coming off the field, standing on the sidelines was difficult for Eric. Aside from special team duties and entering the game as an extra defensive back in passing situations, Eric was relegated to backing up veteran Marlon McCree. "Not starting was my biggest personal challenge as a rookie," Eric said. "It was tough not playing every down, but it motivated me to show the Chargers they were right to pick me. I learned to do as I was told, play as hard as I could when possible, and not worry about what my teammates were doing. I also decided to let the coaches decide what was best, and I focused on film study and preparation. The worst thing you can do is get in there and mess up. It's so much more mental than physical."

## THE HIGHLIGHTS

Toward the end of their college years, Eric received a monthly $700 scholarship check, and Chanel pulled in $300 with her scholarship. After graduation, Chanel worked at an at-risk girls program in Salt Lake City for a short time and earned around $1,200 a month. Eric's first NFL paycheck was $800,000. He also signed an endorsement deal with Under Armour right before the draft. Chanel snapped a photo of the check to preserve the memory.

"The check felt fake," Eric said. "We felt very lucky to be in that position, and we put it right into the bank." The Weddles decided from the beginning to spend conservatively because they didn't know how long Eric's career in sports would last. They bought a comfortable, two-story house in the upscale west side of Escondido, a twenty-minute drive north of San Diego, and made some minor improvements. Eric bought a new car for Chanel but continued to drive their old reliable Honda Accord to work for a few years.

With Escondido less than a hundred miles from his parents' home, Eric's family and friends relished the opportunity to get season tickets and immerse themselves in rooting for the Chargers and their new safety. Beginning in 2007, more than fifty relatives and friends, all wearing their No. 32 Weddle jerseys, arrived early to each game and laid claim to a lane of parking spots near section H3 on the west side of Qualcomm Stadium. A member of the group posted a sign designating the row as "Weddle Way." While a large banner honoring Eric was rolled out, the women spread out the food, which included steak, grilled chicken, barbecued ribs, hot dogs, a Crock-Pot of pork and beans, salads, chips, dip, cookies, brownies, and coolers of ice-cold beverages. A member of the party packed a large-screen TV and a satellite dish so they could watch other NFL games while they awaited kickoff in San Diego. Eventually the group gathered in the 70,500-seat stadium and found their seats in the lower level, where the party continued for another four hours. When Eric entered the game, made a tackle, broke up a pass, recovered a fumble, or delivered a big hit, the Weddle fan section stood on their feet, yelling and waving signs. When Eric stepped in front of a pass by Houston quarterback Sage Rosenfels for his first NFL interception in a 35–10 win over Houston, the Weddle group was first on their feet, roaring with applause and slapping high fives of jubilation. After the game, Eric found his way to "Weddle headquarters" at H3 for a quick hello to everyone. Concerned for Eric's health following a physical game with Baltimore, Grandma Jean Weddle asked Eric, in her raspy voice, how he was holding up after delivering all those big hits. "Yeah, Grandma, I'm good," Eric responded as he tenderly hugged her. "That's what I do for a living."

"For us, it's all about family," Steve said. "Having Eric here in southern California is a dream come true. We thought for sure he was going to Carolina."

After San Diego throttled Baltimore, 32–14, on November 25, Eric joined his family and made time for some young fans from Salt Lake City who were sporting Weddle jerseys. Cole Parkinson, age ten, and his three cousins were huge Weddle fans and had the fortune of stumbling onto Weddle Way, where they met Eric's family before the game. They met Eric's mother, Debbie, and had plenty of questions about how Eric liked the NFL, how much money he made, and who he had a locker next to. After answering their questions, the family invited them to sign the Weddle banner and return after the game to meet Eric. When they returned following the Chargers' win, Cole got an autograph and a few pictures with his hero. When Cole's cousin Riley started singing "Utah Man," Eric and the whole clan joined in. "What a great day!" Cole wrote on his mother Jill's blog. "I will never forget my day with Eric Weddle."

## FOOTBALL AND A BABY

The San Diego Chargers defeated the Tennessee Titans, 16–7, on January 6, 2008, to win their first playoff game since the team played in the Super Bowl in 1995. Weddle played sparingly and failed to record a single tackle in his first postseason experience, but the AFC Wild Card victory would soon become a footnote to an even bigger event.

One day past her delivery date, Chanel endured a long, rainy afternoon at Qualcomm with her mother, Sonya. After returning from the game that evening, Chanel called the hospital to see when her doctor could induce labor. With the win, the Chargers were going to Indianapolis in five days, and she dreaded the thought of Eric missing the birth. To her surprise, she was informed she could check in right away. Eric gave his wife a priesthood blessing before the couple gathered their things and drove to the hospital. They arrived around 1:00 a.m., and within an hour Chanel was lying in a hospital bed, surrounded by nurses. It was almost 2:00 a.m., but their adrenaline kicked in and both Eric and Chanel were full of anticipation and curiosity. What would this experience be like? Would the baby look more like its father or mother? Were they ready to be parents?

They had all night and most of the next day to ponder those questions. Despite the doctor's medical tactics, nothing happened for several hours. They tried in vain to sleep. They watched TV, played games, walked around the hospital, did whatever they could to pass the time. The baby didn't budge.

As they waited, the couple recalled the story of how, around the eighteen-week mark, they had learned the sex of the baby. On the day of the ultrasound, an "inexperienced" midwife announced the Weddles were having a baby boy. "I'm not good at this," the woman had said, "but I'm 98 percent sure it's a boy."

The Weddles were thrilled, especially Eric. They told their family, and Chanel spent about two hundred dollars purchasing boys' clothing and other materials. A feeling of excitement began to build in their home.

More than a month later, the Weddles returned for another checkup—and a surprise. This time their doctor was available, and he performed another ultrasound. As they watched the baby on the monitor, the doctor said, "This is a baby girl."

"What?!" was the couple's perplexed reaction. Once the doctor explained the evidence, the Weddles adjusted. It didn't matter whether the baby was a boy or a girl; Eric and Chanel would love him or her unconditionally. But once Chanel started buying outfits for her daughter, the change in her feelings was complete.

Finally, several hours after labor was induced, Chanel felt the first of many contractions. Thirty minutes later an epidural was administered. Unfortunately for Chanel, their daughter was still hours from delivery.

Finally, after 3:00 p.m., more than fourteen hours after the Weddles checked into the hospital, the baby appeared ready to make her entrance. The epidural had worn off, and the nurse asked her patient if she wanted another, but Chanel said no; she really wanted to end the ordeal. Between pushes, Chanel yelled to Eric to call her mother. But Sonya had left her cell phone behind when she took the dog, Chloe, for a walk, and unfortunately she missed the birth. At approximately 4:10 p.m., an exhausted Chanel delivered a healthy, eight-pound, four-ounce baby girl. To the parents' great alarm, the umbilical cord was wrapped around the baby's neck three times, but the doctor carefully removed it, and Eric accepted the honor of cutting the cord. They named their new daughter Brooklyn Marie Weddle.

"Watching my little baby girl be born was probably the most amazing, most incredible, and most emotional experience I have ever been through. There is nothing else like it," Eric said. "It was a little scary seeing her come out like that, but the doctor acted like it was a piece of cake to unwrap the cord. Because of this baby, our lives changed for the better."

Chanel was completely worn out. When extended family and friends filled the hospital waiting room and wanted to see the baby, it was almost too much for her. The couple appreciated the family support, but eventually hospital personnel had to ask the noisy Weddle clan to go home. Sonya arrived and offered to hold the newborn so Chanel could sleep.

"There was not a San Diego Charger in that room, only a man who loved his wife and daughter," Sonya said. "He was so overcome. He said he could tell right away that baby Brooklyn was a genius. He wanted to do everything right. It had been raining and was a little cold, but we were still in southern California and it was around fifty-five to sixty degrees. When we got home, Eric turned on the heat and started a fire in the fireplace. The house was probably 110 degrees."

Sonya continued to observe Eric during those first days and came away impressed. "Some men are afraid of babies. Eric was not. He changed her, bathed her, and held her. When he came home from practice, it didn't matter how tired he was, he grabbed that little girl," Sonya said.

Eric adapted well to his new responsibilities—which was impressive, because before Brooklyn was born, Eric had never even seen a diaper. Chanel recalled how, after family and friends hosted a baby shower in Rancho Cucamonga, she had returned home with several gifts. She noticed Eric pick up a plastic package of soft, rectangular-shaped objects.

"What's this?" Eric asked Chanel.

"Those would be diapers," Chanel replied with a raised eyebrow and a hint of disbelief. "You've never seen a diaper before?"

When Eric shrugged his shoulders and returned a blank look, all she could do was laugh.

Eric was a quick learner, though. Sonya later observed, "Eric is an amazing football player, but I see more amazing things from him as a husband and father. As impressive as he is on the field, I am more impressed with how he helps his wife and how his kids run to see him when he walks in the door. That is what is important to me. I especially love to see my daughter smile when he walks into the room."

## THE ONE-HANDED PICK

Less than a week later, the Chargers traveled to the RCA Dome in Indianapolis for an AFC divisional playoff with the defending Super Bowl champion Indianapolis Colts. With the Chargers trailing 10–7 just before halftime, Antonio Cromartie intercepted a Peyton Manning pass and weaved his way 89 yards for a touchdown. The play should have had a significant impact on the outcome of the game, but much to San Diego's dismay a yellow flag was thrown and the referee signaled holding on No. 32, Eric Weddle. The penalty nullified the touchdown.

"Anytime Cro got a pick, I was like, go block somebody because it's going to the house," Eric recalled. "When he got the ball and made his move, I found a Colt, got my hands inside and totally pancaked him. My only thought was, 'Yes, I sprung him for the TD.' Then I turned back and saw a flag. I couldn't believe it. The block was legal. I can only figure the referee saw the guy on the ground and thought he was thrown down. If he had seen the play, it wouldn't have been a flag. I was mad and decided I needed to make up for it."

Eric redeemed himself near the 7:05 mark of the third quarter when Indianapolis had the ball third-and-3 on the Chargers' 4. San Diego was up 14–10, but the Colts appeared poised to retake the lead. The ball was snapped, and Manning dropped back beyond the 10 before floating a pass toward running back Kenton Keith. But the pass was high, and Keith tipped it backwards into the right hand of Weddle, who was attempting to fight off the block of Colts center Jeff Saturday. Eric's teammates swarmed him as he carried the ball to the Chargers' sideline. While Manning walked to the opposite sideline, shaking his head in frustration, CBS sports broadcaster Greg Gumbel announced that it was "the rookie Eric Weddle with the pick."

With Tomlinson injured and the offense struggling to score points, the defense talked at intermission about making plays in the second half. Thanks to hours of diligent film study, Eric recognized the Colts' formation and knew a middle screen was coming. Indianapolis had run exactly the same play earlier in the game for a big gain. "I lined up on the running back side and waited for the play so I could make the tackle," Eric said. "Then Saturday comes at me while I'm trying to watch Peyton and keep track of Keith. Just as I was ready to throw Saturday aside and make the tackle, for whatever reason—maybe Peyton was rushed and he threw the ball high—it went off Keith's hands and was right there. I somehow got my hand out there and cradled that sucker in. I felt like I was in college again.

"I thought, 'No way is this happening.' You just don't expect things like that to happen. It was huge because it was in the red zone and took points off the board. Those kinds of plays can win games," Eric continued. "Big players make big plays in big games. That was a big play for me. It's one of my most memorable picks because it happened in the playoffs and helped send us to the AFC championship."

San Diego defeated Indianapolis but lost the following week to the New England Patriots. Eric finished his rookie campaign with 54 tackles, one sack, and one interception in fifteen regular-season games. During his exit interviews with the Chargers coaches, Eric was told to focus on gaining strength in the off-season. He committed himself to five days a week in the gym. Eric also decided to watch film of his mistakes in an effort to clean up his game.

During the off-season, San Diego released McCree in favor of Weddle, a move his teammates favored. "I can't say enough about the kid," teammate Clinton Hart told the media going into the 2008 season. "He's the perfect type of player to play with, a young guy who understands the game and is smart. He lets me get into a groove out there. He's flexible. Nothing against Marlon—he is a good football player—but Eric understands that to be back there with somebody, you've got to be able to work together and let a guy play his game."

Eric gave himself a B grade for his first year in the league. He had made mistakes but had learned in the process. One big lesson he took away from his inaugural season was that there are no shortcuts to success in the NFL. "It's a job and you have to treat it like that," Eric summarized. "You have to mind your Ps and Qs.

There are no off weeks. You must be consistent—don't get too high or too low. Treat teammates like family. Never be satisfied with past success. Keep moving forward and don't look back."

"Now all eyes are on Weddle," said then-general manager A. J. Smith prior to the 2008 season. "That's the name of the game when you're a starter and you haven't been around for very long and don't have a lot of years of experience."

# CHAPTER 13

# BALANCING FOOTBALL AND FAITH

Sunday, September 20, 2009. With kickoff between the San Diego Chargers and the Baltimore Ravens in Qualcomm Stadium less than six hours away, many players were fast asleep in their hotel rooms, while others watched ESPN SportsCenter over breakfast. It was around 8:00 a.m. In a little over two hours, the team would assemble at the stadium and dress for the game.

While most of the team relaxed, one player left the hotel and drove home to change into a white shirt and tie. Before going to work, Eric Weddle, San Diego's starting free safety, needed to feed his soul. It was the first time he had included church attendance in his game day routine, and for Weddle, he had realized after two seasons in the league that it was long overdue.

During his first two seasons, Eric opted for extra sleep over church unless the Chargers played on Sunday or Monday night. He found the justification easy—he had a high-profile job and nobody criticized him for skipping church. But he also started to sense that he didn't feel like the same person spiritually. Eric realized he wasn't meeting the standard he had set for himself when he converted to The Church of Jesus Christ of Latter-day Saints when he was at the University of Utah. If he were going to live up to the spiritual commitment he had made as a sophomore in college, Eric knew that attending church only six months out of the year during the off-season didn't give him the balance he needed. Deep down, he knew he could do more, and he felt compelled to sacrifice sleep in order to maintain spirituality in his life. While attending the LDS Church's full three-hour block of services wasn't possible on game days, Eric decided in his third season that he needed to at least attend the one-hour sacrament meeting— the principal family worship service where members sing hymns, say prayers, take the weekly sacrament (communion), and listen to speakers deliver uplifting messages.

"When I didn't go to church during my first two years in the NFL, I didn't know how it would impact me as a person. It was hard to go six or seven months without church," Eric said. "Going into my third year, I felt like I could do more. Football is important, but my family and faith are also important, and no matter how good a football player I am, I knew I still needed to be a good member of the Church. Having that spiritual connection helped me throughout the season. It brought balance, I felt better about myself, and saw improvements in all aspects of my life."

Making time for church before Charger home games made such a difference for Eric that by his fourth NFL season he decided to include his Sunday church routine on road trips as well. When the Chargers played away from San Diego, Eric located the closest Latter-day Saint congregation that met at 9:00 a.m. and arranged for a cab. Because he was not able to stay for long, Eric would show up in street clothes instead of the customary shirt and tie. He was welcomed warmly at each chapel, although few recognized him. Only after he shook hands and introduced himself did some Church members, usually fans of the local team, recognize his name. For the most part, Eric was pretty anonymous during his short church visits.

Once a month, LDS congregations hold a testimony meeting where members are permitted to stand in front of the congregation and share their personal religious convictions. This is typically done in a member's home congregation where they know most of the people in the audience, but visitors are also permitted to participate. Prior to the Chargers-Raiders game in Oakland in October 2010, Eric realized he hadn't shared his testimony in a while. Dressed in a polo shirt and jeans, he walked to the pulpit in a congregation that met near the Oakland-Alameda County Coliseum and shared his innermost convictions with a chapel full of complete strangers. He didn't introduce himself or talk about football, but he expressed gratitude for the blessing of the gospel in his life. His remarks lasted less than five minutes.

When Eric was finished, he returned to his seat. He was not surprised when nobody seemed to recognize him. Sometimes in other cities, Church members were surprised to learn he was a member of the Church. He didn't get the chance to interact with people very much because he had to leave before the end of the service in order to get back to the stadium. It is unclear how many Raider fans were at church that day, but it was certainly a unique moment in the history of the Chargers-Raiders AFC West rivalry.

"I was glad I bore my testimony," Eric said of the experience. "It's a blessing to know that the Church and the gospel are the same no matter where I go. I can find a church and know the services and feel at home there."

Weddle believes making church a priority has helped bring a balance to his life that can otherwise be lost in the midst of the constant focus on football required during an NFL season. "It has been hard to do, but I make a point, regardless of where I am, to do it," Eric said. "I have noticed a difference in myself spiritually. I have had a better relationship with my wife and kids. It's because I am putting the gospel first. I just wish it hadn't taken me so long to realize it."

## MORE BLESSINGS

Putting religious beliefs before football isn't always an easy or natural thing, even for the most devout members of the Mormon Church. Besides the three-hour block of Sunday meetings, members are expected to pay ten percent of their gross income as tithing to the Church.

After realizing how much ten percent of his paycheck amounted to, Eric struggled a bit when writing his first big tithing check. "It was a lot of money, and it was difficult because I knew what I could buy with that money. But we did it, and I have never second-guessed myself since then," Eric said. "After I joined the Church, a friend told me that no matter how good or how tough times get, if you always pay your tithing you will have what you need. Paying tithing is bigger than the money—it's about the principles of sacrifice, obedience, and humility. The Lord has given me all I have, and it's important to remember that and put Him first."

Even as an NFL player, Eric also volunteers his time in various teaching and leadership positions for his local LDS congregation, or ward. In the summer of 2009, Eric and Travis Stolk, a fellow member of Weddle's LDS ward, were asked to organize activities for the men in their congregation. While coordinating such an activity usually involves a planning meeting, Eric took a different approach the first time he met Stolk. "After introductions, Eric asked if I played basketball," Stolk said. "I said I did. He suggested we meet up at the church, shoot around for a while, maybe play some one-on-one, and then plan our first activity. After playing some ball, we talked about having a video game night or playing volleyball, but then we decided to have a mixed martial arts night. Most of the guys in our group had never watched a match before, and it seemed like it would be an interesting experience. Eric offered to host the activity at his house. We ordered four large pizzas and were pleased to have our biggest turnout ever as more than fifteen guys showed up. Eric was the difference-maker. How often do you get invited to watch an MMA fight in the home of an NFL player?

"To that point, a lot of men in the ward were probably a little nervous to approach Eric, but this activity broke the ice and everyone got a chance to meet and get to know him. It also sparked interest in future activities."

Eric is often invited to speak to groups in southern California and has become a favorite speaker for members of his faith. He is often asked to share his conversion story, among other topics. In the spring of 2010, he spoke to a large gathering of LDS fathers and sons about gospel principles he had learned from his career in the NFL. Eric described the hours of rigorous training and film study that go into preparing for a game, enabling a player to recall an opponent's tendencies and be in the right place at the right time to make crucial plays in key situations. Using personal examples and insights, Eric then compared that discipline to daily spiritual preparation. "If you prepare, study, and do the extra work, you will be a step quicker and make the play," Eric told his audience. "If you put in the extra work doing the little things—saying your prayers, reading the scriptures, attending church—you will be spiritually prepared when temptations present themselves, and you will make the right play. . . . There is nothing like standing up to temptation, looking it in the eye, and conquering it. Have a game plan and be prepared for those situations in life."

On other occasions, Eric and Chanel have spoken together to hundreds of LDS youth. While Eric most often shares his conversion story, Chanel likes to talk about the power of choices and how her decisions led her to marry Eric. Sometimes after their messages are delivered, they allow the youth to ask questions, which is Chanel's favorite part of the event.

"It's interesting to find out what they want to know about us," Chanel said. "They ask if they can take their picture with us, and we can usually do that. They ask how much they should push the gospel message on their friends, and we tell them to be a good example and answer people's questions when they ask, but that pushing the gospel on someone usually doesn't work. One person asked whom we would vote for in the presidential race, and we declined to say. They ask Eric which team he likes to play against the most, and he usually says the Oakland Raiders. One kid asked Eric if he prayed for his team to win each week. He said he doesn't pray for victory, but he prays for the health of each player. They get to see we are regular people, and it's fun to answer their questions."

Eric's LDS membership is common knowledge to his teammates, and he is occasionally asked questions in the locker room. He is careful not to push his beliefs on others, but he is not afraid to stand up and defend his faith.

Adult Mormons who meet standards of worthiness by following the Church's commandments and moral code are allowed to enter the temple. Inside the temple, members promise to live morally pure and virtuous lives. After making those promises, those members wear white undergarments as a symbol and personal reminder of their commitments to God. Because members of the Church consider these to be sacred articles of clothing, they are worn discreetly and are not flaunted publicly. When one of Eric's teammates began joking about Eric's clothing, Eric made it clear he didn't appreciate the joke and told the teammate to knock it off.

A few days later, the same teammate made another wisecrack. This time Eric became so furious he almost punched the player in the face, but he restrained himself.

"How would you like it if I came to your house and made fun of your family?" Eric fired back at his teammate. "Look, man, I don't say anything about you, make fun of what you believe or what you do outside of football. What gives you the right to make fun of what I wear or what I do? If you value our friendship, you will never make fun of my garments again."

The teammate received the message. It didn't happen again.

Many of his coaches, teammates, and friends respect Eric for his ability to stay true to his religion and be a professional football player. Steve Wilks, a former Chargers assistant coach, admires Eric's ability to balance football and his personal life. "He is a great father and family man," Wilks said. "We talk about it a lot. I see a guy who is dedicated to his job but also dedicated in his personal life."

Justin Hansen, Eric's former Utah teammate and close friend, respects Eric's humility. "Eric knows he isn't perfect and has made many mistakes in his life. He doesn't believe he is better than anyone else. He simply tries to make good choices every day. As a result, Eric has seen many blessings flow into his life from striving to be a faithful member of his church."

Eric traces all good things in his life back to one monumental decision. "To this day, joining the LDS Church is the best decision I have ever made. I have never looked back," Weddle said. "Ultimately I became a better teammate, leader, and person overall. Having the gospel makes a difference. You enjoy life and the people around you more. It has put me in a position to have direction, love, and what I want most for my family."

## 2008 THROUGH 2010: A REFINING PROCESS

By midseason of Eric Weddle's rookie year in 2007, he was splitting time with veteran Marlon McCree. By the start of the 2008 season, McCree was gone and Weddle was in position to earn significant playing time and possibly even start. During spring and summer practices, quarterback Philip Rivers said Weddle covered the field so well it was as if he knew what Rivers was going to do.

Weddle was the shortest person in the defensive huddle and the slowest player in San Diego's defensive secondary. His fellow DBs would occasionally tease him for not having a chiseled, herculean physique, yet it was only a matter of time before Weddle would become the Chargers' starting free safety.

"He doesn't look like a football player until he gets on the football field," teammate Quentin Jammer told the media in 2008. "He's going to be special."

A devout student of game film who was blessed with football instincts, Eric played neither small nor slow and always seemed to be around the ball during his first few NFL seasons. "He's got a nose for the football," secondary coach Bill Bradley said. "He plays football with his eyes as well as anyone I've been around. And he does have some quicks. He can run. It doesn't appear that way, but he can."

Although Eric earned his opportunity to start, he knew he still had much to learn if he wanted to become an elite safety in the NFL. From 2008 to 2010, Eric took his fair share of lumps but also proved to be an asset to his team. He won Chargers fans over with his gusto, energy, hustle, team-first attitude, and ability to smell out the ball. He continued to remind himself that the Chargers had traded away four draft picks to get him, and he didn't want the organization to regret its decision.

As the 2008 season got under way, San Diego columnist Kevin Acee compared Eric's defensive duties to an air traffic controller. "Being a free safety in the moments between plays can be like being an air traffic controller—that is, if the air traffic controller were in the middle of the airplanes flying around his screen and the pilots of those planes were having a difficult time getting his instructions.

"The instant one play ends, Weddle must assess the down and distance, which hash mark the ball is placed on, remember a team's tendencies, find out the play, communicate with the rest of the secondary, look at the formation, read the quarterback, and most likely communicate again with the rest of the secondary about changes based on the formation—all this evolving perhaps until milliseconds before the ball is snapped."

Despite his natural instincts for football and meticulous preparation, Weddle still made plenty of mistakes, some in key moments of critical games. In the 2008 season opener, Eric was close enough to prevent Carolina tight end Dante Rosario from catching the game-winning touchdown, but failed to knock the ball away. The following week at Denver, he was partially responsible for the Broncos' final touchdown and then blew his coverage on the game-clinching two-point conversion. When the Chargers hosted the New York Jets in an AFC divisional play-off in January 2010, running back Shonn Greene broke Weddle's tackle late in the game and ran 53 yards for the game-winning score. In the hyperanalyzed world of sports talk radio and post-game call-in shows, it's often the missed tackle here or blown assignment there that is noticed over the body of work by any player or team throughout a game.

"It just comes with the job," Weddle said. "You've got to ex-pect yourself to make those plays. You do it your whole life. In my position, you either make a play or it's a touchdown for the other team."

Usually very sure-handed, Eric dropped at least five intercep-tions in the first twelve games of the 2010 season. As a remedy, Chanel suggested Eric carry a football around all day. "Maybe you'll start catching 'em," she said. For the next two weeks, Eric was seen cradling a pigskin in his arms on the sideline, between drills in practice, as well as in the film room. He even slept next to it. "I was just trying to do whatever I could to get better," Eric said.

Weddle's efforts paid off later that season in a Sunday night game at Indianapolis when he snagged a third-quarter pass by Colts quarterback Peyton Manning and returned the ball 41 yards for a game-changing score. Eric finished the year with two picks.

As he tried to settle into his role on the team from 2008 to 2010, Eric showed promise and made steady improvement.

**2008:** Eric started sixteen games, recorded 127 tackles, 1.5 quarterback sacks, intercepted a Brett Favre pass against the New York Jets, and returned a fumble 86 yards for a touchdown in a week 13 loss to the Atlanta Falcons (Chanel said he was gasping for air afterwards). The Chargers finished the year 8–8, won the AFC West, and upset the Indianapolis Colts in their divisional round game before losing to the eventual Super Bowl champion Pittsburgh Steelers.

**2009:** Weddle missed three games with a knee injury but still made 82 tackles, posted one sack, and earned two game balls—one for his first career interception return for a touchdown in a win against Miami, and another for his performance in a late-season victory at Tennessee in which he picked off a Vince Young pass and made a key tackle for loss on a critical third down against the NFL's leading rusher, Chris Johnson. San Diego had one of its best regular seasons in franchise history, finishing with a record of 13–3, only to be eliminated in the divisional round at home by the New York Jets.

**2010:** In what many consider to be his best season to that point, Eric had 96 tackles, 10 pass deflections, and 2 interceptions, including his pick-6 against Manning and the Colts. As for the team, a slow start to the season resulted in the Chargers missing the playoffs. San Diego finished the season 9–7.

## TWO COACHES

After the 2009 season, Eric Weddle admitted he was conflicted. Personally, Eric was rooting for San Diego defensive coordinator Ron Rivera to land a head-coaching job because he knew the coach deserved it. Professionally, however, Weddle selfishly hoped Rivera would stay with the Chargers. Rivera had not only mentored Weddle in playing the game, but he had also transformed the Chargers into the number-one-ranked defense in the NFL.

During his playing days, Ron "Chico" Rivera was an all-American linebacker at the University of California at Berkeley. Rivera was drafted by the Chicago Bears in 1984, was a member of the legendary 1985 Super Bowl championship team, and went on to play in the league for nine seasons. After a brief stint in broadcasting, he coached in Philadelphia and Chicago and moved on to San Diego in 2007 as the linebackers coach. When Ted Cottrell was fired in October 2008, Rivera was named the new defensive coordinator. Rivera met Eric shortly after he was drafted in 2007 and was impressed with Weddle's energy and work ethic. Rivera said that despite Eric's lack of physical stature, he did an admirable job of recognizing his abilities and using them to his advantage. "He's a smart football player, and the best thing about him is his understanding of the game," Rivera said. "One thing I find impressive about him is how he knows the time and effort you have to put in to be good. He has a lot of self-motivation and a desire to be great. To be good at anything, you've got to have those qualities, and he does. I think he is on the verge of taking the next step."

Eric said Rivera had a gift for motivating his players. He also stressed accountability and being a team player. "'Be a man about what you do. If you make a mistake, be a man about it,'" Eric said, recalling Rivera's words. "It was always about the team—no egos, no individuals."

In January 2011, Rivera was named as head coach of the Carolina Panthers. "It was a long time coming," Eric said. "And he is going to be a great head coach for a long time."

Steve Wilks, who later followed Rivera to Carolina, played college ball at Appalachian State (1987–1991). He was released after training camp with the Seattle Seahawks. He played a season with the Charlotte Rage of the Arena Football League and then decided to pursue coaching. Wilks was a head and assistant coach at several schools (Savannah State, Illinois State, Appalachian State, East Tennessee State, Bowling Green, Notre Dame, and Washington) for eleven seasons before he cracked the

NFL coaching ranks with the Bears in 2006. By 2009, he was in San Diego with the Chargers, coaching Eric Weddle.

"He's a student of the game," Wilks said of Weddle, "very inquisitive . . . always asking what he can do to improve . . . a leader. [He] wants to know what we know as coaches. . . . He's like a coach on the field. You can have all the physical attributes, but if you don't understand the fundamentals, you won't be successful. Eric understands that."

Wilks teaches that being a good person and doing things right is more important than football. He is known for citing inspirational quotes to the players. "I tried to write down hundreds of his quotes," Weddle said. "That's his little deal. He is very detailed, descriptive, and works extremely hard. I admire his values. He's creative and very outside the box. He is always on me about getting better."

## THE ART OF PREPARATION

There is an oft-cited line from Latter-day Saint scripture that Eric lives by: "If ye are prepared ye shall not fear."

Each week he sits down with a well-used spiral notebook with "EDub 32" handwritten in black and red letters on the cover. Eric has filled its pages with personal notes from team meetings and film sessions and code words such as "Zorro," "Bone," and "Ace" in the margins. There are diagrams and formations scribbled in black and red ink, and others highlighted in yellow. There are personal reminders such as "Don't dance so much on the blitz—make a move and go." Another list begins, "Things to remember in the red zone," and next to it, "Formations they will use in the red zone." There are also notes about key players on other teams. Before the Chargers hosted the Patriots in October 2010, Eric wrote, "Know where No. 83 [Wes Welker] is. . . . Get after QB. Tom [Brady] is one of the best because he manipulates defenses, moves around the pocket well, and reads coverages. But there are things they do that, if we recognize them, can help us be successful."

To anyone else, the terminology may well sound like a foreign language. But to Eric it all makes sense. And despite his share of hits to the head, Eric is able to pull these valuable nuggets from his personal database during key moments in games.

During an average week, Eric is at the Chargers practice facility from 6:00 a.m. until after 6:00 p.m. About ten of those twelve hours are spent in meetings, watching film, studying the upcoming opponent's personnel and tendencies and identifying their weaknesses. Chargers players and coaches also study their own tendencies and weaknesses to understand how other teams might attack them. "Needless to say, you can't just go out and play," Eric said. "God-given ability is just not enough. You have to do more than what is asked to be successful. The game is really fast. If you are a step slow, you will get beat. If you are anticipating what is going to happen, you can be a step quicker and make the play."

In 2009, ESPN.com's Bill Williamson asked Eric to break down the Pittsburgh Steelers offense as part of its coverage of Super Bowl XLIII. The Chargers faced the Steelers twice that year, and Williamson wrote that "Weddle . . . has a reputation as being one of the bright, young defensive minds in the league as well as a tackling machine." Eric elaborated for readers on three key areas for stopping Pittsburgh: contain the run, put pressure on quarterback Ben Roethlisberger, and cover your responsibilities on the back side. On the third key, Eric said, "It's important to play strong coverage on the back end of the defense. You have to stay with your guys and within your coverage throughout the play. Ben can make some very difficult plays outside the pocket. He plays well with his feet. He can roll to his left and throw to his right. . . . You have to stay on the strong side when Ben rolls out or when he tries to buy time in general for all spots on the field. . . . He can hurt you."

Eric's analysis was accurate. Arizona's defense held Pittsburgh to 58 yards rushing, but Roethlisberger proved to be elusive in the pocket and led the Steelers on several scoring drives, including an improbable, game-winning drive at the end of the game. True to Weddle's words, when Roethlisberger scrambled, the Cardinals broke down in the secondary and left receivers open, one player in particular. Santonio Holmes caught 9 passes for 131 yards, including his memorable 6-yard touchdown reception in the corner of the end zone with thirty-five seconds left, to earn the Most Valuable Player award and lead Pittsburgh to a 27–23 victory.

When the Colts played the New Orleans Saints in the next Super Bowl, Williamson asked Weddle to discuss quarterbacks Peyton Manning and Drew Brees. At that point, Weddle had faced Manning four times in three seasons and played opposite Brees once in 2008.

"I saw Drew up close when we played them in London, and he played at a high level for the entire game. . . . When he is on his game or in the zone, nothing is going to stop him. He does a very good job of manipulating the defense with his eyes and shoulder movements. The Saints run the ball well as a team, which helps him with his play action and drop-back throws. . . . He understands defenses, where he can drop back, look left the entire time, waiting for a route to clear on the opposite side of the field and gun it in there. . . . He has an elite arm and is seventy percent accurate. . . . He throws the deep ball just as well as the short and intermediate routes.

"Peyton does an unbelievable job pre-snap as to finding out what defense you may be in. He is always checking as to who the

"Mike" [middle] linebacker is so the line will know where the protection will start from. Here are some reasons why it's extremely difficult to get to Peyton: His pre-snap reads, his accuracy, and the scheme and the plays they run so well. They have about four or five plays that are their bread-and-butter plays, meaning they run them so much it doesn't matter what defense you may be in, they will out-execute you. His accuracy, his mental focus of the scheme and defenses, and his uncanny ability to make the right throw make him one of the toughest quarterbacks to go against."

Once again, Eric's observations were insightful. With Manning's leadership and vast experience, Indianapolis was viewed as the favorite in Super Bowl XLIV. But Brees played one of the best games of his life. He completed 32-of-39 passes for 288 yards and 2 touchdowns and had the Saints up 24–17 in the final minutes of the fourth quarter. Despite Manning's pre-snap reads, accuracy, and uncanny ability to make the right throw, he was also human. Hurried by a New Orleans blitz in Saints territory, Manning fired a pass to teammate Reggie Wayne on a slant route. But New Orleans cornerback Tracy Porter broke on the pass first, intercepted the ball, and returned it 74 yards for a touchdown, giving the Saints their first Super Bowl title, 31–17.

For Eric Weddle, preparation precedes performance and eliminates fear.

"If I don't prepare, if I don't do extra work, I won't be successful," Eric said. "It's really the difference between getting from high school to college and college to the NFL—the majority of players don't do the little things to prepare."

Learning how to prepare for opponents and maintain a spiritual balance in his life were essential to helping Eric survive his first four seasons in the NFL. He also couldn't have done it without his wife and children.

# CHAPTER 14

---

# *THE WEDDLE FAMILY CHRONICLES*

C hanel Weddle hates training camp. As July winds down and most football fans and sports talk shows are clamoring for the start of another NFL season, Chanel is dreading the inevitable. Training camp means her husband will be gone for more than forty days, followed by a season that spans five grueling months.

The Weddles' marriage is one of give and take, with Chanel carrying a heavier burden at home during training camp and the football season, while Eric tries to balance his family life and maintain his laser focus on the game.

Following each matchup, Eric and Chanel make it a point to sit on the sofa and review Eric's game film. A former college soccer player herself, Chanel enjoys the one-on-one time with her husband as Eric critiques his own performance, explains what happened on various plays, and hears Chanel's analysis. At the end of the film sessions, Eric rates himself on a scale of 1 to 10, usually, according to Chanel, between a 5 and 7.5. "It's like watching the director's cut or commentary on a DVD," Chanel said. "He explains everything to me—why this player went here, what happened on that play. He likes to scrutinize the defense. Usually he says he didn't do anything great, but he didn't do anything awful either."

Over the years there have been many games to evaluate. One that stands out to Chanel occurred in October 2008, when the Chargers lost to the New Orleans Saints 37–32 at Wembley Stadium in London, England. Prior to the game, Eric and his defensive teammates decided that if one of them made a big play, they would all mimic a different soccer move. They saw it as a way to honor European football, which is the premier professional sport in the U.K. Their opportunity to salute the Euro game came during the fourth quarter when Eric intercepted a pass by Saints quarterback Drew Brees. Eric attempted to wow the crowd by pretending to juggle a soccer ball and perform a bicycle kick, but he slipped and fell. Many family and friends who saw the bizarre display wondered if Eric was trying to dance. ("Obviously he didn't learn it from me," Chanel said of the move.)

The celebration quickly turned sour, however. It is illegal to go to the ground during a celebration, so Eric drew an unsportsmanlike conduct penalty. Then the officials reviewed the play and found indisputable evidence of the ball hitting the ground, so the interception ruling was reversed. Eric was also hit with "a fat fine," Chanel said.

"He will never do it again," she said. "It's unlike Eric to do that, and he wasn't aware of the league rules on going to the ground, but I think he learned his lesson. He felt really bad afterward. On a scale of 1 to 10, that time he said he played a 1."

## FAMILY MOMENTS

In January 2009, as Brooklyn approached her first birthday, Eric and Chanel began to wonder when the timing would be right for a second child. They wanted their children to be close in age, and, if possible, born during the off-season. The more they discussed the issue, the more frustrated Chanel became. "I was starting to get annoyed with the whole discussion, so we turned to prayer for answers," she said. "We just prayed that we would know when the timing was right and that it would all work out."

Within a couple of weeks, Chanel had an impression that the sooner they had their second baby, the better. Her initial reaction was "No way, not that fast," but the feeling persisted, and she decided to tell Eric. At the time, he was across the country in Miami, and, to her surprise, he said he had similar feelings. Eric told her he had been holding his agent David Canter's one-month-old son when an impression came to him. "It had to be the answer to our prayers," Chanel said.

About a month later, Chanel discovered that she was pregnant. At the time, Eric was with the Chargers for a game in Pittsburgh, so she planned a surprise for his return. When Eric walked into the bathroom he saw balloons, a pregnancy test, and a sign that read, "Surprise, baby Weddle No. 2 is on the way."

"He was dead silent. Then he came over to me and said it was the best surprise he had ever had. The news also significantly helped to take his mind off their loss to the Steelers. We were both in shock and talked for an hour before going to bed," Chanel said. "It was meant to be and we were thrilled." The new baby was a boy, whom they named Gaige.

Because Eric Weddle is a recognizable public figure, when the Weddles take their kids out in public, they sometimes experience a unique challenge. While Eric is grateful that fans buy his

No. 32 jersey, and he usually offers to sign it for them, if they ask him when he is with Chanel and the kids, he has to awkwardly juggle fans and family.

Chanel was almost more excited than the children when a trip to the Circus Vargas in Vista, California, was planned with their close friends, the Binghams. The Weddles and Binghams were having a good time watching the different acts when intermission was announced. Chanel and Danie Bingham took the little girls to get their faces painted while Eric and Ryon, a former teammate, took the little boys outside the main tent to stretch their legs.

After a few minutes, Eric's two-year-old son, Gaige, said he wanted to return to his mommy. The story continues in Eric's words.

"So we walked back into the tent. I saw Chanel, and Gaige started walking toward her. At that moment, I felt a tap on my shoulder, and a woman asked if I was Eric Weddle. When I told her yes, she said they were big fans and asked if she could take some pictures. I figured Chanel had Gaige, so I agreed."

After the impromptu photo shoot, Eric found Chanel to make sure she had Gaige. "I started laughing and said, 'That's not even funny, I never had him,'" Chanel said. "When I saw the panic on his face, I knew instantly he was not joking. My next two thoughts were 'We have to find him,' and 'Don't cry.'" As they split up to search for their son, Chanel tried not to blame her husband until she knew the whole story. "But if he was on his phone," she thought, "I am going to kill him."

A security guard at the main gate assured Chanel he had not seen a little boy fitting Gaige's description leave in the past several minutes, so she knew her little boy was still somewhere close, which brought her a small measure of relief. But her heart continued to pound with worry as she darted from place to place, frantically looking around each corner. Chanel prayed fervently in her heart as she looked under the bleachers and in the aisles. Gaige was nowhere to be found, and serious panic was setting in when she saw Eric moving toward her with the little boy in his arms. She instantly took him and held Gaige as tightly as she could and started to cry. Fortunately, another security guard had discovered the toddler when he tried to climb onto the stage.

Normally, Chanel doesn't mind if people ask her husband for an autograph or picture in public, as long as they don't go overboard. "I am supportive of it," she said. "He owes it to the fans. They make him who he is. People have rarely been rude. It's only hard when we have the kids and someone wants him to sign a lot of things."

Although her son was missing for only about fifteen minutes, it was perhaps fifteen of the most frightening minutes in Chanel's life. "Those minutes felt like days. It was in that moment of holding him that I realized a mother's love—my love for my kids," she said. "Words can't explain the feeling of losing one of them."

"I always try to please fans, taking pictures or signing autographs," Eric said. "But that was one of the craziest, scariest moments ever. That's my little man, and it was all my fault. My wife was crying. It won't happen again."

## A KID AT HEART

As dedicated as he is to his craft and his family, Eric is just as much a boy at heart. Before his youngest daughter was born on August 4, 2011, Eric arrived at the hospital with Chanel anticipating some down time. Labor was to be induced that day, but Chanel's past history suggested this trip to the hospital wouldn't be quick. Their first two children, Brooklyn and Gaige, were both delivered more than twelve hours after Eric and Chanel arrived at the hospital.

"We checked in, and they started the inducing medication. As soon as I was settled, Eric asked the nurse, 'What are the plans for the next 30 minutes?'" Chanel said. "I asked him, 'Why? Where are you going?' He said the TV in our hospital room wasn't compatible with the Xbox he'd brought, so he was going to run to Target and buy a new TV that would work. 'Really?' I said. Of course, really."

Weddle left and returned thirty minutes later with a new 40-inch flat screen TV.

"He proceeded to try to set it up, including the Wi-Fi, so he could play *Call of Duty* online with his friends," Chanel said. "He requested help from a nurse, a doctor, the doctor's daughter, and even an anesthesiologist to figure it out. Much to his dismay, they never got it to work. But he got a daughter out of it."

More than thirteen hours and several video games later, baby daughter Silver Jean Weddle finally entered the world, with Eric assisting the doctors in delivery.

Eric's love of video games is somewhat equal to his love for the Christmas holiday. Growing up, Eric's family always had a real Christmas tree and Chanel's family always had a fake one. When Eric and Chanel were first married, they were poor college students and opted for a fake tree, but they agreed that when they were more established, a real tree would grace their living room.

Sure enough, when the Chargers drafted him in 2007 and the couple bought a home in Escondido, Eric reminded Chanel about getting a real tree. Christmas tree farms were scarce in Escondido that year, but the couple utilized the Internet to locate one within driving distance.

When they arrived at the tree farm, the selection was poor

and unimpressive. It was Tuesday, Eric's only day off in the week and thus their only chance to find and bring home a real Christmas tree. They started searching elsewhere and found a Walmart that was selling live Christmas trees. They selected an enormous, eight-foot pine and carried their tree to the car—where they realized they had a problem.

"The tree was too big to put in the back seat, and the windows rolled only halfway down," Chanel said. "Eric said he would lash the tree to the hood. I asked if we needed to go into Walmart and get some string, but he said, 'No, I have this extension cord.'"

Eric wrapped the cord over the tree and around through the rolled-down windows so the cord ran across the inside ceiling of the car and back out to the hood. It wasn't pretty, but it appeared secure. As Chanel with her pregnant belly attempted to get into the car, she realized the cord was preventing her from opening the door. To get into the front passenger seat, she had to enter on the driver's side and crawl across the gearshift. After several minutes of maneuvering, they were finally ready to head home, about six interstate exits away. About halfway there, they began to have more problems. "The tree started falling," Chanel said. "We pulled over to rearrange it, and for the last mile or so Eric drove with one hand on the steering wheel and one hand holding the tree on the hood. We were moving so slow. I told him that I hoped no one recognized Eric Weddle and his pregnant wife with a Christmas tree lashed by extension cord to their tiny Honda! Sometime between then and forever, we made it home."

"I probably didn't think everything through very well," Eric admitted, "but we got the job done, and we had a great first Christmas in our home. I was better prepared the next Christmas."

The following year, Eric bought a truck, which made hauling

large Christmas trees much easier. Eric now tries to find a bigger Christmas tree each year. "It's serious business," Chanel said. "I just get everything out, and he has to decorate it himself. Every ornament has to be hung just right. When our kids got old enough to help, we would let them help hang the ornaments and decorations. But after they went to bed, Eric would go back in and fix everything."

## UNIQUELY ERIC

When Chanel suspected there was a virus on the family computer in June 2008, Eric wanted to fix that, too. Chanel had organized months of photos and videos into several files, and she wanted to know everything was protected. No problem, Eric said.

"Eric, being the man he is, bought an anti-virus remedy at Best Buy instead of calling my cousin Todd, who is a computer professional. When that didn't work, he decided to reboot our whole computer," Chanel said. "To make a long story short, he came to bed one night and told me all our pictures and videos weren't showing up. He said he copied them all onto disks, then wiped the system and reinstalled everything, but for some reason the pictures weren't showing up. I started crying instantly."

Eric assured his wife everything was backed up, but she suspected the worst—that all their family files were gone. "I said he had better figure it out or I would be devastated."

About two weeks later, Todd helped the Weddles recover the lost files. In the Weddle home, the news was received with relief. "I am so happy," Chanel said, "and Eric isn't on the couch anymore."

"She wasn't very happy with me," Eric said, "because it was really important to her. But despite what many may think, I am computer literate, and eventually everything worked out. When she realized that was the case, she told me, 'You are a lucky dog.'"

On occasion, Chanel has awakened to strange sounds in the middle of the night and found her husband sleepwalking. One night, Chanel sat up in bed and heard Eric breathing heavily across the room. The semi-open window blinds provided slivers of light from the street, but her eyes struggled to adjust to the darkness. As her heart rate increased, she flipped on a lamp and went to examine the damage on the other side of the bedroom.

When Eric awoke, he realized his knee was several inches inside the wall of the couple's bedroom. How he got there and how he broke through the drywall was a mystery. The best he and Chanel could piece together was that Eric had tried to tackle the dresser like an opposing player and somehow rammed his knee through the wall. It wasn't the first time he had done something like this.

"Most of the time, we just talk while he is asleep," Chanel said. "But there have been times he has yelled out football plays and lines from movies. Once he threw a suitcase into the wall, creating a hole the size of a softball. Another time he turned on the light and started screaming because he thought he saw someone trying to get into the house. One time he thought there was a huge spider on the wall, and he attacked it with a lamp. He often goes right back to sleep and snores. I really need to record what he does."

## HIGH-PROFILE HUSBAND

Chanel is married to a high-profile athlete but doesn't like to draw attention to it. One of the biggest challenges for Chanel as the wife of an NFL football player is Sabbath day observance. Devout Mormons place a particular importance on attending church on Sundays and avoiding other forms of recreation. Some even shun watching football or other sports on their weekly day of worship. For Chanel, Eric's profession means that during the season there is a weekly tension between attending church with the kids and supporting her husband. Road games are easy because she can record the game and watch it later. For home games, she attends church for an hour and then leaves for Qualcomm Stadium. "It's a struggle, but it's a choice we made, and we try to do our best," Chanel said. "This is how he supports us, but we know he won't play forever. It could all be over in one play. . . . The battle continues to be between putting the family first and supporting the job."

Thanks to their postgame film sessions, Chanel considers herself more informed than the average fan. In 2008, she read *Quiet Strength,* a memoir by former Indianapolis head coach Tony Dungy and writer Nathan Whitaker, and grew to admire Dungy for his character and example.

"I am happy that Eric plays for the Chargers," Chanel said, "but if he could go anywhere else, I would love for him to play for Tony Dungy. It would be an honor. I highly recommend his book. I was pleased to read about not only what a great coach he is, but what a great father, guy, and example he is. All along I told Eric about Tony Dungy and the book, hoping Eric could learn from him."

After the Chargers played the Indianapolis Colts in the 2007 playoffs, Eric told Coach Dungy how much he and Chanel enjoyed his book and how they respect him. When the two teams played again in 2008, Eric said Coach Dungy came looking for him as he walked off the field.

"He called Eric's name and told him what a great player he is," Chanel said. "He told Eric that even though the team [San

Diego] wasn't having a great season, he should stay positive because there was still a possibility of making the playoffs. Eric asked about his family and he asked about our family. They chatted for a few minutes and went their separate ways. Eric was excited about how Tony searched him out, and I'm really jealous that I didn't get to meet the man."

## MORE GIVE AND TAKE

The Weddles know they have been blessed with a good life, yet they don't pretend to be perfect. They have had their share of challenges and faults, but they have been able to laugh at most of them. Chanel's efforts to keep life normal at home have helped Eric to have balance and support.

"Like in any family, sometimes kids are hard and there is no break. We take turns," Eric said. "I don't know how Chanel does it when I am at work. I don't help as much as I should. But she is amazing. She was born to be a mother. She reads to them, plays with them, and makes sacrifices for them. While they sleep, she takes care of the house. Our kids are well behaved and amazing because of her."

Eric says that Chanel also keeps him in line when he needs it. "She supports me and is there for me no matter what. She is understanding but also demands I live up to who I am, a father, husband, and head of the household. At times she reels me back in and helps me keep things in perspective. Everyone has different challenges and problems, including football wives. They are home alone with the kids a lot, and at times it's not easy, but Chanel never complains. She just goes about her work. She is very unselfish, and the more the years go by, the more I appreciate and love her. My family is everything to me."

In February 2010, Chanel had been debating for some time

about whether or not to attend a Utah State University alumni soccer game. She had no desire to play, but the idea of renewing old friendships and seeing the campus in Logan, Utah, again was enticing. She didn't want to go by herself, however. She debated her decision until one day she called Eric and presented her argument for going to Utah for the alumni game.

"Since I always let him do what he wants and support him in things he does, I thought he should come with Brooklyn and me for the weekend," Chanel said. "He said okay, and I was thrilled. I booked the tickets that night before he could back out."

The weekend trip was everything Chanel hoped it would be. They visited friends and ate at Maddox Ranch House, a popular restaurant located about twenty-five miles southwest of Logan, in Brigham City. After some snowmobiling and shopping, they traveled through scenic Sardine Canyon, which winds from Brigham City into Logan and Cache Valley.

Chanel was able to reconnect with many former teammates, tour Utah State's new facilities, and eat at her favorite Mexican restaurant, Café Rio, before the Weddles left Logan. They then traveled south to Salt Lake and stayed with other friends.

"It was so good seeing people I haven't seen in so long, and I'm sorry we didn't get to see everyone," she said. "I'm so glad I decided to go after all."

Charity and community service have always been important to Eric and Chanel. In June 2008, the couple, along with Eric's parents, attended a charity dinner for the Boys and Girls Clubs of San Diego at the downtown Marriott, where Eric was the featured guest. After a seafood dinner, music, entertainment, and an awards presentation, each child had his or her picture taken with Eric. A silent auction followed, with all proceeds going to a charitable cause. Eric wanted to bid on something, but nothing caught his eye. "After the bidding was over, Eric offered himself," Chanel said. "For a donation, someone could spend time with him, doing whatever they wanted, and he would sign a jersey. And what do you think that sold for? $6,000. It was unbelievable. I figured I'd better value my time with my husband more, since I get him for free. It was amazing how generous people were."

"I was already there, but I really wanted to give more, and Chanel was giving me a look," Eric said. "So I offered a day with me, a tour of the Chargers facility, and lunch. A couple of people bid on it, and I ended up hanging out with two guys. It was easy, and I had the time. It felt good to help out the Boys and Girls Club like that."

# CHAPTER 15

—

# *THE AMBASSADOR*

B rian Johnson could not stop smiling.

After a disastrous third quarter, the Utah quarterback had rallied the 15th-ranked Utes to score 11 points in the final 1:30 to defeat Oregon State 31–28 in front of a packed house at Rice-Eccles Stadium. After throwing a 25-yard touchdown pass to Bradon Godfrey with 1:29 left to play and running in the two-point conversion to tie the game at 28–28, the defense held the Beavers to three-and-out. Johnson moved Utah to OSU's 24 and called time-out with two seconds left. Kicker Louie Sakoda trotted out and booted a 37-yard field goal as time expired, to keep the 2008 Utes unbeaten at 6–0. After the game, Johnson told the media it was, "hands down, the biggest win of his career."

In the Utah locker room after the game, Johnson showered, dressed, and checked his phone for messages. The senior's eyes widened when he realized there were more than eighty text messages waiting for him. He wasn't surprised, however, to see they were all from the same number.

"During my senior year, Eric Weddle would text me his play-by-play analysis of each game. I would come back to the locker room and find my phone had blown up with text messages, series by series, quarter by quarter," said Johnson, now Utah's offensive coordinator. "He called once a week and wanted the whole game plan in detail—what we were doing, what the opponent was doing, who are their best players, how we were going to attack them, and so forth. And I told him."

When Johnson explained the defensive tendencies of Oregon State, Eric suggested some pass routes he thought might work. "We were able to work it into the game plan," Johnson said.

As Eric watched the Utah-Oregon State game with his wife, he reacted to almost every play with a text to Johnson. "BJ is one of my boys," Eric said. "He and I became close friends after I went into the NFL. He was a young guy, but wise beyond his years. I wanted to be there for him and mentor him. So I would watch games and text him my thoughts. Chanel would say, 'Why are you doing that? He can't see it. He doesn't want to hear from you.' I defended myself: 'Yes, he does.'"

Back in Utah's locker room after the OSU win, Johnson scrolled through a bunch of his friend's messages. Most made him laugh.

"What play call was that?"

"What is their defense like?"

"What happened on that throw? Got to make the throw on third down."

"Way to not take a sack in the red zone."

"Why did you run that play?"

"Great blitz call by Kalani [Sitake, Utah's defensive coordinator]!"

"Why are so many receivers dropping the ball?"

"It was fun for me. I enjoyed it," said Johnson, now Utah's offensive coordinator. "It meant a lot to me for him to get that into what we were doing. He is truly a great friend who has always been there, and it's nice to have that. We are fortunate [at Utah] to have a group of guys that love coming back and still want to be a part of the program. I don't think that happens a lot when a guy goes to the NFL."

Maintaining close ties with the University of Utah football program and sharing his knowledge with younger players has been an important part of Eric's life even as he has moved on. His experiences at Utah greatly impacted his life, and he maintains a genuine love for people in the program, the university, and its proud athletic tradition.

"It's been great to have him around our guys," Coach Kyle Whittingham has said on many occasions. "He's such a great ambassador for our program. We're very proud that he's an alum."

Eric is a Ute for life, and his mentor/friend relationship with Whittingham is a convenient bonus. Of all the coaches he's had, Whittingham is the coach Weddle looks up to the most. When Eric is hungry for the inside details of the program, the recruits, and coach's observations, Whittingham supplies the inside scoop. For example, after Utah was invited to join the PAC-12 in 2010, Eric wasn't surprised because he had been talking to Whittingham. Sometimes they just want to talk football. "We talk about philosophy, offense, defense—he knows I watch the game," Eric said of Coach Whittingham. "He likes to know my opinion. Coach bounces ideas and questions off me, asks what I see and observe. He's not too big to learn and is always looking to get better. We also talk about our families. We have a great relationship."

Looking back to the time he recruited Eric from Alta Loma, Whittingham is not surprised at what Weddle has accomplished. He has developed into the player that Whittingham envisioned. Along the way, the coach has felt a special bond with Eric. "It's very unique. It goes far beyond the athletic realm," the coach said. "The most rewarding part of this profession is the relationships with players. We get to watch them develop, progress, and grow from eighteen-year-old kids to twenty-two- or twenty-three-year-old men with degrees in hand, and hopefully we teach some life lessons along the way."

The two stay in contact all year long. Any time Whittingham is near San Diego, for recruiting trips or otherwise, he makes time to stop by the Weddle house and visit the family. Whenever they get together, Weddle wants to know everything his former coach will tell him. "He's very inquisitive and has a genuine interest in everything that's going on," Whittingham said. "He wants all the little details. I listen to his interviews with the Chargers, and he is always plugging our program. When he has time, we love having him around our team. If I have played a small role in his life as a mentor, that is great. I've gotten as much out of it as he has."

Eric's ambassadorship for the U officially began in 2007 during his rookie season. As soon as he learned the Utes were coming to San Diego to play Navy in the Poinsettia Bowl, he checked his schedule. He was delighted to see the Chargers would host the Detroit Lions during bowl week. Eric attended Ute practices at the University of San Diego, and he and Chanel spent three nights in the San Diego Sheraton Hotel and Marina with the team. The Sunday before the bowl game, several Utes came to Qualcomm and watched the Chargers throttle the Lions, 51–14.

Eric said the week with his old teammates was a special reunion. "It was amazing to see all the players and coaches again," Eric said. "They are like my family, my brothers. I value any opportunity to show my support."

Kyle Gunther recalled when Eric pulled up to the team hotel in his Honda Accord. "He was still the same guy we all remembered," Gunther said. "I was expecting him to pull up in a brand-new Cadillac Escalade. He had played a full year in the NFL and was still rocking the same Honda Accord, the same car he had in college. No gold teeth, no diamond earrings, and he was still wearing the same stuff he wore at Utah. He sat around and talked to fifteen or twenty guys for twenty minutes, then went to dinner with some of them. You won't find anyone saying they weren't friends with Eric Weddle. I don't think he has ever had an enemy. He hasn't changed from the day I met him. He continues to be very personable. He is just one of the guys."

Eric has made an effort to go to as many of Utah's games as his schedule permits. He has also been generous with his advice to the team and offers helpful tips about improving their games. Often he gives team members challenges and encourages them to do better, sometimes changing the outcome of the game.

Eric was happy when the Chargers earned an AFC wildcard matchup with Indianapolis following the 2008 season but felt a tinge of disappointment because he couldn't fly to New Orleans and walk the sideline during Utah's Sugar Bowl showdown with Alabama.

When Utah played California in the 2009 Poinsettia Bowl, Eric was able to drop by their practice sessions. Then most of the Utes coaches and players came to see Eric and the Chargers defeat the Cincinnati Bengals, 27–24, to secure the AFC West title. Unfortunately, Weddle couldn't attend the Utes' bowl game because the Chargers played the Tennessee Titans on Christmas Day that year.

In 2011, San Diego's bye week happened to be the same week that Utah traveled to Notre Dame in South Bend, Indiana. And the following week, the Chargers hosted the Denver Broncos on *Monday Night Football,* and Eric was able to cheer for his college team in their game against San Diego State on November 20. The Utah defense struggled mightily in the first half of that Mountain West Conference matchup, allowing SDSU quarterback Ryan Lindley to complete 24-of-34 passes for 321 yards and 3 touchdowns. The Aztecs led at intermission, 27–24.

When Utah cornerback Brandon Burton emerged from the locker room after halftime, Weddle pulled him aside and challenged the defensive back to take charge in the second half and inspire his teammates to overcome the adversity. Utah's defense responded, and the Utes pulled out a much-needed victory, 38–34.

"Basically, what he said was, 'Get the defense going,'" Burton told *Deseret News* beat writer Dirk Facer. "'Get out there and make plays. Just do what you know how to do to. Relax—you know you're the best at it.' And I just went out there and tried to do what I had to do, and the defense, we all backed each other up. We all had each other's backs, and we went out and made plays."

When it was announced that the University of Utah was being invited to join the PAC-12 Conference, no one was more proud or excited than Eric. He boldly predicted the Utes would have a conference title within three years. "It was surreal," he said, reacting to the news about the invitation. "Coach Whit had a feeling it was going to happen early, like three or four months before it happened. It's amazing. I dreamed of it when I came up here in 2003, and for it to be a reality, not only for the players now, but for the former players, we're all proud to be part of it and make it happen."

In addition to rarely passing up a chance to attend his alma mater's games, Eric has also developed a tradition of traveling to Salt Lake City for Utah's final spring scrimmage each April. He and other former players like to congregate on the field along the back of the south end zone at Rice-Eccles Stadium to analyze the up-and-coming talent, reconnect with former teammates, and swap stories. When he isn't watching a play, signing an autograph, or posing for a picture, Eric can be found catching up on the news with friends and teammates. "I definitely won't miss the spring game," Eric said. "It's a great time to come back and visit ex-teammates, ex-players that played in the program, and see the future [of U football]."

Many current and former Utah players consider Eric a close friend. Paul Kruger played a major defensive role in Utah's 13–0 run to the Sugar Bowl and now lines up at defensive end for the Baltimore Ravens. The six-foot-four, 265-pound mammoth lineman has always admired the way Eric plays football.

"I am a real big Eric Weddle fan," Kruger said while taking in the 2011 spring scrimmage. "He's consistent and a tremendous competitor on the field. I think he is absolutely one of the best safeties in the NFL. He has proven that over the last couple years. Teams recognize him as a dangerous player. He was great to me when I got here to Utah and gave me great advice when I left. I have appreciated his friendship over the years."

Robert Johnson wore the Utah uniform from 2007 to 2009 and is now a safety with the Tennessee Titans. Johnson recalled feeling flattered when Eric introduced himself at a spring scrimmage in 2007. "We met, and he knew who I was, which made me feel good," Robert said. "He called me 'Ro-Jo.' When an NFL player knows your name, you know he has been keeping up with the team. I watched him in the Armed Forces Bowl, and he was doing everything on offense and defense. I was coming out of junior college and had played a little offense, too, and it motivated me to want to come to Utah with the hope of playing both ways as well.

"Carrying on the tradition of safety pride was a little overwhelming because of some of the great safeties who have played here, like Weddle. It forced me to step up."

Stevenson Sylvester, another anchor at linebacker on Utah's 2008 Sugar Bowl team, is now a six-foot-two, 231-pound linebacker for the Pittsburgh Steelers. He considers Weddle one of his mentors. "I owe Eric a lot for my success. We developed a great relationship," Sylvester said. "With Eric's help, I was able to develop study habits for watching film and keys to reading offenses. With his help, I was able to play my freshman year and for the NFL. His friendship has meant everything. I trust his judgment."

The list goes on. Former teammate Marty Johnson said Eric Weddle saved his life twice. After battling through two DUIs to play running back on the 2004 Fiesta Bowl team and graduate with a degree, not one NFL team was willing to take a chance on Marty. "It was because of my past. I wasn't even offered a free agent contract in 2005," he said.

The twenty-six-year-old was given a chance to play with the Berlin Thunder in NFL Europe. While there, Johnson rushed for 424 yards and 2 touchdowns and caught twenty-two passes for 178 yards and 2 scores.

When he returned to the United States in May 2006, Marty signed a free agent contract with the Denver Broncos and worked out with the team for four months. Johnson felt like he could play at the NFL level, but with players like Ron Dayne and Tatum Bell ahead of him on the depth chart, he never got a real opportunity to showcase his skills. One day after practice that fall, he approached the running backs coach and requested an opportunity to play. He received the news the next morning that the Broncos had released him. "I guess that taught me a lesson: Keep your mouth shut," Johnson said.

The five-foot-eleven, 225-pound back was quickly picked up by the Philadelphia Eagles but played in only three preseason games before being cut again.

His football career over, a disappointed Marty Johnson returned to Utah in 2007 and eventually to his old neighborhood in northern California. He struggled to keep a job and began hanging out with old friends. Old drinking habits returned. He was busted for another DUI and spent a year in jail. These were the lowest of times for Marty Johnson.

"To have your freedom taken away for a year—it was a wake-up call," Johnson said. "I didn't belong there. I felt like I was wasting opportunities."

About a month after Marty was released from prison, he sought out his former teammate and friend, Eric Weddle, and made an emotional plea for help.

"I hadn't heard from him in a while, and he texted me out of the blue," Eric said. "He said he was going through some things then broke down and asked for help. He asked if I could be there for him. I told him we were family, that we were brothers. I told him I would be there for him through the situation, and in the end he would be a better man. I told him he was going to get his life straight and do great things."

Knowing Eric was his brother during that difficult time made all the difference for Marty. "I told Eric I really appreciated his help, and I remember him saying, 'That's what brothers are for.' That really stuck with me. He helped me get back on my feet after some hard times, and I will always look up to him for that."

Today, Marty Johnson is a changed man. He's sober and has a full-time job. He has valuable support around him in fighting his alcohol addiction. Marty and Eric continue to exchange text messages or talk on the phone from time to time as Eric checks up on his brother and monitors his progress. Things are going well.

"I'm happy," Marty said. "I am paying my own bills and working to take care of myself. I'm doing the right things. I changed my whole way of thinking. I'm thinking about the future. It's great to know Eric will always be there for me if I need him."

Taking care of his Utah brothers will always be a high priority for Eric. For him and his family, though, another significant moment was around the corner. The 2010 season was the last on Weddle's rookie contract, and he was about to become a free agent. Despite the 2011 NFL lockout, Eric was about to find out how valued he was by the San Diego Chargers.

# CHAPTER 16

———

# THE FREE AGENT

Following the 2010 season, Eric Weddle's rookie contract expired, and he became a free agent. Would he re-sign with San Diego or sign with a new team?

He would have plenty of time to think about it.

On March 11, 2011, the NFL owners imposed a lockout, suspending the labor deal that was in place at the time, in hopes of creating a new financial structure. Ten players, including elite quarterbacks Drew Brees, Tom Brady, and Peyton Manning, subsequently filed an antitrust lawsuit against the league on behalf of the other players. One of the main issues was how to divide the $9 billion the NFL takes in each year. The labor dispute left Weddle and about two hundred other players frozen in free agency until a new deal was struck. For more than five months, the players were not allowed to train at team facilities or interact with their coaches. Many feared that if resolutions were not reached in a timely manner, the season might be cancelled. It was a long, frustrating summer for everyone involved.

"I tried to keep my cool about it, but it still stunk," Eric said. "You come in, you play well, and hope to get that second contract. I didn't know if I would. That was frustrating. We just had to sit back and wait and hope that things worked out. It was hard being patient. You play yourself into that position, and you want to take advantage of it."

The buzz around the league was that if Weddle could endure the lockout, he was a hot commodity. Bill Williamson, who writes about the AFC West for ESPN.com, posted that Eric was the Chargers' top free-agency priority and would be popular in the market.

ESPN NFL analyst Adam Schefter said of Weddle: "Eric is one of the top young safeties in the game. Some might be bigger, stronger, or faster. But for all-around athletes, Weddle is superb."

Jason La Canfora, a broadcaster for the NFL Network and writer for NFL.com, agreed with Schefter. During the summer lockout, he said, "Eric is without a doubt one of the emerging safeties in this game and someone who, if able to hit the open market, would be reaping substantial rewards. He doesn't go out of his way to self-promote or make it about him, but his play speaks for itself. Whenever he is on the open market, I'd expect him to command a deal similar to what a safety like Antrel Rolle commanded a year ago [five years, $37 million from the New York Giants].

La Canfora added that playing in San Diego and away from a major media market had probably hurt Weddle in terms of name recognition. "He deserved to be in the Pro Bowl last year [2010], but that's a popularity contest with some flaws in the voting system in my opinion. His peers know he is an elite player."

Matt Williamson is an NFL scout for ESPN.com and Scouts, Inc. He also hosts a *Football Today* podcast. Williamson classified

Eric as one of the top ten safeties in the league. "There is an awful lot to like about Eric. He was probably the best player on the San Diego defense in 2010," Williamson said. "His play justifies him to be right below Troy Polamalu and Ed Reed. He will probably only get better. He has tremendous work ethic, the right mindset and I like his versatility. He has a lot of playmaking instincts. He is starting to come into his own and the Chargers should want him back. An awful lot of teams would like to have him."

Weddle's stats through the first four years of his NFL career were comparable to the first four years of production by both Polamalu and Reed, although he grabbed fewer interceptions. From 2007 to 2010, Eric played in 60 regular-season games, had 6 interceptions, made 358 total tackles, and scored 2 touchdowns. Between 2003 and 2006, Polamalu played in 61 games, had 10 interceptions, made 302 tackles, scored 1 touchdown, and qualified for 3 pro bowls. From 2002 to 2005, Reed played in 58 games, had 22 interceptions, made 269 tackles, scored 2 touchdowns, and went to 2 pro bowls.

With his first four seasons, Weddle was proving the Chargers' gamble in the 2007 draft was paying off. San Diego traded four picks to Chicago so they could move up twenty-two spots to draft Eric, and while he was quickly becoming a potential Pro Bowl safety, none of the Bears' four picks were still on an NFL roster by the middle of the 2011 season.

As Weddle continued to wait for the lockout to end and the 2011 season to begin, speculation swirled that the Jaguars, Browns, Vikings, Cowboys, and Texans were interested in signing him. Eric preferred to stay in San Diego but was not afraid to leave for a better offer. Because he couldn't control what was happening, he prepared as if there were no lockout. He decided to try something new. After only two weeks off, he began conditioning himself by running long distances on the treadmill to build his endurance and stamina. "I hoped I wouldn't be so tired during the games, and it made a big difference," he said.

In the back of his mind, he remained optimistic that things would work out. "I'm looking forward to the future," Weddle told San Diego *Union-Tribune* sports columnist Kevin Acee just before the lockout. "I think everything will work out. If I'm here, I'm here. If I'm not, I'm not. I love being in San Diego, but it's not the reason I'll stay. My wife and kids loving San Diego won't keep us here. If it's not where I need to be, I can leave in a heartbeat."

Eric told the media he wasn't trying to break the bank. If the value of another team's offer was close to what the Chargers offered, it would be easy to stay in southern California. Eric had at least three good reasons to stay: He had good chemistry with his teammates, he was comfortable with the organization, and he loved having his family and friends nearby. He was playing less than two hours from where he had grown up.

## CAMP WEDDLE

The ten-year-old boy wearing a No. 32 Chargers jersey simulated the snap, took three steps back, and fired the pass while Eric Weddle, his NFL hero, studied his throwing mechanics. The pigskin sailed 15 yards into the arms of another anxious youth, who caught it and immediately looked at Weddle for approval. Eric nodded in his direction before turning back to the first boy.

"Look at that spiral," Eric said as he patted the kid on the back. "Nice throw."

Weddle moved from drill to drill so he could offer individual attention and encouragement to more than sixty-five kids, ages seven to fourteen, all of whom were attending his first football camp at Sunnyside Park, less than a mile south of the University of Utah football facilities. It was the first day of a three-day camp, with campers divided into four groups to practice their fundamentals.

Eric's top priorities during the lockout included personal workouts and spending more time at home with Chanel and his kids. He also did something he had wanted to do for years—host a youth football camp.

Eric didn't attend football camps until he was in high school. As a kid, he envied the classmates and friends who had the opportunity to learn from players competing at the highest level. Now that he was hosting his own camp, Weddle made personal interaction with each player a priority. He recruited former Utah teammates Sean Smith and R.J. Stanford to help with the camp, and the camp staff also included members of the University of Utah football team, including Dallin Rogers, Westlee Tonga, Reggie Dunn, and Derrick Shelby. "This has been a long time coming," Eric said to a reporter following the first session. "I've always wanted to do a camp up here, but with scheduling, it wasn't possible until now. I wanted to do it in Salt Lake City because I love the people. I couldn't be more excited. We want to teach the fundamentals and techniques, but we want them to compete and have fun, and if they say they had a blast and it's the best camp they've been to, that's what you want to hear."

Cooper Kenney *was* having a blast. His parents, Tim and Carey, drove about six hours from their home in St. George, Utah, to bring Cooper to Eric's football camp. In October 2009, the Kenney family was vacationing on a houseboat at Lake Powell when the boat's generator exploded and flames erupted. Cooper suffered second-degree burns on sixty percent of his body and was given a twenty-five percent chance of survival. The eight-year-old endured several surgeries and, to the doctors' amazement, walked out of the hospital twenty-one days later. His body was covered with scars, but he could still play running back on his Little League football team. Plus, as Cooper likes to tell people, "Chicks dig scars."

The highlight of Eric's camp for Cooper came on the final day when he received an autographed picture previously taken of him with Weddle and Smith. Eric also signed a Chargers football for Cooper with the message, "Keep up the good work. Stay strong. Be humble."

"It was a great camp," said Carey Kenney, Cooper's mother. "Eric and the other players were great with the kids. Our son learned a lot. It was worth it—we had a good time."

Other parents noticed Eric's hands-on approach and down-to-earth personality when working with their kids. "He wasn't 'big-timing' anyone or just going through the motions," said Ben Southwick, whose son was at the camp.

At the end of each session, which lasted about two hours, the kids took a knee and listened while Eric and other players spoke. Eric liked to ask several kids to share something they learned or improved on that day, and he publicly recognized kids he thought went the extra mile. On the last day, Eric asked Smith, Stanford, and the Utah players to each share some advice. When it was Eric's turn, he counseled the kids to trust and obey their parents, work hard in school, be team players, take pride in doing their best, respect their opponents, and always display good sportsmanship.

"Keep doing good, keep being passionate," Eric told them. "People may tear you down, they may say you can't do something, but stick with what you do, stick to your dreams, strive to be great, and you will define what you do in life. I am living proof of that."

## A BIG DEAL

Eric Weddle didn't normally walk the peaceful streets of his Escondido neighborhood around 3:00 a.m., but in the early morning hours of Wednesday, July 27, 2011, he was troubled.

Was he really about to move his family to Houston?

Eric's mind was in overdrive as he hiked across the pavement. Less than two hours earlier, the Texans had expressed serious interest in retaining Weddle's services, and he and Chanel, who was almost nine months pregnant with their third child, had all but decided to accept. Eric's agent, David Canter, was pulling an all-nighter at his Florida home to analyze the numbers. It was the kind of deal any NFL free agent would be thrilled to receive; yet Eric couldn't sleep. So he continued to wander in the dark silence.

The NFL Players Association and the league's owners had recently reached an agreement to end the 132-day lockout, and the free agency frenzy had begun. Canter began monitoring his network and responding to tweets, e-mails, and phone calls.

By Tuesday afternoon, Canter had learned that of the league's thirty-two teams, twelve were interested in the twenty-six-year-old safety. The sports agent had a firm number in mind for Weddle's salary, and when he shared it with the teams, several bowed out, including San Francisco, Carolina, Minnesota, Philadelphia, and Cleveland. Ed McGuire, executive vice president of the San Diego Chargers, made contact with Canter around midday and sent an initial offer around 9:30 p.m., but Canter wasn't impressed. Houston entered the picture shortly thereafter.

Around midnight, Canter and Weddle spoke at length and narrowed the list down to two teams—San Diego and

Jacksonville. Both teams had discussed similar figures, but neither had made an official offer. Eric and Canter wanted to sleep on it. They informed the teams they were shutting down for the night. Around 1:30 a.m., Canter was contacted by a third AFC team—Houston—and the Texans were prepared to battle for Weddle's services. Canter called Eric around 2:30 a.m. to report the unexpected development. While they talked, a Houston front office executive sent a text message to Canter, "We can match the number. We're in it to win it. He is going to love playing here!"

As Eric paced, several thoughts swirled in his mind. He wasn't prepared for how the reality of leaving southern California would hit him emotionally. He tried to imagine playing in a different city, wearing a different uniform, and how the front office personnel and coaching staff might regard him. The idea of leaving family and friends stirred deep feelings. Leaving them would be painful. He was also struggling to shake his loyalty to the team that had drafted him. Eric wanted to give the Chargers a chance to match the offer, even though it seemed unlikely they would try to prevent him from leaving town.

As Eric turned up his driveway and approached the front door, he determined to make at least one more call to his team. "I owed them that much," he said. "I was trying to prepare myself if they weren't going to come close to matching the offer. My wife and I had a long talk and she said that we had to hope for the best but prepare for the worst, and if it didn't work out, we were ready to move on."

The next eight hours went by in a blur. About 8:00 a.m., Wednesday, Canter e-mailed McGuire to inform him of the night's events, and Eric called Steve Wilks, his position coach. "I wanted to be honest with the Chargers and let them know other teams were serious," Eric said. "I didn't want to leave, but they needed to know I might be going somewhere. I wanted to give them a heads-up."

Around 9:00 a.m., an erroneous report began circulating that Eric had agreed to terms with the Jacksonville Jaguars. Using the Twitter hashtag "#signEricWeddle," fans of the Texans, Vikings, Cowboys, and Jaguars bombarded Canter with messages containing reasons why Eric should sign with their teams. During the media melee, the Bengals and the Lions also called to inquire about Eric, but neither made a serious offer.

Amid the chaos, agent and client came up with their contingency plans. If San Diego offered something close to the other teams, Eric would re-sign with the Chargers. They also discussed what to do if San Diego's offer was significantly less than the other suitors.

About 11:00 a.m., the news they were waiting for finally came. McGuire called Canter with an offer that was significantly higher than the previous night's. Canter countered, and some minor tweaks were made. Within sixty minutes, a dream deal was reached. Eric was set to stay in San Diego for another five years and earn $40 million, with $19 million guaranteed. When Canter called Eric with the good news, they were both overwhelmed by a flood of emotions. Weddle continually repeated phrases such as "Did we just get this deal? Did this really just happen?"

"We had come to the conclusion that we were most likely leaving, so to get the offer from the Chargers was incredible," Eric said. "Chanel and I couldn't have been more happy and relieved."

When he hung up the phone, Canter fell to his knees and wept. Knowing how hard Eric had worked over the years, he was happy for him. The feeling reminded him of negotiating similar deals for former NFL running back Stephen Davis. In 2000,

Canter helped Davis sign a nine-year, $135-million contract with the Washington Redskins. In 2003, he negotiated a five-year, $36-million deal for him with the Carolina Panthers. Canter was also grateful for what Weddle's deal with the Chargers would mean for Canter's own family. "I was a puddle of tears," the agent said. "I had my entire company and client list stolen from me in 2001. Eric stood by me every step of the way from the time I signed him in 2007. This contract, what it did for him and his wife, and what it did for my family, was incredible."

The free agent marathon concluded around 1:00 p.m. when Weddle and Canter joined a conference call with San Diego president and CEO Dean Spanos, then-general manager A. J. Smith, and McGuire. Eric was quick to thank the men for showing so much faith in him.

Another Twitter storm erupted when Canter tweeted the proclamation that Eric Weddle was "the highest paid safety in NFL history." In reality, Weddle was the second highest-paid safety. Mike Florio, of NBC's *ProFootballTalk,* reported in an article that in 2010 Kansas City gave safety Eric Berry a six-year, $60-million deal with $34 million guaranteed. Even so, Weddle was trending on Twitter within minutes of the announcement. As NFL reporters and sportswriters via Twitter relayed the terms of Eric's megadeal, everyone had an opinion.

Jim Trotter, a senior writer for *Sports Illustrated,* said in two tweets: "I want to make this clear: congrats to Eric Weddle. But I want to add: life is good if you're one of A. J.'s chosen ones. . . . More power to Eric, but he's not an $8 million per year player."

Kevin Acee tweeted this quote from San Diego teammate Quentin Jammer, regarding Weddle's new contract: "People shouldn't be hating on him. I'm going to give him the biggest hug he's ever had."

Matt Bowen, a former NFL safety and NFL writer for *The National Football Post,* sent this tweet: "This is big money for Eric Weddle or any safety in the NFL. Wow. In the end, the Chargers prevail."

Warren Sapp, a seven-time pro bowler, said via Twitter that the Chargers were paying $8 million to a safety "you couldn't pick out of a lineup."

Pittsburgh free safety Ryan Clark added this tweet: "Congrats to Eric Weddle! He just signed a deal for what the Steelers got [Troy Polamalu] and I for combined! Wow!"

The Weddle deal was a hot topic for fans all over the country, and they sounded off on sports talk shows and the Internet. Many had never heard of Eric and felt he was overpaid.

Not Norv Turner.

"I just know that Eric's on the verge of taking that next step," Turner told the media after the deal was signed. "He's a guy that's gotten better every year. He's got great leadership skills. He's got great understanding, not only of our defense, but of what people are doing. He's got great range. We need to get him to where he catches the ball better. If his interception totals go up, he'll be recognized as a truly elite player."

Tim Sullivan, another columnist for the *San Diego Union-Tribune,* wrote that Weddle was the kind of player who is worth keeping. "Does he belong in the same game-changing class as a Ronnie Lott or an Ed Reed? Not based on what these untrained eyes have seen thus far. Still, some numbers are worth noting.

"In four seasons with the Chargers, Weddle has been credited with 295 solo tackles. During that same span, Pittsburgh's Clark has totaled 194; Polamalu 166; Baltimore's Reed just 135. If Weddle doesn't deliver as many highlight-worthy hits as some safeties, and though he has yet to force an NFL fumble, the

Chargers appear to be more interested in his coverage than his carnage."

Sullivan quoted then-general manager A. J. Smith: "I think he's an outstanding football player that has not scratched the surface. He had a very good year this past year [2010], but more importantly, it's what he will become. We think he's going to be swinging upward tremendously. . . . I've seen the growth from year to year, and particularly in the 2010 season. I think he's going to get smarter, more instinctive, and it grows over time. On top of that, it's part of the package of the entire defense. . . . A lot of people have accused me of being 'old school.' This is a guy I believe will do everything [correctly]. His work ethic is unmatched. He's a good person. You feel comfortable investing in the future of someone like that. . . . Eric is a great kid and an outstanding player. He is exactly the type of player we want to be part of the Chargers organization."

Increased scrutiny followed Eric from the day he signed the contract. Many asked what he would buy first with his new wealth. A sports car? A fancy boat? "Nothing," Eric repeated in several media interviews the day he signed the contract. "Just paying off my house. That's about it. I don't need anything. I'm just putting it away for my kids and my family."

Eric accepts the fact that there will always be fans or critics who consider him overpaid. "That's what the media and fans talk about," he said. "I was grateful for the opportunity. All you can do is work your tail off, get better, and everything will take care of itself. You just worry about what you can control. That's getting better and going out and having a great year. I will do anything to help this team win a championship."

Eric spent the 2011 season doing two things. First, at every opportunity he publicly expressed gratitude to the Chargers for being so generous. Second, he found ways to work harder and do more for his team. Eric already felt he needed to live up to the expectations that came with being traded for four draft picks when his career started. Now, four years later, he needed to live up to the expectations of his humongous new contract. "I want to prove them right," he said.

And he did just that.

# CHAPTER 17

---

# *VALIDATED*

The 2011 football season was both disappointing and deeply satisfying for Eric Weddle.

It was disappointing because the Chargers finished the season 8–8 and missed the playoffs for the second straight year. It was satisfying because the twenty-six-year-old played the best year of his NFL career.

In four years, head coach Norv Turner's San Diego team was never better than 2–2 after four games. That trend was broken in 2011 as the Chargers jumped out to a 4–1 record. But following a bye, San Diego lost its next six games, and the season fell apart. On life support, the Chargers rallied to finish the year by winning four of their last five, but a 38–10 loss to the Detroit Lions in week sixteen terminated their postseason hopes.

Despite missing the playoffs, Eric finished the season as San Diego's third-leading tackler (93), and he tied with New England's Kyle Arrington and Green Bay's Charles Woodson for the most interceptions in the NFL with seven, one more than Weddle's total for his first four seasons. He was named the Chargers' defensive player of the year and was one of four defensive backs named to the third-annual USA Football All-Fundamentals team.

Every interception was a hallmark moment, but two picks stand out for Eric. The first came early in the season in San Diego against Kansas City. With the Chiefs driving to score the game-winning touchdown, Eric read a screen pass and stepped in front of the ball to secure the victory for the Chargers.

Eric's other favorite interception came in a loss against the New York Jets. From his center field position, Eric saw Jets receiver Plaxico Burress get behind Jammer. Eric moved over in time to pick off a pass from quarterback Mark Sanchez at the goal line.

But individual success doesn't matter when your team isn't winning. "The season we had puts a little damper on it," Eric said, "but I put a lot into it and worked my tail off this off-season to make that next jump and become an elite player in this league. I think I've done that. Now it's all about consistency and continuing a high level of play and helping my team win."

Despite the team's struggles, David Canter spoke openly and confidently about his client earning his first trip to the league's annual all-star game in Hawaii. Eric was afraid such talk would jinx his chances. He insisted on changing the topic. "'Quit talking about it, quit talking about it,'" Chanel recalled Eric saying. "He hated talking about it."

About five hours before the Pro Bowl rosters were announced on Tuesday, December 27, 2011, Chanel asked Eric, "Are you ready to celebrate?"

"Celebrate what?" Eric replied.

"Going to the Pro Bowl," she teased.

Eric rolled his eyes.

Less than an hour later, Eric and Chanel were talking in the kitchen when his phone buzzed with a call from his position coach, Steve Wilks. The coach was calling to congratulate his free safety on being named to the Pro Bowl. Chanel said her husband's face beamed with a smile "as big as California" and he pumped his fist with elation. The news was too good to be true.

"I thought I had a chance, but never really believed it would happen. I don't like to get too high [on myself] or overconfident, but I was in shock," Eric said. "In that moment I thought about everything I have done, all the time and work spent in the off-season, all the time and work during the season. I've always felt I was a great player, but this solidified it. As a player you're always trying to earn the respect of your peers. Being recognized as one of the better players in the league and on this team is something I've dreamed about and worked for. It's a big honor to be recognized by teammates, coaches, competitors, and fans this way."

Eric immediately began texting family and friends with the news. Chanel moved to the computer and began checking flights to Honolulu. The couple had already decided that if Eric made the prestigious roster, more than twenty family members—including his wife, three children, his and Chanel's parents, along with a few close friends—were invited to accompany the Weddles to Hawaii. This could be a once-in-a-lifetime opportunity. That night, family and friends gathered at a local restaurant for a celebratory dinner. It was a day that Eric will remember for the rest of his life.

"I try to live in the 'now' and get the most out of today," Eric said. "Who knows if I get back to the pro bowl, so we planned to make it a big deal. Through the highs and lows, the tough times and the good times, I'm grateful for everyone that has been in my life. I wanted to say thanks for helping me get to where I'm at, so we wanted them to come along and enjoy it with us."

Eric received more good news a week later. He had earned first-team All-Pro honors by vote of the *Associated Press*, one of the most respected honors an NFL player can receive in a career. The All-Pro team consists of the best players at each position in the entire league, combining conferences into one squad. The *Associated Press* voted Weddle ahead of elite safeties such as Baltimore's Ed Reed, Seattle's Earl Thomas, and Arizona's Adrian Wilson. Weddle had been named to the second-team All-Pro in 2010.

"Eric has gotten better each year," said Norv Turner, San Diego's head coach at the time. "It was important for us during camp to get him to a long-term contract, and he has certainly made another step in terms of his progress as a football player. You see a young guy who each year has made progress as a player and who's gotten better. When he had a couple situations this year where he didn't play as well as he would like to or we would like him to, he responded the very next week and played his best."

The trip to the Hawaiian Islands was full of highlights, although the water was colder than Eric expected. The Weddles' entourage lounged on the beach, attended a luau at the Polynesian Cultural Center and other fancy dinners, went snorkeling, toured the Dole plantation, met professional surfers, and hung out with other members of the Pro Bowl squad. With grandparents around to tend their kids, Eric and Chanel were able once or twice to escape for dinner and some alone time. One day, Chanel was able to visit the Laie Hawaii LDS Temple. Aside from trying to get their children to sleep, their eleven days in Hawaii were paradise.

Another highlight was becoming acquainted with all the NFL's top defensive backs and safeties. Eric found players such as Pittsburgh's Ryan Clark, Houston's Jonathan Joseph, Denver's Brian Dawkins, and New York's Darrelle Revis to be "regular, cool guys."

"They are really down-to-earth guys with great personalities," Eric said. "We didn't go do anything together, but it was really fun to just sit in a room and get to know them."

Eric bonded the most with Steelers quarterback Ben Roethlisberger. The two found common ground when discussing golf, fishing, hunting, and marriage. Roethlisberger told Weddle about his recent wedding. Eric appreciated Big Ben's sarcastic sense of humor and comedic personality.

When the all-star game rolled around, some players looked like they were going half-speed. Eric was not one of them. He intercepted two passes and recorded five tackles as his AFC team defeated the NFC 59–41. Eric's first interception came off a pass from Carolina's Cam Newton, which he returned 63 yards deep into NFC territory, leading to a field goal.

Eric also intercepted another pass by Newton late in the game. After picking off the deep pass, he returned the ball 27 yards and pitched the pigskin to surprised teammate Derrick Johnson before going down. Johnson then zigzagged and rumbled 60 yards for the AFC's final score.

Eric described his pro bowl experience as "incredible," but he wasn't satisfied with going just once. "I was extremely honored and excited to be part of it, but by no means is it a one-year thing. I want to be consistent and continue to prove that I'm one of the elite players in this league. I know I need to go out and prove it each year."

Winning a Super Bowl is still a top goal for Eric, but to be considered among the elite players in the NFL is a dream come true.

VALIDATED

"Honestly, who would have ever thought I would be where I am today? I was a little, short, white kid who loved sports, who would go out and play, who struggled, who was benched, who was injured, who was not recruited," Eric said. "Every step has molded and defined who I am to this point in my life—a mentally tough man who loves and enjoys every second of the day, who cares for teammates, family, and friends, and who doesn't let the little things get him down. The little things don't affect who I am or what I'm about, but they drive me to do better. It's crazy to think about how everything I've done in my life has gotten me here today. I wouldn't change a thing."

## LOOKING AHEAD

One week after the San Diego Chargers concluded their 2012 season with a disappointing 7–9 record, Eric found himself sitting at his dining room table with San Diego *Union-Tribune* columnist Kevin Acee for his final "Weddle Chat" video interview of the year. Eric was sporting a full beard and a black sailor-style hat with the front brim turned up as the interview started.

"It's a sad day . . . but you are probably happy to be done with the 'Weddle Chat.' Let's be honest, you've already got your off-season hat on," Acee said, prompting laughter from Eric. "This was not the season you expected or wanted. You've had some time to come to terms with it—although a lot has happened since the season was over. What have you been reflecting on?"

"Shoot," Eric said, after clearing his throat, "a lot."

Individually, the 2012 season was the best of Eric's career. The five-foot-eleven free safety followed up his 2011 all-pro season by leading San Diego in tackles (103) and interceptions (3). He was also proud of defending nine passes and forcing two fumbles.

Overall, he was a durable playmaker who also helped to coordinate a much-improved San Diego defense. His actions drew praise from the national media.

"Long after [Ed] Reed and [Troy] Polamalu retire, Weddle will wear the mantle of 'most instinctive safety,'" wrote *Sports Illustrated*'s Peter King.

At the end of the season, Eric wasn't selected to play in the pro bowl, but he was named to the league's All-Pro second team and voted as the Chargers' most valuable player in 2012, which he considered a major compliment.

"It's your teammates, it's your family, your guys you fight for and deal with on a daily basis, so to be honored like that is pretty special," Eric said of the award.

While the individual recognition was well deserved, it was difficult for Eric to find contentment when his team fell so far short of its goal to make the playoffs and compete for a Super Bowl. The end of the long season also sparked major changes in the team's front office. A. J. Smith, the Chargers general manager who was ripped by many for giving up four draft picks to get Eric, and Norv Turner, the only NFL head coach Eric had ever played for, were both fired after the final game. When asked about their departure, Eric expressed respect for each man, recalling how Smith gave him a shot in the NFL and describing his positive relationship with Turner, a coach who prepared diligently for each game and was loyal to his players. He wished them well in their future endeavors.

In the meantime, however, Eric remains in San Diego. He still wants to win games and get back to the playoffs. With a new general manager, head coach, staff, and personnel, Eric anticipates that he'll need to earn his starting job again. He knows the ball will take some unpredictable bounces, and the Chargers will not be favored to win the AFC West division in 2013, let alone make the playoffs.

Once again, Eric and his team are back in their familiar role as the underdog. But that's the kind of challenge Eric lives for in the game that he loves.

"I'm looking forward to the chase, healing back up and getting back at it," he said at the conclusion of the interview. "There are still reasons to be optimistic."

# CHAPTER 18

—

# A PLAYBOOK OF PRINCIPLES

When he entered the NFL as a rookie, Eric wrote or erased "EDub 32" into the cover of a small collection of spiral-bound notebooks and took them with him to every team meeting and film session. In the lined pages, he scribbled copious notes on every offensive formation, opposing team, coach, and player. He has kept these notebooks at home and refers to them when they might provide relevant information.

"You play the same teams over and over again, so you can look back at previous notes and get a jump start by looking at what they did, what they like to do, etc.," Eric said. "The same offensive coordinators end up coaching at different teams, but run the same systems. It's good to have information on certain guys. Everyone comes to meetings with a notebook, but not everyone takes notes. I do what works best for me."

When coaches or speakers are invited to address the team, they often share motivational material or inspirational quotes. Eric has written some of these motivational thoughts in his notebooks. They have become themes of his life. Reflecting on his experiences, what he stands for, and the things that motivate him, Eric has identified several principles in his personal playbooks that inspire him. If he were sitting down with you for a face-to-face talk, these are, in his words, the themes of success the all-pro safety would share.

**Adversity Makes You Stronger.** Adversity affects everyone at some point. There is something powerful about someone telling you they don't like you or that you can't do something. What gives them the right to judge you? It drives me to prove them wrong, to show them I am better than they thought I was. Ever since I played in Pop Warner, I've been told I'm not big enough or fast enough. Along the way, I've made mistakes, missed tackles and dropped interceptions. But the past makes me stronger. I like the words of former college football coach Lou Holtz, who said, "Adversity is another way to measure the greatness in people."

**Conquer Your Fears.** General George Patton said, "Courage is fear holding on a minute longer." People are far too concerned these days with what others may think or say about them. Listening to the critics opens you up to fear. Fear robs you of blessings. Fear justifies giving up. Fear leads to defeat. The only way to conquer fear is to tackle it head on. Forget the critics and don't be afraid to take a risk or make a mistake. Find the courage to conquer your fears.

**"Decisions Determine Destiny."** This is one of my favorites from Thomas S. Monson, President of The Church of Jesus Christ of Latter-day Saints. He said, "I can't stress too strongly that decisions determine destiny. You can't make eternal decisions without eternal consequences." Your decisions will lead you to either victory or defeat, joy or disappointment. Winners choose to work hard. Winners choose good friends with good values.

Winners choose education. Winners honor their parents and family. Winners care more about their teammates than individual accolades. Be a winner by making good choices.

**Pay the Price.** Bud Wilkinson, former Oklahoma head football coach, said, "If you are going to be a champion, you must be willing to pay a greater price than your opponent." NBA legend Larry Bird said, "A winner is someone who recognizes his God-given talents, works his tail off to develop them into skill, and who uses them to accomplish his goals." Author and motivational speaker Brian Tracy said, "Move out of your comfort zone. You can only grow if you are willing to feel awkward and uncomfortable to get better." To get better today, you must demand more than you did yesterday. Winners pay the price to reach their goals.

**Carry Yourself with Confidence, Character, and Class.** These are the "three Cs." Throughout my career, the greatest men and women I have known all have these characteristics. They believe they can do great things. They have integrity and do the right thing when no one is watching. When they fail or succeed, they do it with sportsmanship and class. You should always strive to do the right thing and live the right way, whether you are on the winning end or the losing end of life.

**Team Is Everything.** Legendary Green Bay Packers coach Vince Lombardi said, "People who work together will win, whether it be against complex football defenses, or the problems of modern society." Football is not an individual sport. It is the greatest team sport. If I play great and my team loses, what good have I done? Whether you are on a sports team or not, strive to surround yourself with good friends or teammates who will support you in making good decisions, lift you up when you are down, and cheer you on to success. Be loyal to these teammates. I have been blessed in my life to have many great friends who are there for me no matter what, and I will be there for them no matter what. Former Los Angeles Lakers coach Phil Jackson said, "Good teams become great ones when the members trust each other enough to surrender the 'me' for the 'we.'" Team is everything.

**Honor Your Parents and Love Your Family.** One reason I am the person I am today is because I had unbelievably great parents. They loved me. They were strict. They taught me how to live the right way. They taught me how to be humble and respectful. They taught me how to be a good person. Listen to your parents. Sometimes you get mad at them, but realize they want what is best for you. Sometimes we think we know it all, but we don't. Your parents have been through life. Lean on them for wisdom and advice. I also have a wonderful wife and kids to lean on. Your family is your greatest support.

**Be a Sponge.** Education is important. As hard as you work to be successful in sports, you should work even harder in academics. It's difficult to get any job today without a high school diploma or college degree. Take pride in being a good student and absorb information from every positive source. I was blessed in my life to have several great coaches and mentors who helped me stay grounded and who taught me true principles. Identify those people in your life and humble yourself to learn from them.

**Lead by Example.** LDS Church President Thomas S. Monson said, "A good example is more effective than good advice and, I might add, more easily and willingly followed." If you aren't willing to be great when no one is watching, then you don't deserve the chance to be great when everyone is watching. When you take shortcuts or cheat, you are only hurting yourself and the team. Mark Twain said, "Do the right thing. It will gratify some people and astonish the rest." A great leader inspires others to do great things by first being a good example.

**"If Ye Are Prepared Ye Shall Not Fear."** I took this from Doctrine and Covenants 38:30. Vince Lombardi said, "The will to win is not nearly as important as the will to prepare to win." Someone else said, "Today's preparation determines tomorrow's achievement." One way I gain an advantage over other players and opponents is how I prepare before a game. It's important to do your homework, study your opponent's weaknesses as well as your own so you know where they might attack. It's the same with life. Success is not going to just happen; you must have a game plan for it. If you are prepared, you shall not fear.

**Never Give Up.** Thomas Edison, famous inventor, said, "Many of life's failures are men who did not realize how close they were to success when they gave up." B. C. Forbes, journalist and author, said, "Triumph often is nearest when defeat seems inescapable." A winner never gives up.

**Play with Heart.** Regardless of your abilities or talents, circumstances or challenges, everyone has been blessed with a heart. Playing with heart means doing whatever it takes to get the job done. When it's late in the fourth quarter and the outcome hangs in the balance, at some point your heart takes over because you are going the extra mile. Even if you are not the strongest or the fastest guy, you know you will get the job done because you have heart. Live life with passion. Live and play every day like it's your last.

**Dream Big.** Life coach Tony Robbins said, "I believe life is constantly testing us for our level of commitment, and life's greatest rewards are reserved for those who demonstrate a never-ending commitment to act until they achieve." Remember that all things are possible, no matter how big or fast you are. Don't keep your dreams in your eyes; keep them in your heart so that every heartbeat reminds you to fulfill your desire. Set goals, formulate a plan to obtain those goals, and then make it happen. If your mind can conceive it, you can achieve it.

# AFTERWORD

The story behind this book started with a text message. On the morning of February 17, 2010, my cell phone vibrated, and the name *Eric Weddle* popped up as I sat at my cubicle on the fifth floor of the old Deseret News building, located at 30 East and 100 South in downtown Salt Lake City, Utah.

I don't normally receive a lot of texts, so I immediately reached over and flipped open the phone to read the message. The San Diego Chargers safety and former University of Utah all-American was willing to grant a special interview. I smiled with satisfaction.

"Hey, Mr. Toone, this is Eric Weddle. Morgan [Scalley] gave me your number to talk about a piece you want to do. Would you like to call me tonight so we can talk?"

I don't interact with NFL players very often, so my initial reaction was that of a typical sports fan—*wow, Eric Weddle personally just sent me a text.* I suppressed my urges to parade my celebrity text message around the newsroom and texted back that

# AFTERWORD

I looked forward to the phone call. Little did I realize how that small message, less than 150 characters long, would eventually send my life in a new, unexpected direction.

As a lifelong football fan, the idea of interviewing an NFL player was exhilarating, but football was not the angle for the article. My purpose in tracking Eric down was getting him to share the details of his decision to be baptized a member of The Church of Jesus Christ of Latter-day Saints in 2004.

Religious conversion stories often include powerful, compelling, and life-changing experiences that strengthen faith and deepen testimonies. Brigham Young, second president of the LDS Church, once said that he "would rather hear men tell their own experiences . . . than hear any kind of preaching" (*Discourses of Brigham Young,* 335). Outside of Eric's family, friends, teammates, and some others, few were likely aware of his baptism prior to his sophomore season at the University of Utah. It wasn't a secret, but it isn't in Eric's friendly nature to go around broadcasting or pushing his religious convictions on others. Eric Weddle's conversion story was one he was pleased and eager to share. I was thrilled that he trusted me enough to let me publish it. With added insight from his parents and additional details from a few former Utah teammates, the 2,200-word story was published in *Mormon Times,* a section of the *Deseret News,* on March 24, 2010.

Eric's story must have hit the mark with readers because the response received from this single article was off the charts. E-mails and comments from impressed BYU Cougars, loyal Utah Utes, and many others flooded in, expressing admiration and respect for the former all-American. A mother living in the Tongan Islands was touched by the details of Eric's conversion story and couldn't wait to share it with her nine children. A man from Provo, Utah, wanted to know more about Eric's life. He was not alone.

In the days that followed, I continued to marvel at the reader reaction and contemplated what else I might write about Eric. Then one night as I drove home, I was hit with a crazy idea. What about a book on Eric Weddle? Almost as instantly as the idea came, I shot it down. Why would Eric allow me—a journalist who had never written a book and someone he has never met in person—to tell his story? I was sure he would politely listen to my idea and say, "No thanks, bud."

Despite my doubts, after two sleepless nights I was unable to shake the idea. I planned what I might say. I knew I could utilize my reporter skills and gather information, interview, write, edit, and revise as well as the next journalist. I had followed Eric's college and professional football careers as both a sportswriter and a fan, and I believed his story was compelling. It boiled down to the matter of having the courage to ask him. While I expected him to decline, I knew that if I didn't at least pitch the idea, I would regret it for the rest of my life. I really had nothing to lose.

I also considered the fact that Eric was only twenty-five years old at the time, and still somewhat young in his NFL career, with many great years ahead. Wouldn't it make more sense to wait? Even so, something pushed me forward. The next day at work I typed a short e-mail to Eric, clicked "send," and waited expectantly.

Eric responded a week later with the message, "Hey, bud, sorry it took so long to get back to you. U serious about doing a book?" That was it. Did this mean he was actually considering the project? I fired back a message to assure him I was eager to tackle the task. Another week crawled by. When his name finally popped into my inbox, I was prepared for rejection. Instead, I read the words, "Yeah, I think we can definitely do something.

# AFTERWORD

I want you to call my agent, David Canter. Great guy. How are things with u?"

All at once I felt honored, thrilled, and terrified. Now I actually had to go through with it. I wasn't sure where to start, but I called Eric's agent and plowed forward nonetheless. I wanted the book to be an honest on-the-field, off-the-field portrait of Eric Weddle. Nobody had a problem with that. We shared the hope that the book could somehow inspire young people to work hard and overcome adversity on the way to achieving their dreams. Thus began my adventurous excursion through the life of Eric Steven Weddle.

Our first face-to-face meeting took place Friday, June 11, 2010, at his southern California home. Two of the Weddle children, Brooklyn and Gaige, played with toys on the living room floor while my wife, Lisa, and I visited with Eric's wife, Chanel. That's when Mr. Weddle himself entered from the garage, dangling keys and a sack of Subway sandwiches and chips. He wore a bright yellow Lakers T-shirt, long athletic shorts, and sneakers. A well-groomed beard covered his face but couldn't hide his big smile. After warm introductions, we sat at the kitchen table and unwrapped sandwiches. Three months earlier, I had never even spoken with Eric—now here we were eating together in his kitchen.

Eric's first comment to his wife was probably not typical of many how-was-your-day-at-the-office-honey conversations, but it was typical in the Weddle household. "I picked off Philip again today," Eric said with satisfaction. He was talking about all-pro San Diego quarterback Philip Rivers. Chanel smiled. It was business as usual.

We discussed several topics as we became acquainted over the next thirty minutes. Between bites of our subs, I learned quickly that Eric is a huge Lakers fan, and Kobe Bryant is his favorite player. One of Eric's lifelong dreams is to play one-on-one with the L.A. hoop star. He predicted the Lakers would defeat the Boston Celtics by game six of the 2010 NBA finals.

Another of Eric's aspirations is to someday play a round of golf with Tiger Woods. Nothing is more relaxing to Eric than getting out on a beautiful green course with friends and his bag of golf clubs—Chanel permitting, of course.

After polishing off half of his foot-long sub, Eric asked where I went to college. I was proud to inform him that Lisa and I both graduated from the University of Utah. He grinned with approval. In an instant we moved from being new friends to kindred spirits. No former player supports the University of Utah football program more than Eric Weddle.

Later that night, after the kids went to bed, Eric and I sat up late talking about his childhood, his days at Alta Loma High School, the University of Utah, and how he courted Chanel. Four hours flew by, and we were both exhausted.

The next morning I was invited to climb into Eric's black 2010 SS Camaro, a.k.a. "Black Beauty," for an hour's drive north on Interstate 15 to tour his hometown of Alta Loma and other parts of Rancho Cucamonga. Sporting manly shades, Eric drove his car with his left hand on the wheel and his right hand on the gearshift, as if he were a stunt man in *The Fast and the Furious.* As we cruised north, engine purring, R&B music pulsing through the speakers, the NFL safety thoughtfully shared experiences regarding football and his life. In Rancho Cucamonga, we drove past Alta Loma High School, Chaffey College (where the Alta Loma Braves played home football games), practice fields and ballparks, his parents' home, and Chanel's family's former residence. At one red light, Eric rolled down his window for a quick hello to some Latter-day Saint missionaries who were walking by.

I watched and listened with fascination, doing my best to absorb and document everything. I snapped photos with my digital camera and typed notes on my laptop. A digital recorder was also capturing our conversation from the cup holder next to the stick shift. Before we left Rancho Cucamonga, we stopped for lunch at Popeye's Chicken and Biscuits. This time Eric asked the questions about my life. His personable nature and genuine interest put me at ease.

On the drive back to his home, I learned that Eric has a tendency to sleepwalk, he loves to play all kinds of video games, and he lives for action movies with sword-fighting warriors and epic battle scenes. For added game day inspiration, he has downloaded to his iPod memorable dialogue from films such as *Braveheart, Troy,* and *The Lord of the Rings.* The well-rounded Weddle has also read Stephenie Meyer's *Twilight* series and favors werewolves. "Jacob is so much more real than Edward," he explained.

After Eric and I fought traffic on the way back to his home, my wife and I were invited to the home of Eric's friend and former San Diego teammate, Ryon Bingham, where we enjoyed a barbecue in Bingham's tropical paradise of a backyard.

The weekend concluded the following morning as we attended LDS Church services with the Weddles. We arrived a few minutes late but found an open bench in the middle of the chapel. While Chanel pulled out picture books and a plastic container of animal cookies for their kids, Eric grabbed the LDS hymnbook and showed me his two favorite hymns—"Have I Done Any Good?" and "Praise to the Man." As the hour-long service carried on, Eric listened attentively, laughed at an occasional joke, and helped his wife manage the kids. When we noticed a frustrated parent carrying a screaming child out the side exit during the final speaker's remarks, Eric watched sympatheti-cally. "Ouch," he said.

Before leaving for the airport, we met Eric's parents, Steve and Debbie. Steve was decked out in Chargers gear, a common occurrence according to his family. Eric's dad also had a Lakers T-shirt on hand for the L.A.-Boston NBA finals game that after-noon. Like any proud father, Steve was more than willing to talk about his son's achievements. Debbie fussed over her grandchil-dren and made pleasant conversation. It was easy to see why Eric thinks so highly of his parents.

During the 2010 season, access to Eric was limited due to his schedule. As the months passed, I held extensive interviews and informal chats with more than sixty other people—members of Eric's family, friends, current and former teammates, coaches, current and former opponents, and other acquaintances.

A second trip to beautiful, sunny, southern California came the weekend of October 24, 2010, when the Chargers played the New England Patriots. The game provided an opportunity to ex-perience the NFL atmosphere in San Diego, as well as to watch Eric and the San Diego defense square off with the Pats' MVP quarterback Tom Brady. It was the first NFL game I had ever at-tended. I had never witnessed tailgate parties or pregame festivi-ties like this before. Canopies and vehicles surrounded Qualcomm Stadium and stretched in every direction. The smell of barbecue sauce and sizzling meat on the grill wafted in the breeze. "Weddle Way" was easy to find by following the No. 32 jerseys.

Inside Qualcomm Stadium, the Weddle fan base sat in the lower level near the north end zone. While Chanel and a friend entertained three-year-old Brooklyn and one-year-old Gaige, more than 68,000 fans watched the Chargers stage a thrilling fourth-quarter comeback that fell short when a 50-yard field goal attempt by San Diego kicker Kris Brown smacked off the right-side upright. The Patriots won 23–20. Weddle recorded five tackles in the game. Afterward we rendezvoused at the Weddle home, where family and friends gathered to visit with the sore NFL player. Eric found time to speak with everyone.

There are approximately 750 miles between Eric's home near San Diego and my home in Utah, so we communicated mostly through phone calls and text messages through the duration of the project. On a few occasions when he came to Utah, we arranged to meet for breakfast. He loves a hearty breakfast, followed by a workout. I also tagged along as Eric strolled the sidelines at the 2011 Utah spring red-and-white football game at Rice-Eccles Stadium. More than nine months into the project, I thought I knew most of the relevant details of Eric Weddle's life. Then he surprised me again. As we talked over breakfast at The Original Pancake House in Salt Lake City one April morning in 2011, he related another experience I had never heard before about his off-the-field relationship with former Utah teammate Marty Johnson. Feeling in awe of the story yet a little frustrated, I remarked that if this book was ever going to be written, he had to stop holding out on me. He grinned as he replied, "You got to remember—I do bang my head for a living."

Several months later, I saw another side of Eric when I attended the press conference announcing offensive lineman Kris Dielman's retirement at Chargers Park, the team's headquarters. Prior to the press conference and far from the media, I witnessed Eric's genuine concern for his teammate as he sought out Dielman and his family for a hug before the emotional announcement. The next day I tagged along in Weddle's golf cart as he played eighteen holes with two San Diego teammates, wide receiver Vincent Jackson and center Scott Mruczkowski. Eric had a nickname for everyone, and in between drives and putts there was good-natured sparring and teasing going on. Everyone laughed when Eric spontaneously invented a song and dance. If he finished the hole with par, he would walk low to the ground, pump his arms, and sing, with an R&B beat, "riding the par train." If he recorded a double bogey, he was "riding the bogey train" and he needed to "get off." Regardless of where he is or what he is doing, you can be sure Eric is competing and having fun to the fullest.

One of my greatest moments in this journey came when I challenged Eric to a game of "Madden Football" on the Xbox at his house. He, of course, selected the San Diego Chargers, while I was the Philadelphia Eagles. Fortune shone on me first when his defensive back tipped a pass into the hands of my wide-open receiver for a touchdown. I didn't say anything because the last thing I wanted to do was motivate him to beat me. The weirdest part was seeing Eric Weddle, sitting on the couch, playing the game as Eric Weddle. More than twenty-five minutes later, I trailed 14–13 late in the second half when Chanel announced it was time to head for the airport and my return flight to Utah. Eric told me I had one final drive to beat him. What could I do? I ran the same play five times in a row—with all four receivers running short routes—in hurry-up offense mode. With Michael Vick as my QB, I drove the Eagles down the field and scored the winning touchdown on a short pass to receiver Jason Avant. When he crossed the goal line, I wanted to scream out, "I just beat Eric Weddle!" but I didn't feel it would be appropriate. I stole a glance in his direction and noticed a slight look of disbelief on his face. Honestly, I was lucky to even compete with him.

"Thanks for letting me win," I said to Eric. "You're a generous host."

He smiled as if to say, "Sure, Trent."

Early on in the long process of putting the puzzle pieces of Eric's life story together, his father, Steve, pulled me aside and got right to the point. He asked the question many readers may be wondering: "Why write a book about my son, Eric? He is only twenty-five years old."

Steve had a point—we don't see a lot of hour-long specials on ESPN or books published about five-foot-eleven, 205-pound blue-collar safeties. What really sets Eric apart from the others?

I didn't have a good answer for Steve that day, but I've had a few years to ponder his question. Although Eric will be the first to acknowledge his weaknesses, I hope his experiences demonstrate the basic themes of family values, goal-setting, faith, sportsmanship, and courage amid adversity. To me, these and other qualities are evidence of Eric's inspirational example. Most of all I admire his drive to prove the critics wrong.

"There is something about someone telling you they don't like you or that you can't do something," Eric has explained. "They judge you. For me it's added motivation to prove those people wrong. I'll show them I am better than they thought I was, and I am not a guy who forgets easily."

Who wouldn't respect a man who has achieved success all on his own merits? I respect the fact that Eric has earned everything he has through dedication and honest hard work without taking shortcuts.

As talented an athlete as Eric is on the field, he is also a difference-maker off the field. What I find refreshing about Eric is that while he is devoted to the LDS faith, he doesn't wear his religion on his sleeve. You might not ever suspect he's a Mormon in a casual setting. But you would quickly see that he is an individual with a set of principles, and he lives by them. Aside from being an active member of his church, his top priority is taking care of his family.

Eric finds joy in serving others, whether it's through charitable events in the community or teaching a youngster how to tackle at a football camp.

He is a great example of humility. His friends, family, and old teammates admire him for not developing an ego with his success. "He is still the same, fun-loving Eric," they agree. He is so unassuming that he blends right in with the crowd. Few fans even recognize him when he eats at a restaurant with his family.

Weddle has a genuine ability to tune out the world and make the person he is talking to feel as though their conversation is the only one that matters, even when it's somebody he just met. He has a way of making those he interacts with feel important and part of his inner circle.

Finally, the saying, "Live each day like it's your last," Eric's daily motto, was evident in every experience he shared.

We can all take a lesson from that.

# ACKNOWLEDGMENTS

The gratitude first comes to rest on Eric Weddle, for trusting me enough to tackle this project, which was an honor.

I am incredibly thankful for the patient assistance of Chanel Weddle, who provided hospitality and wonderfully detailed interviews while taking care of her energetic children. She deserves a beautiful bouquet for all she did to make this happen.

A special thanks goes to David Canter, Eric's agent; Eric's parents, Steve and Debbie Weddle; his sister, Kathleen; Chanel's parents, Ron and Sonya Blaquiere; along with friends, coaches, and teammates, for offering their time, insights, and memories.

Personnel from the San Diego Chargers and the University of Utah were accommodating and helpful, especially Utah head coach Kyle Whittingham and former Utah sports information director Liz Abel. Members of the media in the Salt Lake City and San Diego markets also contributed necessary information.

This book would not be possible without the folks at Shadow Mountain. I express my gratitude to Cory Maxwell, Chris

Schoebinger, Lisa Mangum, and the rest of the team, for assisting this rookie.

In my journalism and writing career, more mentors have influenced me than I can possibly name. But I must credit the late Terry Munns, Bear River High School; Greg Madson, publisher of the *Tremonton Leader;* Ron Bennett, retired communications professor, BYU–Idaho; Jim Burton, sports columnist at the *Standard-Examiner;* Dave Greiling, *Standard-Examiner* city editor; Brad Rock and Lee Benson, *Deseret News* columnists; and Aaron Shill, *Mormon Times* and Features editor at the *Deseret News,* as well as my many friends and coworkers, for each teaching me something unique about writing and how to tell a story.

A special tribute goes to my friend, Derek Jensen, who died tragically in a June 2012 bicycling accident shortly after an early draft of the manuscript was completed. Derek, a former journalist with a resourceful mind, read the manuscript twice in the early stages and offered many beneficial tips and editorial suggestions. His contributions proved to be invaluable and will never be forgotten.

Finally, the completion of this project could not have happened without the unconditional support of my wife, Lisa, who kept faith in me through the countless late nights and early mornings; my children, Trevin, Kalen, and Elise, for loving their father even on the hard days; and my sweet parents, Greg and Connie Toone, along with many other family members, for your kind words and prayers that sustained me in reaching this incredible goal.

# SOURCES

*Note:* Except where indicated, all direct quotations in this book come from personal interviews with the author. The following books, periodicals, and Internet sources provided useful information. University of Utah video footage, shared by KSL Television and the Mountain Network, was also immensely helpful.

## BOOKS

The Book of Mormon: Another Testament of Jesus Christ. Salt Lake City: The Church of Jesus Christ of Latter-day Saints, 1981.

Call, Jeff. *Roaring Back to Glory.* Provo, UT: Spring Creek Book Company, 2008.

Facer, Dirk. *BCS Breakthrough: Utah's Historic 2004 Season.* Savoy, IL: KCI Sports Ventures, LLC, 2004.

Hinckley, Shane. *University of Utah Football Vault: The History of the Utes.* Atlanta, GA: Whitman Publishing, LLC, 2010.

Martin, Buddy. *Urban's Way: Urban Meyer, The Florida Gators, and His Plan to Win.* New York, N.Y.: St. Martin's Press, 2009.

# SOURCES

Sheltra, Patrick. *100 Things Ute Fans Should Know and Do Before They Die*. Chicago, IL: Triumph Books, 2011.

Young, Brigham. *Discourses of Brigham Young*. Compiled by John A. Widtsoe. Salt Lake City: Deseret Book, 1954.

## PERIODICALS

*Atlanta Journal-Constitution*

Billick, Brian. Quoted in Don Banks and Jon A. Dolezar, "2000 NFL Playoffs: Notebook," *CNN Sports Illustrated*, January 7, 2001, accessed February 28, 2013, http://sportsillustrated.cnn.com/football/nfl/2001/playoffs/news/2001/01/07/nfl_notebook_ap/.

CBSSports.com

*Deseret News*

*Ensign,* November 2008

ESPN.com

GQ.com

Inland Valley *Daily Bulletin*

Inland Valley *Voice*

*North County Times*

profootballtalk.nbcsports.com

*Sports Illustrated*

*The Los Angeles Times*

San Diego *Union-Tribune*

*Salt Lake Tribune*

Wikipedia

## OTHER

KSL Television

The Mountain Network

# INDEX

# INDEX

# INDEX

# INDEX

# INDEX

# INDEX